hotels • restaurants • shops • spas

englandchic

hotels • restaurants • shops • spas

englandchic

text ferne arfin • brandon lee

thechiccollection

publisher'sacknowledgements

Finally—after 23 editions in The Chic Collection—welcome to *England Chic*. We started with *Mexico Chic* and have been gradually making our way closer to home ever since. The following pages give you a look at some of the most chic hotels in England—a very impressive selection as you will discover. Maybe this book would not have been viable 10 years ago—I doubt we would have found 50 chic hotels in England.

Author Ferne Arfin has done a fantastic job in selecting and describing the chic in England; from Northern Style to Stately Homes to Dining Out in the Southwest. Thank you Ferne.

Yet again the team at Editions Didier Millet has pulled out all the stops and worked through the night to produce *England Chic*. My thanks go to Melisa, Suzanne, Meia, KC and Bobby for their commitment to the cause. In England I would like to thank my colleagues James, Helena and our friend in the north, Margaret. Thank you all—and also to our many co-publishers who have taken The Chic Collection to different countries, in (at last count) 6 different languages.

Most of all, I must thank the properties that you will see in the following pages for their support and belief in *England Chic*. It has taken 24 Chic editions and almost 24 months of effort to get here, so thank you all for your commitment. Finally to you, the reader, a huge thank you and please take time to register with us at www.thechiccollection.com so that we can send you some great special offers in these and other chic properties around the world. If you are reading this in England, I hope *England Chic* makes you want to get out and explore your own country; for those elsewhere in the world, come and see for yourselves!

Nigel Bolding
publisher

executive editor
melisa teo

editor
suzanne wong

assistant editor
meia ho

designer
chan hui yee

production manager
sin kam cheong

first published 2008
the world's best hotels ltd
the studio, 27 high street
godalming gu7 1au, united kingdom
enquiries : nigel@thechiccollection.com
website : www.thechiccollection.com

designed and produced by
editions didier millet pte ltd
121 telok ayer street, #03-01
singapore 068590
telephone : +65.6324 9260
facsimile : +65.6324 9261
enquiries : edm@edmbooks.com.sg
website : www.edmbooks.com

©2008 the world's best hotels
design and layout © editions didier millet pte ltd

Printed in Singapore.

isbn: 978-981-4217-39-2

COVER CAPTIONS:

1: The windows of a black cab reflect the lights of Piccadilly Circus on a rainy evening.
2: England's modern art scene is flourishing.
3: Fine dining and top service at Brown's Hotel.
4: A university student about to go on a leisurely punt down the River Cam, in Cambridge.
5: A high-street shopper laden with carrier bags.
6: Birmingham's Selfridges store at The Bullring.
7: Celebrity chef and restaurateur Gordon Ramsay.
8: The spectacular show-jumping at Cheltenham.
9: Fine cuisine at The Landau at The Langham.
10: An art installation exhibit at the Tate Liverpool.
11: 30 St Mary Axe, designed by Sir Norman Foster.
12: A stunning pair of stilettos by John Galliano.
13: A studious gargoyle perched on an Oxford wall.
14: Sandringham House, the royals' country home.
15: The Light Bar at St Martins Lane Hotel, London.
16: Luxurious baths at Le Manoir aux Quat' Saisons.
17: Sunrise over Stonehenge at the summer solstice.
18: A sumptuous guestroom at Strattons Hotel.
19: Shopping at Piccadilly Arcade, London.
20: The acclaimed restaurant at Gidleigh Park.
21: Gidleigh Park offers spa relaxation at its finest.

THIS PAGE: *The London Eye against grey winter skies.*

OPPOSITE: *An item on every visitor's itinerary—the changing of the guard at Buckingham Palace.*

PAGE 2: *A model is silhouetted in smooth shades of fuchsia on a high-profile London catwalk show.*

PAGE 8 AND 9: *A night view of Westminster Palace.*

contents

london 40

thesoutheast 94

Atlantic Ocean

NORTHERN IRELAND

REPUBLIC OF IRELAND

Irish Sea

Celtic Sea

england

SCOTLAND

North Sea

WALES

ENGLAND

London

France

Strait of Dover

N

Legend
⊕ Airport
◯ Lake
⬤ Urban Area
Below Sea Level
1000–1500 m
500–1000 m
200–500 m
100–200 m

0 km 25 50 75 km

introduction

the world on an island

Love them or hate them, you can't deny that the English have a certain style. When Napoleon called them a nation of shopkeepers, it's safe to assume he intended insult. But the descendents of seafarers, pirates and adventurers who populate more than half of Britain—the Celts, Britons, Romans, Norsemen, Danes, Angles, Saxons and Normans who together gave rise to the English— just carried on with what they had been doing for hundreds of years, sniffy remarks from across the Channel notwithstanding. While other Europeans divided up the world for religion and power, the English ventured out in search of customers.

Along the way, they created an empire of which it was famously said the sun never set. By the time it did, the English language and culture had spread well beyond its boundaries and turned England into one of the most unselfconsciously cosmopolitan destinations in Europe.

Today's England is a magnet for citizens of the world. In its cities and towns, on its streets and in its markets, the tastes, colours, music, designs and accents of India, Africa, the Caribbean, Asia, the Mediterranean and the Pacific Rim jostle for attention. And though the country had to be dragged, kicking and screaming, into the European Union, the influences of Spain, France, Italy and Eastern Europe are now familiar elements of England's 21st-century cultural mix.

The wonder is that while visitors always comment on England's international ambience, the English themselves hardly even notice. Instead, England's style setters adapt, absorb and tame the foreign and exotic with an offhand nonchalance.

city mouse country mouse

England is urban and densely populated: about 85 per cent of the population of the British Isles is concentrated in England, which occupies about 50 per cent of the land area. Nearly 60 per cent of them live in cities.

London was once the only city that mattered, the centre of the English universe and the arbiter of all matters of taste and style. Visitors, too, once overlooked the rest of England to soak up all that London had to offer.

Now things are changing. The colourful cities of the north are catching up fast. Places such as Liverpool—the 2008 European Capital of Culture—that lost population and status in the 1990s, are growing once again. And they are once again enriching the vibrant mix that is English style. Indie music, anarchic comedy and hip bars;

THIS PAGE: A Bollywood-style mural appears in Trafalgar Square, reflecting the cultural heterogeneity of the country.

OPPOSITE: Dancers whirl about the floor at a gala Viennese Ball in Liverpool's St George's Hall, commissioned specially for the city's status as 2008 European Capital of Culture.

...a pointedly wicked taste for the outrageous...

amazing architecture and radical art; gritty theatre, film and literature; jewellery and chic designer shopping—come to England and all across the country you'll never for once find yourself at a loss for things to do. Cities such as Birmingham, Newcastle, Sheffield, Liverpool, Nottingham, Manchester and Leeds are all close behind London's premier position as the country's creative engine.

Ask a roomful of trendsetters to define English style and you'll wait a long time for them to come to a consensus. Yet, as is the case with so many other undefinable abstractions, most will know it when they see it. England's cities give rise to the cultural trends. But it is in the English countryside—in the dwindling but jealously protected greenbelts, the rolling patchwork of fields and moors, heaths and fells, the thousands of miles of varied coastline, the country estates and the weekend bolt holes—that urban edge is transformed into English style.

from bold and independent...

It's a bold style that starts out hip, anarchic, independent and fluid. Its artists and designers are almost always controversy-courting iconoclasts—some, like Vivienne Westwood who elevated street punk to high fashion, stay that way.

From the gritty films of its home-grown cinema industry to the myriad collections of deconstructed clothes that march aggressively down its catwalks during London Fashion Week, England's aesthetic sensibility trades heavily on a much vaunted sense of irony as well as a pointedly wicked taste for the outrageous. Its freshest comedy is frequently shocking and always provocative, its newest music easier to shout than to sing. When artist Damien Hirst's displays of sheep and sharks suspended in formaldehyde became old news, it didn't take him long to come up with a new angle on his pet theme—Death. In recent years he has produced a diamond-encrusted skull called *For the Love of God* (the title attributed to Hirst's mother, who summed up popular sentiment by exclaiming 'For the love of God, what are you going to do next?') and the pretty-in-pastels 'Butterfly Paintings', made of hundreds of real butterflies trapped in paint.

THIS PAGE: The sun sets over the Dorset coast, bathing some of England's loveliest landscapes in the day's last golden rays.

OPPOSITE: Damien Hirst's animals in formaldehyde shocked the art scene when they were first exhibited—less controversial were his 'spot paintings'.

English architect Richard Rogers was the first to put a building's insides on the outside, bringing the style to London and changing people's attitudes about architecture and design with his still controversial masterpiece, the Lloyds Building. Today, England's installation artists also expose the inner to shocking effect—think Tracey Emin's unabashed *My Bed*, Rachel Whiteread's *House*—a casting of the inside of an empty house, or Cornelia Parker's *Cold Dark Matter*—an exploded view of a garden shed, blown up for her by the British Army.

While elsewhere in Europe, the trendiest and most stylish people value sophistication and soignée elegance, England chic is radical, noisy, political, and one suspects more often than not tongue in cheek. And yet...

...to subtle as the landscape

Existing in such close urban proximity with other city dwellers, one cannot possibly live it large, as the English say, all of the time. Come the weekend and even the most dyed-in-the wool clubland vampires will head for the hills to chill out in the country, particularly in the warm summer months, when the heat in the cities can easily rise into the high thirties. There, it is peaceful, sparsely populated and, for a landmass that would easily fit into the state of Texas five times over, surprisingly varied.

Yet, as England's countryside segues from storybook-pretty Kent, with its aerial pastoral patchwork of velvety fields and hedges, to the bleakly beautiful moors of North Yorkshire, as immortalised in Emily Brontë's *Wuthering Heights*, it does not challenge with extremes. England is not a land of towering peaks and thundering cataracts, neither does it overwhelm the senses with an onslaught of vibrant colours and heady scents.

The colours of the countryside are as soft and sublime as the vague contours of the English landscape: tints of heathers, mossy stones and slates; the muted wildflower hues of a Cotswolds meadow, a hundred shades of mist-soaked green hidden in the dewy folds of an Exmoor glade. Even in the Lake District, England's only true mountain region, the topography is more about long perspectives and the imperceptible blending of browns, golds, greens, purples and greys, set amidst a graceful sprawl of mirrored lakes, meres and waters, than it is about jagged peaks and breathtaking vertical drops.

Like the Japanese, another people who crowd the cities of a small, densely populated island, the English are able to foster an aesthetic that encompasses both radical excess and sophisticated refinement. Alongside the most street savvy English trends is another kind of style based on subtle distinctions of quality, texture, colour and taste. Together, they constitute what is undefinably yet unmistakably English.

THIS PAGE: Living for the weekend takes on new meaning if you are doing it out in the country.

OPPOSITE: Kayakers paddle across a glassy lake in the serene and picturesque Lake District.

...the Lake District, England's only true mountain region...

fashion + design

the london launchpad

When French first lady Carla Bruni accompanied her husband, France's President Nicholas Sarkozy, on their first state visit to England, the English press judged her entire wardrobe a diplomatic example of the entente cordiale. Nobody missed the fact that it was also an example of the far-reaching influence of English fashion ideas. All her clothes for the visit came from **Christian Dior**. But Dior's head designer, who chose and made them for her, was John Galliano, an English-boy-made-good and fashion graduate of **Central St Martins School of Art and Design**. As they like to say in England—didn't he do well.

It must be something in the water, but there is definitely a kind of catwalk madness that is particularly English and that is so contagious it regularly invades the well-established fashion houses of Paris, New York and Milan. Every year, Central St Martins, along with its stable mates at the **London's University of the Arts— Cordwainers College** and **London College of Fashion**—sends a fresh crop of world-beating designers out into the fashion realms. Besides Galliano, the triumvirate, along with the **Royal College of Art**, have also fostered the talents of such fashion wunderkinder as **Stella McCartney**, known for her relaxed shapes in beautiful fabrics, and released the mad, futuristic tailoring of **Alexander McQueen**. Rifat Ozbek, **Bruce Oldfield**—famously a favourite of Princess Diana, **Jaques Azagury**, Clements Ribeiro, Alice Temperley, loopy knitter **Julien Macdonald**,

Hussein Chalayan, milliner **Philip Treacy** and shoe designers **Jimmy Choo**, **Patrick Cox**, and **Joseph Azagury** all developed their highly distinctive styles in London.

fast forward

During the London Fashion Week shows, in September and February, the newest talents jostle to share precious catwalk time with dozens of England's well-established designers. The classics—household names such as **Ben De Lisi**, **Betty Jackson**, **Amanda Wakeley**, **Caroline Charles**, **Jaeger**, **John Rocha**, **Nicole Farhi**—can always be relied upon to offer stunning collections of grown-up elegance in gorgeous fabrics.

When she chooses to show, as she did in 2008, **Vivienne Westwood**, the doyenne of the English fashion world, can be counted upon to shake things up. But it's the younger set of designers who are the usual suspects when it comes to headline grabbing. In September 2007, enfant terrible **Gareth Pugh** sent a model down the catwalk with her head completely encased in a sparkling cube—nor is the rest of his portfolio particularly known for keeping within the bounds of practical wear. **Christopher Kane** combined the sugar-spun delicacy of beaded and paillette-spangled chiffons with heavy, cable-knit cardigans and Roman centurion sandals, while **Osman Yousefzada**'s elegantly retro, sheathed models wore bag lady knee-highs to emphasise their short skirts and bare knees. Meanwhile, fashionistas flock to the Central St Martin's MA show for a chance to witness the

school's rawest new talents before they are tamed by the commercial realities of having to sell clothes that women will actually wear.

Although access to the shows themselves is limited to retail buyers, show sponsors, the fashion press, celebrities and this year's crop of press-worthy clothes horses, the international fashion tribe, filling the clubs, cafés and shops, sets the rest of London abuzz. Special fashion events, featuring top English designers, draw the rest of us into London's most directional retailers—**Harvey Nichols** (109–125 Knightsbridge), **Liberty** (Regent Street at Great Marlborough Street), **Selfridges** (400 Oxford Street), **A La Mode** (10 Symons Street, South Kensington)—for a taste of things to come in the world of fashion.

beyond london

If London still leads in the catwalk stakes, English cities elsewhere are pulling ahead on other design fronts. Nowhere is this more apparent than in the explosion of cutting-edge architecture in the former industrial cities of the North. A new crop of 21st-century architectural visionaries are moving in on territories once held almost exclusively by Britain's world class builders **Norman Foster** and **Richard Rogers**.

Manchester, in the northwest, has been virtually transformed in the last decade, by futuristic expressions in steel and glass. **Urbis**, by architect **Ian Simpso**n, stands on an island of green where, in 1996, one of the last IRA bombs in mainland Britain ripped the heart out of Manchester's city centre. Clad in 2,200 individually

THIS PAGE (CLOCKWISE FROM TOP LEFT): Amanda Wakeley's classic style on the London catwalk in autumn 2007; backstage, a model has her makeup expertly applied just before a show; headline-making fashion from the industry's iconoclast Gareth Pugh.

OPPOSITE (CLOCKWISE FROM TOP LEFT): Head-turning stilettos from Galliano's recent Spring 2008 collection; Stella McCartney, February 2008; John Galliano exhibited at the V&A; Sarah Jessica Parker, at the Sex and the City London premiere, stays in character in McQueen and Treacy.

shaped glass units, the urban exhibition centre has a shimmering and constantly changing sculptured surface. Also rising in the city centre, Simpson's steel and glass **Beetham Tower**, at 171 m (561 ft), is Europe's tallest residential building and one of the world's thinnest skyscrapers. Reportedly, the architect himself has purchased the penthouse. Other notable Manchester structures include **Daniel Libeskind**'s **Imperial War Museum** (The Quays, Trafford), and Sussex architect **Michael Wilford**'s **Lowry Centre** along Salford Quays. The new **Manchester Civil Justice Centre**, a series of transparent, cantilevered glass boxes that are a tour de force of mind-bending physics, won Australian architects **Denton Corker Marshall** their country's highest architectural prize.

Gateshead, across the Tyne from Newcastle in the northeast, is rapidly becoming another hotspot for architectural daring. The **Gateshead Millennium Bridge**, by architects **Wilkinson Eyre**, looks a bit like a giant eyelid—especially when the bottom tilts open to allow passing marine traffic. Beside it, **Baltic**, a grain silo and flour mill converted to a huge, modern gallery by **Ellis Williams Architects**, has a constantly changing programme of exhibitions. One of the building's most striking features is a multi-story, wing-shaped fabric 'door', made of Teflon glass fabric, that slides across the façade to control light entering the galleries.

London, of course, won't be left behind for long. It adds astonishing bits and pieces to its cityscape all the time. Norman Foster's **30 St Mary**

Axe—Londoners call it the Dill Pickle and other, ruder names—looks like a rocket, about to take off from the heart of the financial district. Already, planning permission has been granted for architects **Herzog & de Meuron**'s addition to the **Tate Modern** on the South Bank, a virtual explosion of glass and structural forms that will sprout from the river side of the gallery in a converted power station. And, in Stratford East, a whole new city of stunning arenas and public venues is taking shape as London prepares for the **2012 Olympics**.

home is where the art is

Splendid architecture cries out for beautifully designed furnishings and accessories. Remarkably, 1970s style guru **Terence Conran** (The Conran Shop, 81 Fulham Road) and interior designer **Tricia Guild** (Designers Guild, 267-277 Kings Road), both of whom have influenced entire generations of nest-builders with furnishings, home accessories and fabrics, are still going strong. The bold simplicity of their signature styles are easily adaptable to the 21st century.

Newer to the scene, but already well established, is designer **Kelly Hoppen** (175-177 Fulham Road), who mixes Eastern and Western influences with a sharp, graphic edge to create striking and luxurious interiors.

For the house-proud and design-aware, a head-spinningly wide array of design genres that ranges from the fantasy shoe drawings of **Manolo Blahnik** to **Jean Prouvé**'s historic modernist furnishings are exhibited at **London's Design Museum**, at Shad Thames, beside Tower Bridge.

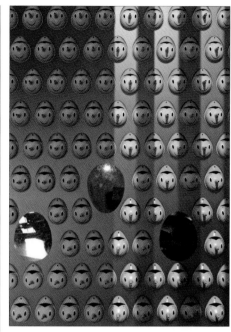

THIS PAGE (CLOCKWISE FROM TOP LEFT): Strips of light and shadow interplay on a wall hung with decorative funnels; lush fabrics from Designers Guild; Matthew Williamson at a Design Museum exhibit in October 2007.

OPPOSITE (FROM TOP): Gateshead's tilting Millennium Bridge on the Tyne; Daniel Libeskind's Imperial War Museum in Manchester.

the art scene

challenged by the britpack

To take the temperature of the contemporary art scene in England, one need only consider the annual shortlist of the ever-controversial **Turner Prize**. The prize, named after 19th-century pre-Impressionist JW Turner and organised by the **Tate** galleries (**Britain**, **Modern**, **Liverpool** and **St Ives**), can be relied upon to provoke ridicule in the tabloids and to get the so-called chattering classes into heated debate.

Works that the prize has gone to in the past include an empty room with changing lights (Martin Creed, 2001), a 24-hour Psycho in which Hitchcock's film is slowed down to fill one whole day (Douglas Gordon, 1996), collages liberally enhanced with elephant dung (Chris Ofili, 1998), animals afloat in formaldehyde (Damien Hirst, 1995), and a faithful re-creation of a well-publicised anti-war display (Mark Wallinger, 2007). In 2006 the prize even courted public controversy by being awarded to a painter (Tomma Abts), for the first time in about 10 years.

English contemporary art is often about gesture, performance and a sense of fun, with installations and video having a significant presence in the major public and private galleries, not to mention the streets. Keep a lookout for the often satirical, stencil-like graffitti creations of internationally known—yet still anonymous—**Banksy**. His work can crop up anywhere in England's cities.

It is also about craftsmanship and provocative imagery. The fleshy explorations in paint of the late **Francis Bacon** and **Lucien Freud**'s unsentimental, warts-and-all portraits virtually dare the spectator to look. Painter **Peter Doig**'s surreal images and saturated colours are like haunting, surreal dreams. Sculptor **Anish Kapoor** explores colour, surfaces and space with installations based on intense pigments, clear resin, fibreglass and mirror polished metals. In 2002, he filled the entire enormous Turbine Hall of the Tate Modern, on London's Bankside, with **Marsyas**, a genuinely awe-inspiring installation construction of coated fabric and steel frames.

With two Tate galleries (Modern and Britain, across the Thames from the Modern on Millbank) as well as several notable private galleries—Jay Jopling's **White Cube Galleries** (East at 48 Hoxton Square and West in Mason's Yard, St James's), **The Saatchi Gallery** (opening near Sloane Square on the King's Road in summer 2008) and the **Lisson Gallery** (52 -54 Bell Street)—London is a very good place to explore England's contemporary art scene. But it isn't the only place. The **Baltic** on Gateshead Quays, across from Newcastle-upon-Tyne is a huge and flexible public art space. In Birmingham, the new **IKON Gallery** in Oozell's Square, Brindleyplace, is a small gem of a venue with a singing performance art piece in the lift. And the **Tate** in Liverpool, on the Albert Docks, focuses on the contemporary art scene of the north.

the beat goes on
Classical, jazz, folk, rock, pop, dance, alternative, indie—the music scene in England is a feast and the tables are set all over the country. Tickets for

THIS PAGE (FROM TOP): The surprise of guerrilla London street art by Banksy; Anthony Gormley's Lost Horizon *at East London's White Cube Gallery.*

OPPOSITE: Acclaimed artist Damien Hirst's Beautiful, Shattered, Mellow, Exploding Paint Filled Balloons .

concerts and gigs are usually easy to get at short notice though the opera, both at **Glyndebourne** in East Sussex, and **The Royal Opera Covent Garden**, the big rock festivals and major tours of global stars, remain plan-ahead-book-ahead events.

England has at least five world class symphony orchestras—the **London Symphony Orchestra**, the **Royal Philharmonic Orchestra**, the **Royal Liverpool Philharmonic Orchestra**, the **BBC Symphony Orchestra** and the Birmingham-based **Hallé Orchestra**. There are also dozens of chamber and early music ensembles, chorales, and professional cathedral choirs. Connoisseurs of classical music are spoilt for choice, any time of the year but never more so than during the summer months when the **Royal Albert Hall** on Kensington Gore in South Kensington is taken over by the world famous concert series, the **Proms**.

International jazz stars and fans make their way to the venerable **Ronnie Scott's Jazz Club** in London's Soho for dinner and sophisticated, cool music. And jazz sets the tone for the early part of England's festival season, with a clutch of first-class jazz events on the **Isle of Wight**, in **Nantwich** near Crew in Cheshire and in **Cheltenham**.

For several decades the most directional music in Britain has come from its provincial cities. Manchester gave rise to alternative superband **Oasis**, indie singer-songwriter **Badly Drawn Boy** and pop act **Simply Red**. Also Manchester sounds—seminal 80s band **The Smiths** (and their vocalist turned solo act **Morrissey**) and rock band **The Stone Roses**. **Jimi Hendrix** busked in Newcastle which also spawned the **Animals**, glam rockers **Duran Duran** and **Sting**. And Birmingham can justifiably call itself the birthplace of heavy metal; both **Judas Priest** and **Black Sabbath** were local, Brummie bands.

Today, it's a mixture of new wave, post-punk that is pouring out of the north—**The Arctic Monkeys** from a Sheffield suburb, **The Kaiser Chiefs** from West Yorkshire. Not to be left behind, London always has something

to add to the mix—more recently **Babyshambles** (with Kate Moss's on-again-off-again bad boy squeeze Pete Doherty), **Coldplay**, dance diva **Alison Goldfrapp** and acclaimed yet troubled bluesy jazz singer **Amy Winehouse**.

By the time the bands hit the country's massive rock festivals—**Glastonbury**, **Isle of Wight**, **Bestival**, **V Festival**—they are already old news. Real trend setters keep up with this rapidly changing scene and constantly changing, coolest venues through the hip Muso mag **NME** (New Music Express) or its online blogs.

lights, camera, action

The global influence of England's film industry far exceeds its size. English actors, directors and craftspeople are familiar winners at the Oscars and the world's prestigious film festivals.

England at the movies is the character-based observations of **Mike Leigh**, the politically driven oeuvre of **Ken Loach** and the heritage industry of **Merchant Ivory**. But it is also the James Bond franchise and the light romanticism writer/director **Richard Curtis** has represented since *Four Weddings and a Funeral*. Overseas, Brit directors such as **Sam Mendes** (*The Road to Perdition*, *American Beauty*) and the late **Anthony Minghella** (*The English Patient*, *The Talented Mr Ripley*) have taken skills from British theatre to mainstream American film.

The British Film Institute's **London Film Festival** in October satisfies sophisticated international cineastes with 300 films, from 60 countries. Throughout the year, the BFI shows films in modern screening rooms, a Mediatheque and an IMAX theatre.

THIS PAGE (CLOCKWISE FROM TOP): Red carpet glory at the London Film Festival; Daniel Craig plays the latest Bond; Russian film The Banishment *at the London Film Festival in October 2007; the festive, popular last night of the BBC Proms at the Royal Albert Hall.*

OPPOSITE (CLOCKWISE FROM TOP LEFT): The Proms live broadcast in Hyde Park; the ever-glamorous Alison Goldfrapp; The Kaiser Chiefs at Glastonbury.

shopping

england puts on the style

Dedicated shophounds need never worry about suffering withdrawal pains in England. Except perhaps for the very remotest corner of the Lake District, you'd be hard-pressed to find anywhere more than half an hour away from a good selection of shops or a picturesque market.

The days when London was the only place for smart shoppers in England are history. Wherever fashionable people choose to live, there are stylish shops—and plenty of them. Since the millennium, a Chic explosion has created dozens of fashion and boutique hot spots.

Liverpool, **Leeds**, **Manchester** and **Bristol** have new or revitalised shopping areas stuffed with top national brands, the best fashion department stores, local independents and designers. The meandering lanes of **Bath**, **Chester**, **York** and **Harrogate** are studded with independent boutiques, bursting at the seams with desireable goodies. In **Brighton**, the historic area known as **The Lanes** is a maze of alleys, hidden squares and passages lined with antiques, designer jewellery, art galleries and fashion shops.

look out for...

Harvey Nichols, made world famous by the television program *Absolutely Fabulous*, has branched out and offers high fashions for men, women and the home at **The Mailbox** in Birmingham; **107-111 Briggate**, Leeds; Manchester's **Exchange Square** and, by autumn of 2008, **Bristol**. **Selfridges**, which once invited English artist Sam Taylor-Wood to wrap its

London exterior in the world's largest photograph, makes extravagant and stylish statements with its façades. Its futuristic-looking Birmingham branch, in **The Bullring**, is based on a 1960s Paco Rabanne dress. Selfridges' winning retail concept mixes mid-market goods, gourmet food halls and wine selections with selected top designer collections.

If they don't have their own shops in a town, English luxury brands set out their wares in departments of the best local stores. Keep an eye out for **Mulberry** leathers—belts, bags, luggage and accessories for men and women in edible, colours—as well as scarves and brilliantly flash sunglasses styled for them by legendary London maker **Cutler&Gross**. Try **Jo Malone**'s fragrances and candles, packed in black and white. **Links** of London, in the best shopping areas around the country, sells modern gold and silver, set with the occasional gemstone. **Boodles**' dazzling gems—fancy a 21-carat sapphire for £116,000?—are available in Chester, Manchester and Liverpool as well as London.

Burberry, one of England's largest luxury brands, with a flagship at 157-167 Regent Street and **Aquascutum**, across the road at number 100, both about 150 years old, have added to their collections upmarket, up-to-the-minute luxury fashions well worth seeking out. There's not a hint of the familiar tan, red and black Burberry check in Prorsum (the Latin means forward), the modern, wearable line by Royal College of Art designer Christopher Bailey. The menswear is often more adventurous than the women's collections. And alongside

its sturdy and reliable trademark raincoats, **Aquascutum** (since 2005) is showing two collections—a year of colourful, structured suits, dresses and coats. In various shops around the country, look for **Fenn Wright and Manson**, **English Eccentrics** and **Nicole Farhi** ready-to-wear as well.

bespoke in britain

Having clothes, sporting accessories, jewels and lingerie custom made, or bespoke as they say, is not a quaint, charmingly Edwardian service in England. Nor is it dying out, as it has in other world centres in the West. In fact, bespoke is growing in popularity, with more available than for many years. **Aquascutum**, for example, recently added personal tailoring for women the first time. And the traditional suit and shirt makers of **Jermyn Street** and **Savile Row** are welcoming stylish women customers into their hushed shops and fitting rooms. A new generation of chic consumers is discovering the refined pleasures of being personally looked after by a tailor, a perfumier or a private dressmaker.

It is possible to be outfitted top to toe—and from the skin out—in bespoke garments. **James Lock & Co** at 6 St James' Street in London, a traditional men's hatmaker that has been in business since 1676, has a new designer making bespoke women's hats. Custom-fitted smalls? Some bespoke shirtmakers will create boxers for Sir while women can buy made to measure lingerie from the Queen's favourite, **Rigby & Peller** (2 Hans Road, Knightsbridge and 22A Conduit Street, Mayfair).

THIS PAGE (CLOCKWISE FROM TOP): Home of Birmingham's Selfridges, The Bullring echoes a 60s Paco Rabanne dress; late-night shopping in London; exclusive, 19th-century Burlington Arcade, located in London's Mayfair.

OPPOSITE: Icon of a reinvented London classic—Burberry in Knightsbridge.

THIS PAGE (CLOCKWISE FROM RIGHT): *Choice designer togs from London-based roubi l'roubi's latest collection; a roubi l'roubi handbag in bold red; the line-up of tailors on Savile Row.*

OPPOSITE (FROM LEFT): *Street market style can go straight to shoppers' heads; the arcade at Covent Garden Market.*

Designer **Ozwald Boateng** (30 Savile Row, London) became one of the exclusive Savile Row community of bespoke tailors in the mid-nineties (in the arctic pace of the street, he's still seen as the new kid in town) and immediately began to shake up the place with sharp modern styles in brilliant colours and exclusive fabrics. The look, as seen on Jamie Foxx in the 2006 Hollywood blockbuster *Miami Vice*, is anything but traditional.

There are shoes—**John Lobb** on Jermyn Street or **Caroline Groves** (by appointment only in London's West End); colourful women's suits and sexy, red-carpet dresses from City of London-based, exotic private designer **roubi l'roubi** (13 Norton Folgate); the irresistibly pretty bespoke bikinis of **Biondi** in Chelsea (55B Old Church Street), and luggage custom made—to fit the boot of the Aston Martin or the rack of the Morgan perhaps?—by the traditional British purveyors of leather goods **Swaine Adeney Brigg** (54 St James's Street, London).

the buzz on the street

London's markets—**Portobello Road, Camden Locks, Spitalfields, Brick Lane**—are laboratories of street style, humming with the next hot catwalk trends. Savvy designers are inspired by them; fashion students sell their fledging efforts in them. **Borough Market**, named the best market in Britain by a national newspaper, is where the southeast's foodies buy hand-dived scallops from Cornwall, Spanish Pata Negra ham, English wild fish and game, handmade chocolates and cheeses driven up from Italy's Piedmont that very morning.

Most English towns have equally colourful street markets. In an age of global multiples, they are refreshing outlets for individuality and quirky enterprise. Forget what's on sale— half the fun is the buzz.

Jewellery designers, fashion shops, and a wonderful dried flower seller share **Oxford Covered Market** with sloping piles of fruit and vegetables— produce doesn't get much fresher than this—fishmongers, cheesemongers and ethnic grocers. In **York**'s market square a vendor sells traditional Yorkshire flat caps to trendy young girls and old geezers alike. The **Rag Market** in Birmingham, where today exquisite wedding saris are for sale, has been in the same place for 700 years. At **Swaffham**'s Saturday market in Norfolk, you'll find plucked pheasant and French cheeses alongside plastic bins and cheap CDs. In **Lincoln**, **York**, **Bath** and **Birmingham**, Christmas markets sparkle after dark through November and December.

eat + drink

In the 21st century, the English attitude towards food and the quality of their restaurant dining have undergone a revolutionary change. Nothing could be more dated than the old European joke in which Hell was a place where the chefs were British. Today, British chef-owners regularly make it onto international lists of the world's top dining establishments.

The **Roux brothers**, **Albert** and **Michel**, led an avant garde of French chef-patrons who woke the British palate up in the late 1960s. Michel's Michelin-starred **Waterside Inn** remains a top dining destination. **Raymond Blanc**, another pioneer, opened his romantic hotel/restaurant, **Le Manoir aux Quat' Saisons**, in the mid 1980s. While earning several Michelin stars himself, he helped to train a new generation of British chefs who have taken exceptional dining across the country. **Paul Heathcote** (**The Longridge** near Preston, Lancashire), **John Burton-Race** (**The New Angel** in Dartmouth, Devon) and **Michael Caines** (chef-director of **Gidleigh Park** in Devon), count amongst them.

At Bray, a tiny village which is—for its size—prodigiously blessed with great restaurants, **Heston Blumenthal** cooks up experiments in **The Fat Duck**. *Restaurant Magazine* regularly selects Blumenthal for the top of its list of the top 50 restaurants in the world.

In 2007, he placed second for his scientific cuisine. In 2008, adventurous diners might find salmon poached in liquorice gel, artichokes and vanilla mayonnaise or 'Nitro-scrambled' egg and bacon ice cream with pain perdu and tea jelly on his tasting menu.

When he isn't bawling out other chefs, would-be chefs or soon-to-be-ex-chefs on his television outings, the infamously profane Oxford United footballer turned chef/entrepreneur **Gordon Ramsey** supervises a small empire of restaurants, including the eponymous ones on **Royal Hospital Road** and at **Claridges**, as well as **Boxwood Café**, **Maze**, **The Maze Grill**, **Petrus**, **Foxtrot Oscar** and **Plane Food**, in Heathrow's new Terminal 5. Menus are modern British with continental influences—roast Barbary duck breast with creamed Savoy cabbage, quince, chestnuts and Madeira jus; roast wild Scottish halibut with Cromer crab, caviar, crushed new potatoes and a basil vinaigrette.

Rick Stein owns four restaurants and an inn in the Cornish seaside town of **Padstow**, having reintroduced the English to the riches of their own waters. Fresh locally caught seafood—oysters, smoked eels, langoustines, scallops, squid, monk fish, sea bass and gurnard—gets an international treatment on the original menu of his simply named **Seafood Restaurant**. Recent selections included Singapore chilli crab; hot shellfish with parsley, chilli, olive oil, garlic and lemon juice; monkfish Vindaloo, Plateau de Fruits de Mer, char-grilled Dover sole and locally caught cod and chips.

In the Midlands, chef-patron **Andreas Antona**, together with his executive chef **Luke Tipping**, has earned Michelin stars for **Simpsons** in Edgbaston, Birmingham. And **J Baker's Bistro Moderne**—with its emphasis on a grazing menu of simple food—has helped turn York into one of the top dining cities in England.

THIS PAGE (FROM TOP): Seafood magnate Rick Stein is based in Padstow; Gordon Ramsay is as feared by his underperforming kitchen staff for his notorious temper as he is loved by gastronomes for his cooking.

OPPOSITE (CLOCKWISE FROM TOP LEFT): Heston Blumenthal fuses hard science and the culinary arts at The Fat Duck; the romantic and elegant Le Manoir aux Quat' Saisons in Oxfordshire; Raymond Blanc is a pioneering chef who has also trained other young up-and-coming stars in the industry.

museums + galleries

Archaeologists, explorers, aesthetes and eccentrics followed in the wake of England's merchant and military empire builders. The storehouses of treasure they carried home are now showcased in some of the world's greatest museums.

The **British Museum**, located in Bloomsbury, is the controversial guardian of the **Elgin Marbles**, a set of classical Greek marble sculptures originally from the Parthenon; also the **Rosetta Stone**, a vital artefact in hieroglyphic studies; a Babylonian tablet recording a delivery of gold to King Nebuchadnezzar; the elaborate wrappings of Egyptian mummies, and thousands of other fascinating objects illuminating human history by theme, location or culture.

Just a few miles away, in South Kensington's **Victoria and Albert Museum**, applied art and design exhibits include costumes and couture fashion, textiles, jewellery and decorative objects. Stop for tea to enjoy the **Green Dining Room**, extravagantly decorated in ceramic tiles by **William Morris & Co**, with painted panels and stained glass by **Edward Burne-Jones**. A Dale Chihuly chandelier in the entrance hall is a striking reminder that the museum is renowned for its glass collection. Look out for the tiny **Frost Fair mug**, a souvenir from a fair held on the Thames ice when the river froze in 1683. Visit **The National Gallery** on Trafalgar Square for an encyclopaedic tour of Western European painting, and the **Tate** establishment (**Tate Britain**, **Tate Modern**, **Tate Liverpool** and **Tate St Ives**) for the national collections of British art.

The smaller galleries reflect the various collecting passions of private individuals and families. In **Somerset House**, off The Strand, **The Courtauld Gallery**'s selection of impressionists and post-impressionists includes **Edouard Manet**'s iconic paintings *The Bar at the Folies Bergere* and *Dejeuner sur l'herbe*. And there is something that is almost intimate in the way the **Wallace Collection** of 18th-century French paintings, furniture, porcelain, Old Masters paintings and even sets of antique arms and armour are all crammed into an unprepossessing townhouse in the West End.

Not all of the best museums and galleries are found in London. The 19th-century industrial tycoons of the Midlands had a taste for the romantic and decorative. As a result, alongside Canalettos, Gainsboroughs, Picassos and Lowrys, **The Birmingham Museum and Art Gallery**, in the city centre, boasts the world's largest collection of Pre-Raphaelite works. The **IKON Gallery**, in Birmingham's canalside Brindleyplace district, hosts eclectic exhibitions of contemporary art reached via a singing lift, itself a performance art installation.

The prestigious universities of Oxford and Cambridge both have world-class museums. For example, Oxford's **Ashmolean Museum** is one of Britain's oldest. Its wonderfully wide-ranging collection of art and antiquities includes the **Alfred Jewel**, a gold, enamel and rock crystal ornament with links to Anglo-Saxon King Alfred the Great. **The Fitzwilliam** in Cambridge holds highly extensive collections of Chinese, Japanese and European art and antiquities.

Kettle's Yard house, located in Cambridge, is the kind of eccentric small gallery that lucky visitors can stumble across in England. Once the home of Jim Ede, a former Tate curator, it houses his 20th-century English and European art collection, mostly acquired through personal friendships. In 1966, Ede left both the house and his collection to the university. The gallery has been extended from the original private dwelling, but it still maintains its charmingly informal atmosphere. Knock on the door most afternoons and you can have a look around.

THIS PAGE (FROM TOP): The V&A Museum is a South Kensington landmark; an intimate encounter with the Old Masters at the Wallace Collection.

OPPOSITE (CLOCKWISE FROM TOP LEFT): The legendary Rosetta Stone—a highlight of the British Museum's collection; the V&A's focus is fashion and design; The British Museum in Bloomsbury.

stately homes

For sheer quantity alone, England's historic houses and stately homes are unique in Europe. There are châteaux in the Loire but they are little more than unoccupied museums. There are also magnificent private homes in Italy and Switzerland. But no place else in Europe has so many historic estates with original furnishings and art collections intact, surrounded by magnificent gardens and visitor attractions, that are open for viewing to the public yet often still occupied by the families who built them.

Perhaps several hundred years of a stable monarchy may have had something to do with it but it is probably also a general tradition of greedy nosiness about how the most stylish people live that has made the English such enthusiastic protectors of their great houses. As early as the 18th century, practically any 'person of fashion' or status, could drop in on a stately home—to be shown around by the housekeeper—whether or not the owners were in residence at the time. When Elizabeth Bennet and her aunt and uncle first visit Pemberley, Mr Fitzwilliam Darcy's country estate, in Jane Austen's beloved classic *Pride and Prejudice*, it is on just such a sightseeing excursion.

The original owners of England's stately homes were looked upon as the trendsetters of their own periods. Their myriad personal contributions to the evolution of style and fashion in the country make visiting the grand homes they created an unexpectedly chic diversion. In addition, a number of them offer exclusive out-of-hours and behind-the-scenes private tours. Here's just a small selection:

Was it Mr Darcy or his house? Jane Austen ensured that we were never absolutely certain of what clinched the romance for Lizzy and Darcy but when the BBC made its classic version in 1995, the producers must have plumped for the house, because they chose the jaw-droppingly gorgeous **Lyme Park** in Cheshire to stand in for Pemberley. Originally a Tudor hunting lodge, it was turned into an Italianate Palazzo in the 18th century by the Venetian architect, Leoni. It's filled with 17th-century tapestries, English clocks and entire rooms of carved panelling by famed 18th-century woodcarver Grinling Gibbons. Lived in as a family home until 1942, it is now owned by the National Trust, who will arrange exclusive, out-of-hours tours.

At their elegant Bakewell seat in Derbyshire, **Chatsworth**, the Dukes of Devonshire have spent more than 400 years building one of the best private art collections in Europe, and they've been inviting the public to the house and grounds of Chatsworth to see it almost since the day the house was completed in the early 17th century.

The Devonshires are definitely not collectors of the old and dusty. Every generation have been patrons of contemporary work. The current and 12th Duke of Devonshire is no exception. In 2006, he joined with Sotheby's to stage a sale of major modern and contemporary sculpture around the gardens and the splendid waterworks. A Niki de St Phalle Nana cavorted on the lawns, *Le Cheval majeur* by Raymond Duchamp-Villon overlooked a pond and Robert Indiana's *LOVE* in giant pink and blue

THIS PAGE (FROM TOP): The painted hall at Chatsworth is an indication of the art treasures scattered throughout; the grounds of England's stately homes often feature fine sculpture.

OPPOSITE: A tree-lined avenue at Chatsworth House invites strolls.

stately homes

THIS PAGE (FROM TOP): Castle Howard's restored dome, the first to ever grace a private home in Britain; Woburn Abbey, where afternoon tea is said to have been invented.

OPPOSITE: The Queen Anne library at Blenheim Palace is an impressive space that combines comfort with a luxurious air of grand tradition.

letters was installed in the estate's famous cascade. Beyond Limits, a similar show in 2007, included Marc Quinn's *Sphinx*, a statue of Kate Moss in an extreme yoga pose, and Damien Hirst's pregnant *Virgin Mother*.

The Duke likes to poke around the estate chatting with visitors, who can regularly mistake him for a grounds keeper. Your chances of encountering the Duke of Devonshire, unbeknownst, are pretty good.

There has to be a certain cachet in taking afternoon tea where this quintessentially English meal was invented. Back in the 1840s, the then Duchess of Bedford, chatelaine of **Woburn Abbey**, decided the wait between lunch and dinner was too long for her house guests, so she began the custom of a light meal in the late afternoon. Woburn Abbey, in Bedfordshire, is still the family home of the 15th Duke and Duchess of Bedford as well as a grand estate where you can play championship golf, admire the Canalettos, have a spectacular private party, shop for antiques in the biggest antique centre outside of London and, yes, take afternoon tea.

If **Castle Howard**, on the edge of York, seems vaguely familiar, perhaps you've already been there before—at the movies, or on the telly. One of England's most spectacular homes— and, remarkably it still is the home of the Howard family—the house has been used as the backdrop of several landmark dramas, including Peter Ustinov's *Lady L* with Paul Newman and Sophia Loren, Stanley Kubrick's *Barry Lyndon*, and *Brideshead Revisited*, the 1980s British television classic. A remake of *Brideshead* set for cinema release in October 2008 has, once again, used this astonishing house as a backdrop. Where but in England could you find a family home owned by 'commoners' that took 100 years to build and has its own artist-in-residence?

Blenheim Palace, in Woodstock, Oxfordshire, has long been associated with heroes. John Churchill, the first Duke of Marlborough, was given the house by Queen Anne, in the early 18th century, for winning a famous victory over the French in the Spanish Wars of Succession. A more modern Churchill hero, Winston, was born at Blenheim Palace. When built, the social-climbing Duchess was so keen to ensure she obtained the best of everything that, eventually, the Queen grew tired of paying for it all. Nevertheless, Blenheim stands as testament to the height of fashion (circa 1705), devised by English architect Vanbrugh and Capability Brown. Today it is both a UNESCO World Heritage Site and the family home of the Dukes of Marlborough.

Waddesdon Manor, situated near Aylesbury, Buckinghamshire, on the other hand, only looks like it has centuries of history. Baron Ferdinand de Rothschild built the faux French Renaissance château in the late 19th century to use as a play house for weekending with his friends. Drop by to admire the 18th-century Sèvres porcelain and furniture, the paintings by Reynolds and Gainsborough. Then stay to for a wine tasting or a wine and food matching masterclass featuring the Rothschild wines that are always available in the estates shops and restaurants.

the season

The English are very specific about the way they use their native tongue. Trousers are not pants, nor are they slacks. Buying cream involves choices among pouring cream, jersey cream, whipping cream, spooning cream, clotted cream—and more. So when the English upper classes talk about The Season, you may take for granted they're not referring to meteorological phenomena. The Season identifies a particular series of sporting events, social occasions and exhibitions that take place between May and the end of July, mostly concentrated in London and the Home Counties.

The Season is a holdover from the Victorian era when members of English high society moved from their country houses to the city for socialising, entertaining, discreet marriage brokering and, for the men, an annual visit to one's tailor, a spot of horse trading or a casual wager on a rowing team. The 100-day season was meant to take advantage of the best London weather, before the noisome Thames made hanging around London well-nigh unbearable in the August heat.

The Thames is cleaner these days and there are other smart events in other parts of the country throughout the year. But the tradition carries on, blending parties and balls with a set of public events at which English and European society, social wannabes and almost anyone so inclined, can show off their finery, mingle with royals and make the most of the sunshine—if it comes and while it lasts.

The season gets underway in early May when the **Glyndebourne Festival Opera** opens on an estate in

Lewes, East Sussex. By the time the Royal Horticultural Society's **Chelsea Flower Show** begins (Chelsea Royal Hospital, London SW3) in late May, the season is in full swing. Also in May, the **Royal Windsor Horseshow** in the private Home Park of Windsor Castle—Her Majesty usually attends—and a flurry of gala charity balls.

Royal Ascot, the world-famous flat racing meet over five days in June, occurs at the midpoint of the season. **Ascot Racecourse** (Ascot, Berkshire) was established in 1711 by Queen Anne, and royals have supported thoroughbred racing here for almost 300 years. Her Majesty Queen Elizabeth is certainly no exception. The Queen and other members of the royal family arrive in great ceremony in open carriages. **Ladies' Day**, Thursday of Royal Ascot, is when millinery takes the spotlight.

June also sees the running of the **Derby** at **Epsom Downs** (Surrey), **Wimbledon Tennis Championships** (The All England Lawn Tennis Club, London SW19) and the Royal Academy's **Summer Exhibition** (Burlington House, Piccadilly, London), a huge juried art show and sale.

Come July and it's the **Henley Royal Regatta** (Henley-on-Thames), a rowing event that's as much about champagne picnics as it is about sport. At month's end, the Queen watches the Prince of Wales play polo at the **Cartier International Polo** held in her own backyard, Windsor Great Park.

Glorious Goodwood (Goodwood Racecourse, Chichester, Sussex), five days of flat racing at the end of July, traditionally marks the end of The Season and a last chance for summery dressing up until next year.

THIS PAGE (CLOCKWISE FROM TOP): Crowds line the banks of the Thames for the Henley Royal Regatta in July; the Chelsea Flower Show in May; everyone's an art critic at the Royal Academy's Summer Exhibition.
OPPOSITE: Roger Federer sees off Rafael Nadal at Wimbledon Centre Court.

london

Westway A40

Paddington

Paddington

Paddington Station

Eastbourne Terrace

Edgware Road

Edgware Road

> The Caesar
> The Royal Park

Lancaster Gate

Bayswater Road

Marylebone

Gloucester Place

Baker Street

Portland Place

Mortimer Street

Goodge St

Tottenham Court Road

> Artesian at The Langham
> The Landau at the Langham
> Brown's Hotel

Tottenham Court Road

Oxford Street

Oxford Circus

Bond Street

Marble Arch

Grosvenor Square

New Bond Street

Old Bond Street

Albemarle Street

Regent Street

Soho

Shaftesbury Avenue

Mayfair

Picadilly Circus

Hyde Park

The Long Water

The Serpentine

The Round Pond

Kensington Gardens

Park Lane

Park Lane

WoBo

Shepherd Market

St James's

Sofitel London St James <

Carlton House Terrace

The Metropolitan <
The Athenaeum <
Theo Randall at the InterContinental <
London Park Lane

Old Park Lane

Piccadilly

Hyde Park Corner

Green Park

The Mall

St James's Park

Kensington Road

Knightsbridge

Knightsbridge

Buckingham Palace

Westminster

St James' Park

Buckingham Gate

> 51 Buckingham Gate

South Kensington

Sloane Street

Victoria Street

> The Gore
> Number Sixteen

Brompton Road

Victoria + Albert Museum

Jumeirah Lowndes Hotel <
The Cadogan Hotel <
Draycott Hotel <

Pont Street

Cromwell Road

Gloucester Road

Gloucester Road

South Kensington

Old Brompton Road

Cadogan Street

Sloane Square

City of London

Moorgate

Moorgate

Liverpool Street

Liverpool Street

London Wall

Andaz Liverpool Street London <

Old Broad Street

Bishopsgate

> The Cranley
> Sydney House Chelsea

Fulham Road

Sydney Street

Chelsea

King's Road

Bank

Threadneedle Street

0 km   0.45   0.9 km

N

Legend

Highways
Main Road
Other Road
Water
Park
Underground Line
Underground Station

0 km   0.4   0.8   1.2 km

london

global confluence

People from all over the world have been drawn to London for nearly 2,000 years. When the Romans, nominal founders of the city, marched up to the Thames at a strategic crossing point near the current site of London Bridge, they found tribes of Britons already trading there at a primitive market fair. The spot, known as Borough, has been a market ever since. It may have changed with the times and fashions and moved a few hundred yards this way or that, but Borough Market, London's oldest food market, is today one of England's trendiest sources of ingredients for chefs, gourmet shoppers, and grazing tourists.

Angles, Saxons, Danes and Normans followed the Romans and the international influx has never stopped. London's current population of 7.5 million includes about 2.2 million people born abroad. One in every four Londoners is from an ethnic minority. At least 300 different languages are spoken, and more than 50 different national cuisines are served in London restaurants. Since the last census, Eastern Europeans from an expanded European Union have made London an even more cosmopolitan city.

faces of london

Visitors and Londoners alike will often notice a village-like atmosphere in different parts of London—especially when it comes to the various residential districts. This is not a nostalgic or literary illusion. Historically, London as an entity spread outward rather than upward, incorporating neighbouring towns and villages as it expanded in its ever-growing sprawl. The process explains a lot about London, from the way it looks to its host of myriad personalities. The city is actually still a collection of separately governed local communities, as opposed to being a cohesive whole. Unlike other capital cities of comparable status such as New York and Paris, where the mayor is a powerful gubernatorial and civic figure who represents the city on the world stage, London has only had a real mayor—as opposed to a ceremonial one—since the millennium, and the role is still being defined today.

The way London developed also accounts for its variegated skyline, a multi-persona of jagged peaks and low-roofed townhouses. With the exception of the financial centre—called The City—and its millennial adjuncts Canary Wharf and the Docklands, skyscrapers are a rarity in London. Less rare are parks and open areas, corners of fresh verdure and breathing spaces in this hectic

THIS PAGE: Borough Market is London's oldest food market and also one of its trendiest.

PAGE 40: An enduring London icon—the red double-decker.

city. London has a grand total of eight royal parks, 3,240 hectares (8,000 acres) of public parkland and hundreds of private garden squares. It also has pockets of style, chic districts and cool neighbourhoods—each with its own atmosphere and its own 'tribe' of locals—scattered all over its 1,580 sq km (609 sq miles).

Notting Hill and Holland Park have their Yummy Mummies, such as Gwyneth Paltrow, who emerge from their rows of dazzling white townhouses for a leisurely spot of lunch and some boho-chic shopping in the tiny, exclusive boutiques that dot the fringes of Portobello Road and its immediate surrounds. Over on the King's Road, Chelsea's Trustafarians (an ironic term for the area's privileged youths who immerse themselves in the various latest 'causes') do the Saturday promenade, window shopping, checking out each other's style and stopping into the local pubs for a gossip or a rehash of the latest charity event. Fashionistas wear their shoes out dipping in and out of international designer shops in Knightsbridge and Mayfair.

In Westminster, civil servants and politicians dodge tourists in a series of intricate manoeuvres, all part of the local scene. This is iconic London—the city of Big Ben, Buckingham Palace, Westminster Abbey. It's the heart of royal, ceremonial and official London. For first-timers, it is irresistible, but perhaps also a little bit predictable.

into the millennium

Cross the Thames from Westminster, where the London Eye rises up to signal the post-millennial revival of the Southbank, and 21st-century London gets well and truly underway. The South Bank, a concentration of national theatres, concert halls, art galleries and film theatres, once nearly sank under the weight of its 1960s brutalist architecture. Since 1999, when the first grim, windswept concrete walkway was demolished, hundreds of millions of pounds have been spent transforming the riverfront centre and its buildings (£111 million on the Royal Festival Hall alone).

THIS PAGE AND OPPOSITE: Tower Bridge stands guard at the entrance to the Pool of London, the deepest stretch of the Thames, while Norman Foster's London Assembly Building is one of the city's newest landmarks.

Today, the cluster of arts venues starts as a lively riverside promenade of restaurants, cafés, shops, outdoor amphitheatres and terraces, that stretches from Waterloo Bridge, eastward past the Tate Modern and Shakespeare's Globe Theatre in Southwark to London City Hall, the glass-clad work of architect Norman Foster, which some have compared to an egg and some to a Jaguar headlamp.

Foster's influence is much in evidence in this part of London. His Millennium Bridge, modelled, he said, after a bridge of light he remembered from old Flash Gordon serials, sweeps across the river from the Tate Modern to the St Paul's, Christopher Wren's masterpiece. Rising up beside it in this snapshot view of The City (the financial district) is one of the newest additions to the London skyline, Foster's 30 St Mary Axe. Also known as the Swiss Re Buildings, most Londoners refer to this rocket shaped tower, covered in swirling lines of glass panels, as The Gherkin.

all eyes east

Fashionable London's centre of gravity, once found west of St Paul's, has lately been tipping east with revivals of the once run-down districts that ring The City. In the 1990s, young professionals discovered the spacious lofts of Clerkenwell, and a swell of restaurants, nightclubs and art galleries were close on their heels. Now, a wide swath of hip, arty and only slightly gentrified districts stretches eastward along Clerkenwell Road and Old Street with concentrations of cafés, shops and bars in Hoxton Square, around Shoreditch and Whitechapel, Spitalfields and Bethnal Green. Where West London's style is sleek and expensive, East London's is rough-edged, urban, young and alternative—but getting more expensive all the time.

The march eastward continues along the Thames Estuary. Canary Wharf, a post-modern city of towers, links the old City with the new Docklands area. Developments sprout like swift-growing mushrooms amidst the converted warehouses and wharves. North of the Thames, the Docklands Light Railway, its stations looking more like space ports than extensions of the London Underground, connects hotspots that are still in the process of coalescing into the London of the future. And, south of the river, within sight of it all, the 2012 Olympic Park will soon begin to rise.

Visitors who can pry themselves way from London's insistent history will find a capital of directional style-with-attitude; where art, architecture, design, theatre and music are always on the boil and where the next big thing changes faster than the traffic lights in Piccadilly Circus.

THIS PAGE (FROM TOP): Nightlife in London often begins the same way it does in countless other towns around the country—with a pint in one's local pub; bright neon colours reflected in the windows of a black cab crossing Piccadilly Circus, heart of the entertainment district.

OPPOSITE: 30 St Mary Axe, one of Norman Foster's contributions to modern London's skyline.

...one of the newest additions to the London skyline...

up west vs out east

Whatever else changes about London, the **West End**—along with nearby West London districts such as **Mayfair** and **Knightsbridge**—still has a firm hold on its position as the glittering centre of chic and expensive nightlife. During the day, **Soho**, **Covent Garden** and **Shaftsbury Avenue**, which make up the majority of the West End, are at the epicentre of London's glamour industries—television, film, music, magazine publishing, theatre and advertising. Come nightfall, this is where the A-list and the fashionable crowd drink, dine and dance when they are in look-at-me mode.

Dinner, in the dining room of an award-winning chef, or at a popular celebrity haunt requires booking well in advance. Try one of Gordon Ramsay's restaurants, such as **Petrus** (Wilton Place, Knightsbridge SW1) or **Maze** (10–13 Grosvenor Square, W1), Richard Corrigan's **Lindsay House** (21 Romilly Street, Soho), or **Tom Aikens Restaurant** (34 Elystan Street, Chelsea, SW3). At **The Ivy** (1–5 West Street, WC2), **Scotts** (20 Mount Street, W1)—where Ian Fleming is said to have witnessed his first Martini 'shaken, not stirred'— and **Sketch** (9 Conduit Street, W1), the people-watching is just as important, if not more so, as the food.

Stylish drinks and dancing is late (after 10.00 pm or even midnight) and often in members-only bars: **Annabels** (44 Berkeley Sq, W1), **Chinawhite** (6 Air Street, W1), **Met Bar** (The Metropolitan, Old Park Lane, W1), **Kitts** (7–12 Sloane Sq, SW1), or **The Glade** at Sketch.

Exclusivity is the byword at these places, but the best hotel concierges can usually see that guests get on the door lists. Otherwise, there's no membership requirement for **The Light Bar** at **Asia de Cuba**, (45 St Martin's Lane) and the DJs Thursday through Saturday are among London's best and the scene is jumping until 3.00 am every night but Sunday.

London's East End scene is as different from the West End as day is from night. What nightlife there is in **Hoxton**, **Clerkenwell** and **Shoreditch**, is casual, gritty and local. Here, the chic scene is a daylit phenomenon—a cruise of the galleries filling the 19th-century warehouses and factories of Clerkenwell, 17th-century almshouses and the madhouses of Hoxton and Shoreditch. This neighbourhood is one of the most happening areas for contemporary art in Europe.

The intersection of Clerkenwell Road and Farringdon Road is a SoHo-like concentration of contemporary art spaces. From **The Eagle Gallery/ EMH Arts** (159 Farringdon Road), turn onto Clerkenwell Close for **Hoopers Gallery** (5), then Clerkenwell Road for **Rainbird Fine Art** (114) and on to Great Sutton Street for the **Kowalsky Gallery** at **Dacs** (33). Further east, Clerkenwell morphs into Hoxton and Shoreditch— there's the **Whitecross Gallery** (122 Whitecross Street) and **Flowers East** (82 Kingsland Road). The glass-roofed **White Cube**, where it all began in Hoxton Square in 2000, has a policy of one exhibition per artist, ever— even among such contemporary BritArt stars as the Chapman Brothers, Gilbert and George, and Mona Hatoum. Owner Jay Jopling recently bridged the divide between the East End and traditional West End fine arts by opening a **White Cube** in **Mason's Yard**, St James.

THIS PAGE (FROM TOP): Anthony Gormley's Firmament at Hoxton's White Cube; Paolo Giardi's Why Can't I Be You at Clerkenwell's White Cross Gallery; the exclusive Met Bar on Park Lane; magenta and fuchsia lighting sets the mood at Kitts, Sloane Square.

OPPOSITE: The exceptionally slick and popular Light Bar at Asia de Cuba.

london theatre

Every season, at least one Hollywood star makes a London theatrical debut, accompanied by a great commotion in the press. If British actors covet roles on Broadway for the exposure to the lucrative American market, American film and television actors crave roles in London's West End for the legitimacy it offers their careers.

The British take their 500-year-plus theatre tradition seriously and support it in both commercial and subsidised theatres, auditoriums and intimate fringe venues. Nowhere in England is this more evident than in London where a record-breaking 12.35 million people attended plays in the West End in 2006.

The area has been London's theatre district since 1663 when the first theatre opened on Drury Lane. That was a mere three years after the Restoration of theatre-loving monarch Charles II and the lifting of Cromwell's theatre ban. The first theatre on Drury Lane featured the King's mistress, Nell Gwyn among its stars. The oldest theatre still in operation, the **Theatre Royal Haymarket**, dates from 1720.

Now calling itself Theatreland, the West End is the prime Central London district for mainstream, commercial theatre. Forty theatres are located in an area centred on Shaftsbury Avenue, bounded by The Strand to the south, Oxford Street to the north, Regent Street on the west and Kingsway to the east. Hotel concierges should be able to make recommendations and organise tickets. Or make a stop by **TKTS**, the only freestanding building in Leicester Square, where The Society of London Theatres sells half-price and last-minute tickets.

Find newer, more daring work in the subsidised or sponsored theatres, scattered around London. **The Royal Court**, is a writing venue in Sloane Square, Chelsea, that claims to have launched modern British theatre with John Osborne's Look Back in Anger in the 1960s. Kevin Spacey is the artistic director of **The Old Vic** at The Cut, Waterloo, where new productions alternate with challenging revivals. Just along the road, **The Young Vic** (66 The Cut, Waterloo, SE1) showcases younger artists in a flexible new theatre space. **The Almeida**, off Upper Street in Islington (Almeida Street, N1), started off as a lecture hall where Egyptian mummies were first shown in London, then taking subsequent turns as a music hall and then a derelict building. Now the theatre space hosts some of London's most exciting work. While in the heart of the West End, the 250-seat **Donmar Warehouse** in Covent Garden (41 Earlham Street) is where Oscar-winning director Sam Mendes served as artistic director before launching his Hollywood career.

On the South Bank, the **National Theatre** complex is England's repertory showcase for major productions of new work, experimental theatre and classic revivals. Top international and British acting talent perform on three separate stages—the **Olivier**, the **Littleton** and the 300-seat **Cottlesloe**. About half a mile further east on Bankside, **Shakespeare's Globe Theatre**, near the Tate Modern, is an accurate reconstruction of an Elizabethan theatre staging open-air productions of the Bard as well as other period and modern writers.

THIS PAGE (FROM TOP): The National Theatre complex on the South Bank; 2007 revival of the classic Boeing Boeing at the Comedy Theatre.

OPPOSITE (FROM TOP LEFT): Hairspray, The Musical onstage at the Shaftsbury; Dirty Butterfly, an example of new, exciting writing at the Young Vic; the feel-good factor comes into play with a production of crowd-pleaser Grease at The Piccadilly Theatre.

london shopping

Where you shop in London depends on your shopping style—or at least your shopping style for the day. For European designer brands, head for **Sloane Street**, heading north from Sloane Square towards **Harvey Nichols'** corner (109-125 Knightsbridge). **Prada** (43–45), **Giorgio Armani** (37–39), **Dior** (29), **Marni** (26), **Fendi** (20–22) and **Gucci** (18) line the west side of the street. Cross over for **Yves Saint Laurent** (172), **Valentino** (174), **Dolce & Gabbana** (175), **Hermes** (179), **Versace** (183–184), and English designer **Nicole Farhi** (193). The collection of fashion shoe and luxury leather shops tucked in between may be one of the best in the world. Try A-list party girl's choice **Giuseppe Zanotti** (49) or the avant-garde styles at **Walter Steiger** (48).

Of the major department stores, the venerable **Liberty** (on the corner of Great Marlborough Street and Regent Street) is a dark horse. Behind its Arts and Crafts façade, its elaborate carved lintels and stained-glass windows, is one of the best places to find new designers, directional fashion and one-of-a-kind accessories for both men and women.

An instinct for personality-driven fashion will lead shoppers to **Mayfair** where British designers **Vivienne Westwood** (44 Conduit Street) and **Alexander McQueen** (4–5 Old Bond Street), as well as their international coevals **Donna Karan** (new flagship, 46 Conduit Street) and **Issey Miyake** (52 Conduit Street) all have boutiques. The array of jewellers along **Old and New Bond Streets** is just blinding. On the west side of New Bond Street, (163–180), the side-by-side line up includes **Boucheron**, **Asprey**, **Bulgari**,

THIS PAGE (FROM TOP): Hushed, discreet shopping in Piccadilly Arcade; London's streets beckon to chic shoppers from all over the world.

OPPOSITE (CLOCKWISE FROM TOP RIGHT): The Louis Vuitton store on Bond Street; Nicole Farhi collections on show; Fenwick showcases European design; Liberty of London holds up among the multitude of London shops.

Harry Winston, Moussaieff, Chanel, Chaumet, Cartier, Boodles, Mikimoto and David Morris. Tiffany & Co is the next one along as the street changes its name (25 Old Bond Street). Across the road, between 6 and 15 New Bond Street, find Graff, Van Cleef & Arpels, Breguet, Chopard, Georg Jensen and Patek Philippe.

In an independent mood? Small, independent boutiques with carefully edited collections are London's forte. Because they are independent, you might not find them on the most familiar shopping streets, but they are well worth winkling out. Joan Burstein's Browns (23-27 South Molton Street), first opened in 1970, is still an advanced shoppers' destination and now fills several adjacent townhouses with designer clothes, shoes and accessories for men and women. Up in Primrose Hill, Anna Park of Anna's (126 Regents Park Road, NW1) virtually created the 'shabby chic' look and grown-up girly dressing for her young celebrity clientele. The Portobello and Notting Hill area is fertile territory for independents. Try Lebury Road (Paul & Joe at 39-41, Ross+Bute at 57, One at 30) and Kensington Park Road (Nancy Pop at 19, Couverture at 188).

The wildest fashion is out east, where young, aspiring designers test the waters with stalls at Spitalfields Market and an assortment of shops in the streets that link Spitalfields with Brick Lane Market. The hip designers are at the Sunday UpMarket at the Old Truman Brewery (91 Brick Lane). Very hit-or-miss and urban grunge, but, like the vintage clothing end of Portobello Road Market, popular with those who like to discover up-and-comers.

andaz liverpool street london

THIS PAGE (FROM LEFT): Some open-plan suites creatively combine their bedroom and sitting area; the hotel displays a daring sense of style and modernity.

OPPOSITE (FROM LEFT): Lounge in front of the striking Wall of Mirrors, a cosy Living Room takes the place of the customary lobby.

The image of a boutique hotel is one where the rules of the industry do not necessarily apply. In these small establishments, personal service is paramount, and guests are made to feel more at home than if they actually were at home. Large hotels that bend the rules are the exception, with most making do with various facilities, dining opportunities, and the like. One new hotel that takes the best of both approaches to hospitality is the ANdAZ Liverpool Street London, part of the Hyatt Group's latest luxury concept brand.

The ANdAZ is all about interacting with guests on a personal level while still operating on a grand scale. To allow this seeming contradiction, it does a number of things in unexpected ways. For one, every staff member is involved with guest service, with all of them sharing the title of 'ANdAZ host', as opposed to traditional fixed roles such as Manager, Concierge, or Receptionist. In fact, doing away with rigid conventions is key to how the ANdAZ Liverpool Street, London puts the focus on its guests. There are no large, impersonal desks in the lobby. Instead, the first thing guests see is a stylish 'Living Room' space where they are personally greeted by their ANdAZ hosts. Check-ins can be processed anywhere, over a drink at the bar or even en route to the guestroom.

Charges, too, are handled in a transparent manner. Rates include the use of all facilities, including the minibar, in-room movies, local calls, laundry, and breakfast every morning. Menus are set with as few numbers as possible to make things easier; a single price applies to all main courses, for instance. That kind of thoughtfulness is the last thing many would expect from a hotel of this size, but then again, nothing here is ordinary. Each room features an Eames EA 106 chair at an oversized work desk lit by a Jacobson lamp. The luxurious beds by Relyon are partnered with lush organic cotton sheets, and selected suites have leather seating by B&B Italia. In place of a bathrobe, one finds its traditional Japanese counterpart, the yukata.

If any doubt should remain as to whether a London hotel can be both big and boutique at the same time, consider that out of the 267

rooms
244 rooms • 23 suites

food
1901: modern European • Miyako: Japanese •
Catch: seafood and crustacea • Eastway: all-day
dining • George Pub: traditional pub fare

drink
1901 • Champagne Bar • George Pub • Eastway

features
health club • boardroom and meeting facilities •
iPod and PSP lending service • shops • valet
parking • wireless Internet access

nearby
Bishopsgate underground station • Hoxton •
Shoreditch • Spitalfields • art galleries

contact
40 Liverpool Street
London EC2M 7QN, United Kingdom •
telephone: +44.20.7961 1234 •
facsimile: +44.20.7961 1235 •
email: info.londonliv@andaz.com •
website: www.andaz.com

rooms, no two find themselves alike. Suites on the lower floors have Victorian-period features and high ceilings, while the loft-style upper floor suites are as modern as the high-tech amenities found in all rooms, from ubiquitous wireless Internet access to iPods and PSP game systems available on loan.

When the time comes to dine, it's as uncomplicated a pleasure as anything else at the ANdAZ Liverpool Street London. The hotel's five restaurants and four bars enjoy street-level entrances and distinctive personalities, offering everything from Japanese and fresh seafood to European fine dining. The food remains first-class, but service is refreshingly warm and far from pretentious. Private dining arrangements are also possible at the Andaz Studio event room—complete with showcase open kitchen and a separate entrance.

A modern presence in a historic London building dating back to 1884, the new ANdAZ Liverpool Street London hotel is a collection of beautiful contradictions surely headed in the right direction. Combining grand intimacy and casual luxury, it is a unique new entity well worth exploring.

brown's hotel, london

THIS PAGE: *Named for the famous author Rudyard Kipling, the Kipling Suite is lushly appointed.*

OPPOSITE (FROM LEFT): *The rooms are given a bright and airy feel through their tall windows and soothing colour schemes; dine at The Albemarle, which offers classic seasonal British cuisine in an elegant setting.*

When James Brown, Lord Byron's former butler, opened Brown's Hotel in 1837, it was the very first of its kind in the capital. Built on Albemarle Street in the prestigious Mayfair district, the landmark establishment earned a sparkling reputation for its dedication to service. A number of noteworthy guests have done their own parts in placing the hotel on the map. This was where Alexander Graham Bell initiated the world's first phone call, and while staying as a guest of Brown's Hotel, Rudyard Kipling wrote his masterpiece, *The Jungle Book*.

Originally comprising of just four houses, the property has since expanded to fill 11 beautiful Georgian townhouses. Following a £24 million renovation, it now offers 117 luxurious rooms and suites, outstanding dining, a relaxing spa and a buzzing bar. Olga Polizzi, Rocco Forte's Director of Design, has worked her magic in preserving the classic English charm for which the hotel is known, while adding contemporary touches and state-of-the-art conveniences to appeal to the modern traveller. Every room and suite

rooms
88 rooms • 29 suites

food
The Albemarle: classic British •
The English Tea Room: light meals and
afternoon tea

drink
The Donovan Bar

features
gymnasium • spa • complimentary packing and
unpacking • 24-hour business centre • wireless
Internet access • laundry • iPod docking
stations in all suites

nearby
Bond Street • Buckingham Palace • Burlington
Arcade shopping • Green Park • Piccadilly Circus •
Royal Academy of Arts • West End theatres

contact:
Albemarle Street, Mayfair
London W1S 4BP, United Kingdom •
telephone: +44.0.20.7493 6020 •
facsimile: +44.0.20.7493 9381 •
email: reservations.browns@
roccofortecollection.com •
website: www.roccofortecollection.com

has been individually decorated using soft colours and light fabrics, and it is this attention to detail which sets this hotel apart.

Guests of Classic, Deluxe, Presidential and Royal Suites also benefit from a wide range of additional luxuries such as unpacking services, in-room check-in, and complimentary pressing of the suit they are wearing. Bedrooms are custom prepared with a choice of different pillows, duvet weights, and mattresses fitted with 100 per cent Irish linen or fine Egyptian cotton. Not to be outdone, suite bathrooms are lavishly fitted with televisions at the end of the bath and Penhaligan toiletries.

Brown's Hotel was home to the first ever restaurant to open within a hotel, and it has recently seen an exciting change with the launch of The Albemarle. Executive Chef Lee Streeton has created an outstanding menu featuring British classics alongside lighter

seafood dishes, all using carefully sourced seasonal ingredients. Experiencing the daily lunch-time carving trolley is a must. Brown's Hotel is also home to The English Tea Room, where novelist Agatha Christie penned *At Bertram's Hotel*. Intimate and cosy, it has been consistently voted one of the top afternoon tea venues in London. At The Donovan Bar, guests can indulge in a wide range of cocktails while relaxing to live jazz. The Spa is another perfect choice for winding down, with its soothing therapies and three private rooms, including one designed for couples.

Steeped in history, the Brown's Hotel virtually gave life to London's hotel industry. While many things have changed over the last two centuries, the hotel's core philosophy has not. It remains committed to the pleasure of its guests, a fact one suspects no amount of time could ever change.

sofitel london st james

This ultra upscale, delightfully downtown London property occupies the former site of the Cox and Kings Bank—a Grade II listed building on 6 Waterloo Place, on the corner of Pall Mall in the prime district of St James. The style quotient of its stately neoclassical façade is impeccable even today, 85 years after it was designed by E Keynes Purchase and Durward Brown. The hotel's neighbours include a number of the capital's major landmarks, including Buckingham Palace, St James Park, and Trafalgar Square.

Opened in 2002 after an extensive refurbishment of the interiors, the 11,613-sq-m (125,000-sq-ft) hotel boasts 186 luxurious rooms appointed to the high standards of the Sofitel brand. To realise the contemporary style fused with local significance that the Sofitel name is renowned for in all its global properties, the services of French interior designer Pierre-Yves Rochon were secured. Best known for his work on such five-star hotels as the Four Seasons Hotel George V in Paris, Rochon has also been involved in some of the highest-profile Sofitel projects to date.

The scheme developed for the Sofitel London St James takes into account the rich history of the former Lloyds subsidiary, and retains elements of the Cox and Kings' coat of arms. Rochon's work is an informed reinterpretation of many of the building's original features, and the result is at once traditional and modern. From the leather panels to the repurposed furniture from the

THIS PAGE (FROM LEFT): The St James Bar offers an elegant setting for drinks and conversation; savour French classics in the warm and airy Brasserie Roux.

OPPOSITE: A large engraved glass plaque in the lobby pays tribute to the building's long history.

original bank's boardroom, the Sofitel London St James proudly combines a classic British elegance with the French brand's hallmark art de vivre and savoir faire principles.

Upon entering the lobby, one is first surprised by the cavernous space, with a mezzanine hovering overhead from which pianists play in the evenings. Subsequently, finer details emerge—large windows with iconic beige and green blinds, polished marble flooring, and a quantity of incredible art by English and French artists. Features such as a 21st-century glass and chrome clock contrast with the dark green marble of the reception counter, while lively arrangements of fresh-cut flowers add colour. The spatial interplay suggests dissonance, but ultimately comes off as a masterful symphony.

Taking the combination of modernism and the Old World to each of the guestrooms, Rochon has harmoniously combined fabrics in solid chocolate and olive shades with spacious mahogany-furnished living areas to create a unique look and feel. Each en-suite bathroom features Hermès toiletries, Rowe rain showers, and even hands-free telephone lines. All rooms and suites feature the latest in entertainment technologies, as well as automatic minibars and thoughtful touches such as safes large enough for a laptop.

One single opulent Royal Suite on the second floor is the hotel's largest room. The Royal Suite is made up of a large bedroom, separate lounge area, dining room, hallway, and kitchen. The bedroom's centrepiece is a striking four-poster king-sized bed, and like the rest of the suite, it is decorated in a palette of red and canary yellow in a series of unique print textures. Guests in the lounge area are entertained by an oversized plasma television, and the dining room is large enough to accommodate eight diners.

Larger parties would do well to try the superb 100-cover Brasserie Roux on the ground floor, located in what was once the main banking hall. Marked by three 5-m- (15-ft-) high arching windows, the restaurant is bright and airy with buttercup-yellow walls and refined deep red furnishings. Serving a selection of classic French brasserie fare inspired by Albert Roux, Brasserie Roux aims

The nine Junior Suites come in either single king-sized or twin queen-sized bed configurations overlooking Waterloo Place. Within the bedroom are generous lounge and study areas, with the latter having access to a large working desk, ISDN lines, and a cordless telephone. The décor is pure pleasure, rich with dark woods and soft wool carpeting, arranged around large period wardrobes.

Six larger Executive Suites have separate seating areas, and all come with comfortable king-sized beds accompanied by Bose CD alarm clocks. Corner suites offer views over both Pall Mall and Waterloo Place, while the others are situated on single sides of the building. Throughout all the suites, rooms and public areas of the hotel, wireless Internet allows guests to stay connected.

THIS PAGE (FROM LEFT): All rooms are decorated with fine fabrics and rich mahogany furniture; bathrooms are appointed in sleek black marble and chrome.

OPPOSITE (FROM LEFT): Enjoy a slow cup of tea at The Rose Lounge; the hotel occupies what was once the Cox and Kings Bank.

rooms
170 rooms • 16 suites

food
Brasserie Roux: classic French brasserie •
The Rose Lounge: afternoon tea •
Bar: light dishes

drink
St James Bar: gentlemen's club lounge

features
24-hour room service • boardroom and meeting
facilities • business centre • concierge • leisure
centre with gym and massage room • high-
speed wireless Internet access • private dining

nearby
Buckingham Palace • Jermyn Street • The Mall •
St James Palace • St James Park • Trafalgar
Square • West End theatres • shops • city centre

contact
6 Waterloo Place
London SW1Y 4AN, United Kingdom •
telephone: +44.020.7747 2200 •
facsimile: +44.020.7747 2210 •
email: H3144@accor.com •
website: www.sofitelstjames.com

for a simplicity that hearkens back to the roots of French cooking. The restaurant uses only seasonal ingredients from renowned suppliers in England and France, and offers a wine list which is both robust and affordable.

The Sofitel London St James also boasts two meeting places where the traditions of yesteryear may be relived. Fashioned after a gentlemen's club, the St James Bar offers fine whiskies and champagnes to accompany conversation by the bar or fireplace. The Rose Lounge, on the other hand, is a feminine affair in pink and cream where guests may enjoy a traditional English afternoon tea. The Rose Lounge is also where the hotel's library may be found. It offers a wide selection of books, many dedicated to the French and English cultures. None are the equivalent of simply experiencing the hotel, however. From the intricate décor to the service and cuisine, to stay at the Sofitel London St James is to see first hand what happens when two ways of life, both renowned for their love of grandeur, come together in concord.

51 buckingham gate

Sharing a street with royalty would be enough to launch any hotel into the upper reaches of award tables, but the three townhouses that make up 51 Buckingham Gate stand on the strength of their own achievements, making the hotel a noted establishment in its own right. At one point in the last millennium, the buildings played home to the British War Office, but in the past two decades they have been better known for hosting celebrities, foreign dignitaries, and presidents.

Standing seven stories tall, the Victorian-era townhouses enjoy views of the St James Park, Green Park, and the city's rooftops as far as the Houses of Parliament, Big Ben, and Whitehall. Within, they encircle a beautifully kept courtyard garden anchored by a fountain reputedly donated by Queen Victoria herself. Guests will find 51 Buckingham Gate to be amongst the most conveniently located hotels in London, with Buckingham Palace only three minutes away on foot and a number of central underground and railway stations within five minutes by taxi.

The hotel offers a total of 86 generous accommodations. Starting at 51 sq m (550 sq ft), they are easily the largest rooms in London, and make the most of their living spaces with stylish interiors decorated in cool tones. Suites are available in a number of configurations, from the smaller Junior Suites to residential-style apartments with up to four bedrooms, a well-equipped kitchen, and a full complement of business tools in spacious work areas.

Residents of the suites enjoy all the same facilities as the other guests, and even more. This includes around-the-clock room service, twice-daily Knightsbridge and Bond Street

THIS PAGE (FROM LEFT): *Bistro 51 offers fine French and British cuisine; the hotel's staff are dedicated to presenting the best holiday experience to their guests.*

OPPOSITE (FROM LEFT): *Stylish artworks and neutral shades characterise the hotel's decoration scheme; the atmosphere at the hotel is one of dignity and elegance.*

rooms
86 suites and apartments

food
Bistro 51: French and British classics • The Library: breakfasts, light lunches and afternoon tea • Quilon: modern Indian • Bank Westminster: modern British

drink
Zander Bar • The Hamptons

features
gymnasium • spa • butler service • 24-hour room service • concierge • child-friendly facilities • meeting rooms • business centre

nearby
Buckingham Palace • Hyde Park • Apollo Theatre • Houses of Parliament • National Gallery • London Eye • shopping

contact
51 Buckingham Gate
London SW1E 6AF, United Kingdom •
telephone: +44.020.7769 7766 •
facsimile: +44.020.7233 5014 •
email: info@51-buckinghamgate.co.uk •
website: www.51-buckinghamgate.co.uk

retail shuttles, and the superb personal butler service that begins every stay with a British tea presentation and sees to all additional needs. Children are also made to feel entirely welcome at 51 Buckingham Gate, enjoying a selection of games, family films from the DVD library, and other amenities.

Three Signature Suites provide the highest levels of indulgence, and are suited for a few friends or accommodating an entire family. The Chairman's Quarter is a three-bedroom suite with three lounges, a boardroom, and a full kitchen. The Chancellor's Suite has just one bedroom, a reception room, and kitchen, but expands to its full potential when joined with the superlative Prime Minister's Suite via a spiral staircase. That combination yields a magnificent five-bedroom residence with three study rooms, four reception rooms, and separate living and dining areas.

Private dining may be served in all rooms from the hotel's three superb restaurants, or top restaurants nearby. In-room menus and catering are handled by Brian Henry, Executive Head Chef of the hotel's ground-floor Bistro 51. Guests of the suites may enjoy an organic breakfast served every morning at The Library, while the Michelin-starred Indian cuisine at Quilon is an excellent choice for lunch and dinner. If there is one thing which can be said about 51 Buckingham Gate, it is that even the highest of luxuries soon begin to feel natural.

the athenaeum

THIS PAGE (FROM LEFT): *Named for the exquisite rose, Damask dining room is an ideal place to savour the hotel's fine English food; recently renovated, the hotel's décor is comfortable and stylish.*

OPPOSITE (FROM LEFT): *All rooms are fitted with opulent furnishings; relax at the spa after a day of exploring London's attractions.*

The West End is undoubtedly London's nerve centre of entertainment, containing the city's greatest attractions, superlative shopping and of course, its world-famous theatre venues. With its acres of generous parklands and the wide public squares in the vicinity, it is also where one may experience some of London's quietest, most relaxed moments. For that reason, discerning visitors to the city will surely be familiar with The Athenaeum, a boutique hotel perfectly placed in the midst of the West End's natural and architectural splendour.

The hotel overlooks Green Park from its perch on Piccadilly, and lies moments from Hyde Park Corner and the Green Park subway station. Buckingham Palace and Berkeley Square are just around the corner, with the rest of the city only five underground stops away. All of this, and the majestic London Eye, can be seen from many of the 111 guest rooms, with the 10th-floor Presidential Suite offering the most panoramic of views.

Rooms are fitted with Continental-style furnishings and the very best of modern technological amenities. Bang & Olufsen televisions display a range of live and on-demand content, and DVD players are also provided. For connected getaways, email and web access is made a pleasure through high-speed Internet ports, while two separate telephone lines facilitate the most intensive of business needs. Of course, in this or any five-star luxury hotel, comfort is the order of the day, and The Athenaeum goes over the top with dream-inducing Hypnos beds fitted with Egyptian cotton linens and spacious bathrooms equipped with power showers.

Proud of the fact that it remains family owned, The Athenaeum differentiates itself from the mass of chained business hotels in the city with its exquisite suites. All of them sport an individual design, and the antique furnishings found throughout the single-bed and open-plan suites are equally unique. Adjacent to the hotel, The Athenaeum's serviced apartments offer similarly high standards of luxury with even greater privacy for long-term guests. Long a favourite of Hollywood actors filming in London, they have been homes away from home for such distinguished talents as Natalie Portman, Michael Douglas, and Samuel L Jackson.

rooms
111 rooms • 12 suites • 33 serviced apartments

food
Damask: classic English

drink
The Garden Room: lounge bar • The Study: intimate bar space • The Whisky Room: featuring over 250 rare whiskies

features
spa and fitness centre • meeting rooms • hair salon • children's welcome package • 24-hour room service

nearby
Buckingham Palace • Royal Academy of Arts • Bond Street • Green Park • Piccadilly Circus • theatre district • London Eye • Covent Garden

contact
116 Piccadilly
London W1J 7BJ, United Kingdom •
telephone: +44.020.7499 3464 •
facsimile: +44.020.7493 1860 •
email: reservations@athenaeumhotel.com •
website: www.athenaeumhotel.com

Another reason for The Athenaeum's popularity with international celebrities may lie in its gloriously English food, full of the flavour with which the nation defines itself, from hearty classics such as steak and ale pies to Sunday roasts with Yorkshire puddings and the afternoon tea ritual. The elegant Damask dining room is an ideal place to enjoy the ever-changing menus offering only fresh seasonal foods, but guests may also elect to dine in their rooms at any time with around-the-clock room service.

Unusual in a Central London hotel, but a perfectly natural fit for The Athenaeum, is a fully equipped spa with soothing treatment rooms, a jacuzzi, sauna, steam rooms, and a 24-hour gymnasium. Experienced beauty therapists help tense bodies unwind with soothing wraps, facials, and deep tissue massages, while a professional hair salon in the basement makes sure guests look perfect for a truly glamorous stay.

Recently voted by *Travel + Leisure* as one of the '500 Top Hotels in the World', The Athenaeum prides itself on seeing guests leave with more than they arrived with. Given a stay in the heart of the city, surrounded by beautiful scenery and sensual indulgences, that extra something might just be a sense of profound fulfillment.

the metropolitan, london

In 1997, the renowned COMO Hotels and Resorts group opened the first Metropolitan hotel in London with the aim of bringing together the finest in luxury, hospitality, and entertainment. It was soon met with widespread acclaim from virtually all quarters, with one sure reason being its central location on London's premier Park Lane thoroughfare, a short crossing away from Hyde Park Corner.

The hotel's sleek aesthetic identity by Keith Hobbs and Linzi Coppick was certainly another cause for celebration. Featuring all the charms of a traditional English hotel pared down to contemporary perfection, it also displays subtle design influences and antiques from the East.

Over ten expansive floors, the hotel offers 150 rooms and suites of varying proportions. More than half face the park, with the remaining City Rooms and Deluxe City Rooms overlooking the peaceful rooftops of nearby Mayfair. All rooms are comfortably decorated and boast state-of-the-art features such as interactive satellite TV, music and movie selections, and complimentary Internet access.

The Metropolitan's signature Penthouse Suite is one of the most distinctive in London. An impressive 110 sq m (1,184 sq ft) in size, it boasts unique design touches such as a Japanese rock garden displayed outside the windows. The floor-to-ceiling windows in both the stylish living area and the bedroom offer an abundance of natural light and unspoiled 10th-storey views of Hyde Park.

Similarly towering over London's dining scene is the hotel's Michelin-starred restaurant, Nobu. Opened by renowned chef Nobuyuku Matsuhisa, the restaurant offers an original blend of Japanese and Peruvian flavours. Hotel guests are also welcome to spice up their evenings at the exclusive members-only Met Bar, one of London's hottest nightspots. A team of expert mixologists ensures that all drinks, from classic cocktails to customised concoctions, are perfectly prepared.

As a counterpoint, the COMO Shambhala Urban Escape spa offers moments of calm relaxation with yoga, massages, and other therapies inspired by Asian traditions. Two spacious treatment rooms, a gym, and steam rooms help alleviate jet lag and sore muscles.

One of London's most recognized travel and dining destinations, The Metropolitan has a reputation for cool, graceful design, but its charms don't stop there. Energetic service, fine dining, and a wondrous view of the capital make it a classic worth revisiting.

THIS PAGE (FROM LEFT): The Penthouse Suite offers views of Hyde Park through large bay windows; the sleek and exclusive Met Bar offers a wide range of cocktails.

OPPOSITE (FROM LEFT): Displays of art in the lobby add to the hotel's chic and modern atmosphere; bathrooms come with luxurious COMO Shambhala amenities.

...all the charms of an English hotel pared down to contemporary perfection...

rooms
150 rooms and suites

food
Nobu: Japanese Peruvian fusion ·
The White Room: breakfast and private dining

drink
Met Bar · The Lobby Lounge

features
COMO Shambhala Urban Escape spa ·
IT Butler · business centre · concierge ·
5 event rooms · gym

nearby
Hyde Park · Mayfair · Knightsbridge · Piccadilly ·
Victoria station · shops · restaurants

contact
19 Old Park Lane, London
England W1K 1LB, United Kingdom ·
telephone: +44.020.7447 1000 ·
facsimile: +44.020.7447 1147 ·
email: res.lon@metropolitan.como.bz ·
website: www.metropolitan.como.bz

the cadogan hotel

THIS PAGE: Large windows allow rooms to enjoy plenty of light and views of the surroundings.

OPPOSITE (FROM LEFT): Langtry's offers English cuisine in an elegant and intimate dining room; details from the hotel's history, such as the ornate fireplaces, have been carefully restored.

Great moments in history often immortalise the places where they occurred, from the birthplace of Shakespeare to the Tower of London. Over the last century, a small hotel in central London has seen two sensational events unfold within its walls, guaranteeing its place in the annals of national history.

Located on Sloane Street, The Cadogan Hotel was built in 1887, subsuming the home of beautiful actress and courtesan Lillie Langtry. Continuing to live in her old bedroom within the hotel, she began an involvement with Edward, the future King of England, an affair which did not escape public notice. Around the same time, the police were seeking playwright Oscar Wilde on grounds of indecent behaviour. Ignoring advice to flee, he remained at the hotel until being led away from Room 118 in handcuffs. John Betjeman would later write about the incident in his poem, 'The Arrest of Oscar Wilde at The Cadogan Hotel'.

These days, The Cadogan Hotel has moved past the drama of its Victorian years, but has kept the sense of style and luxury that

rooms
65 rooms and suites

food
Langtry's: English fine dining

drink
Bar • Drawing Room

features
24-hour business centre • private gardens • tennis court • fitness room • wedding and event venue

nearby
Buckingham Palace • Natural History Museum • National Science Museum • Knightsbridge • Hyde Park • Harrods • Green Park • shops

contact
75 Sloane Street
London, SW1X 9SG, United Kingdom •
telephone: +44.020.7235 7141 •
facsimile: +44.020.7245 0994 •
email: info@cadogan.com •
website: www.cadogan.com

so endeared it to the distinguished figures of that era's society. Its prime location between Knightsbridge and Sloane Square has only appreciated with time, and the exclusive hotel now counts designer labels such as Prada, Gucci, and Armani amongst its neighbours.

Experience history with a stay in one of the hotel's three landmark rooms. The Lillie Langtry room is 28 sq m (300 sq ft) of gentle, feminine pastels, complete with an original period fireplace. Oscar Wilde's infamous Room 118 overlooks the fashions of Sloane Street through its large floor-to-ceiling windows. With its powder-blue walls and stripes of chocolate over cream, it is a bold design worth savouring. Lastly, and fit for a king indeed, is the Edward VII Suite. Regal in every sense, with

accents of royal red over dark wood, it is also thoroughly relaxing, conjuring images of a bygone era where wealth, power, and playfulness coexisted in perfect grace.

Rounding up the experience in a way that many other small hotels do not is a trio of food and beverage destinations within the hotel building. The opulent Drawing Room offers a distinguished afternoon tea service, while the Bar makes for cosy drinks before dinner at Langtry's, a romantic English restaurant. Stepping through the doors of The Cadogan Hotel is akin to visiting another time and place, where every moment, no matter how seemingly insignificant, lives on in memory for years afterwards—just the sort of place for a special holiday.

the draycott hotel

Amidst London's relentless hustle and bustle, The Draycott Hotel distinguishes itself by welcoming guests as if they were staying at the home of an attentive and impeccably elegant friend. From their practice of displaying a handwritten calling card with the guest's name on the room door, to the teddy bear placed on the bed after the room has been serviced, the hotel has mastered all the niceties that make for an unforgettable stay.

Located in the fashionable Chelsea district, The Draycott Hotel comprises three adjoining Edwardian townhouses, combined to provide a quiet refuge that evokes the reassuring air of a pleasant English manor. There is no hotel sign outside, and stepping through the crisply restored main entrance, flanked by urns, is an invitation to shake off the dirt of the city and be immersed in a warm, intimate retreat.

Inside the fully refurbished building, the classic high ceilings and ornate fireplaces are accentuated by Victorian antiques and wall hangings. Each guestroom is named after a theatre legend and decorated accordingly with prints, posters, photographs and even a miniature biography of the room's namesake. The Ellen Terry room is reminiscent of a Victorian stage star's dressing room, and the J M Barrie room bears designs and prints based on Kate Greenaway's children's books.

While some guestrooms look out onto the residential street, those at the rear of the property enjoy a gorgeous view of a private garden—particularly enchanting when the cherry trees are in full bloom, but retaining its allure all year round. An evening walk in the gardens is the perfect end to a London day, especially when capped with a glass of complimentary champagne. Other treats include afternoon tea and hot chocolate before bedtime, all served in a traditional English fashion in the drawing room.

Adding to the intimate and historic feeling, each room has a beautifully bound guestbook, which guests may freely add to. An archive of completed guestbooks, filled with the signatures and scrawls of previous visitors, is available in the hotel's drawing room.

The hotel has flexible accommodations to suit families. Some rooms, such as the Draycott Suite, are large enough to sleep four comfortably. Others, such as the Lawrence, adjoin smaller rooms with single or bunk beds, some decorated in a playful, nautical theme. The details of a child's stay are carefully tended to as well, with teddy bears and children's gift packs, special children's breakfasts and even a PlayStation console.

For groups who prefer more privacy, Number 22 Cadogan Gardens offers a self-contained complex of nine suites, a boardroom and a private dining room. The building has its own separate street entrance, making a stay here feel even more like a private visit.

With the thoughtful care that takes personalised service to a whole new level, The Draycott Hotel is undoubtedly one of the leading lights on London's hotel scene.

...a quiet refuge that evokes the reassuring air of a pleasant English manor.

rooms
24 rooms • 11 suites

food
Breakfast Room: international breakfast

drink
complimentary champagne at 6.00 pm

features
24-hour reception • 24-hour room service • chauffeur service • concierge service • meeting room • wireless Internet access

nearby
Cadogan Hall • The Saatchi Gallery • Victoria and Albert Museums • Knightsbridge • Sloane Street • Kings Road • Royal Hospital Chelsea

contact
26 Cadogan Gardens
London SW3 2RP, United Kingdom •
telephone: +44.020.7730 6466 •
facsimile: +44.020.7730 0236 •
email: reservations@draycotthotel.com •
website: www.draycotthotel.com

sydney house chelsea

THIS PAGE (FROM LEFT): Clean lines and neutral tones characterise the hotel's modern interior décor; rooms are fitted with all-wood floors, comfortable furniture, and tasteful displays of art.

OPPOSITE (FROM LEFT): Rooms have an airy feel which puts one at ease; the hotel is a perfect blend of contemporary and traditional.

Located in the vibrant Chelsea neighbourhood, this charming boutique townhouse hotel of just 21 rooms is ideal for stylish shoppers and gourmets alike. Sydney House Chelsea boasts beautiful Georgian architecture in a Grade II listed building just moments away from Knightsbridge and Fulham Road, where some of the largest names in fashion can be found.

Sightseeing visitors enjoy convenient access to the South Kensington underground station which, at mere yards away, puts most of London virtually at their doorstep. Owing to Sydney House Chelsea's central location, however, many major attractions are already close by and within walking distance. These include the Chelsea Physic Garden, Hyde Park, Kensington Palace, and the Victoria and Albert Museum among others. Several world-class dining destinations make the neighbourhood a microcosm of culinary delights. There's the fine French dining of Gordon Ramsay's eponymous restaurant, the modern Italian fare of Daphne's, and authentic Portuguese cuisine at Tugga on King's Road.

To suit the tastes of discerning travellers, the modern interiors behind the hotel's original façade have been tuned to contemporary sensibilities. Owned by Andrew and Christina Brownsword, Sydney House Chelsea's design philosophy is reminiscent of their Gidleigh Park and Bath Priory properties. Built on the idea of an elegant private home and furnished with clean lines and exclusive accessories, the atmosphere within is intimate and original.

Guestrooms feature a minimalist design scheme which keeps their walls bare, save for an extraordinary piece of modern art or two, while gentle lighting creates an airy and inviting feel. The concept of uncluttering extends even to the lack of curtains on either side of the enthralling street views. Instead, pull-down blinds create privacy in an instant.

The guest experience is the paramount concern, as evidenced by the large Vi Spring mattresses which are the embodiment of comfort when covered in fine Frette linens and fluffy goose-down quilts. Wooden floors are adorned with rugs woven from Scottish

...ideal for stylish shoppers and gourmets alike.

rooms
21 rooms

food
breakfast lounge · 24-hour room service

drink
cocktail bar

features
boardroom · concierge · airport transfers · high-speed Internet access

nearby
Hyde Park · Kensington Palace · Knightsbridge · shops · museums · restaurants

contact
9-11 Sydney Street, Chelsea
London SW3 6PU, United Kingdom ·
telephone: +44.020.7376 7711 ·
email: info@sydneyhousechelsea.com. ·
website: www.sydneyhousechelsea.com

lambswool, while individual air-conditioning maintains a comfortable temperature at all times. Sleek glass bathrooms are a joy to use, equipped with power showers and luxurious toiletries by the White Company. A full range of modern amenities are provided; unobtrusive but readily available when needed. Flat-screen televisions with DVD players come as standard, while laptops may connect directly to high-speed Internet access ports.

The best room on the premises is literally named 'The Room at the Top'. Essentially a penthouse suite, it enjoys access to a private rooftop garden from which its residents can enjoy sweeping views over the houses of South Kensington while enjoying breakfasts, mid-afternoon flutes of Gosset champagne, or romantic dinners under the stars, all made possible by 24-hour room service.

The house restaurant and bar serves one of London's best traditional English breakfasts, cooked from organic ingredients. Late risers need not worry, as breakfast is served all day. Also of note: the deluxe Continental breakfast with freshly baked pastries from renowned French boulangerie, Poilâne. It is attention to details like these that make the Sydney House Chelsea a uniquely lavish experience.

number sixteen

In recent years, Chelsea has become the de facto neighbourhood of choice for hip, well-connected visitors to London, as the number of quality boutique hotels has risen to match the high glamour quotient conferred by countless instances of designer shopping and eating springing up in the area. One of the very first of these small hotels to open in defiance of the large Park Lane establishments which were the norm in the 1980s, Number Sixteen was revived by Tim and Kit Kemp of lauded group, Firmdale Hotels, and remains a very compelling option today.

Located in South Kensington, the hotel enjoys all the benefits of being close to one of London's most dynamic districts, where the bustle of busy bars, restaurants, and shops spill out onto the streets at all times of day—without the noise and interruptions that entails. Serenely tucked away in a row of white, Victorian stucco townhouses, Number Sixteen enjoys the kind of peace and quiet associated with residential neighbourhoods.

With its conserved façade on the tree-lined avenue, few signs suggest its nature as a centrally located hotel. And yet it is, with the beauty of Kensington Gardens and Hyde Park, the shopping of Knightsbridge and Brompton Cross, and the museums of Exhibition Road all within walking distance. World-renowned restaurants populate the vicinity of Number Sixteen, leaving very little else to be desired. Greater London lies within easy reach courtesy of the nearby underground station.

Stepping into the lobby, the first thing one notices is the marvelously unexpected interiors by Kit Kemp. Classic and modern in a single breath, they embrace the hotel's history and situation with aplomb, drawing the eye from one boldly colourful feature to the next. Floor-to-ceiling windows on the first floor flood the two public living rooms with natural light, creating a bright and airy

rooms
42 rooms

food
light menu in conservatory · 24-hour room service

drink
honesty bar

features
private garden · high-speed Internet access · DVD library · concierge · business services

nearby
Brompton Cross · Knightsbridge · museums · shops · restaurants · parks · health club

contact
16 Sumner Place
London SW7 3EG, United Kingdom ·
telephone: +44.020.7589 5232 ·
facsimile: +44.020.7584 8615 ·
email: sixteen@firmdale.com ·
website: www.firmdalehotels.com

atmosphere that continues throughout the 42 guestrooms. The drawing room and library are also enhanced by pieces of contemporary art, drapes and furnishings with textures that range from the floral to the geometric, and unusual additions such as hanging mobiles.

Each room is a masterpiece of design, having received individual attention to evolve into a space that is separate from the others with its own theme, colours, and layout. They encompass all the elements of modern British style and achieve an inviting warmth with unique character. All the comforts of a luxury hotel are present, with large beds, sumptuous en-suite bathrooms in granite and oak, and extra touches such as Tivoli radios and heated towel rails. The latest flat-screen televisions are provided for entertainment, with satellite channels backed up by a solid DVD selection.

The hotel offers excellent 24-hour room service in lieu of a restaurant, as well as an honesty bar in the ground-floor lounge. The loveliest thing, however, might be the private garden that runs the length of the entire hotel. Shaded from view by tall trees, it offers a place where breakfast, drinks, and light refreshments may be enjoyed in splendid, leafy seclusion. Along with its remarkable location and heritage, the touchstones of any great city hotel, Number Sixteen claims a slice of London for itself with its natural sanctuary and utterly original design.

the cranley

Almost like a summer home in London's ultra-desirable South Kensington district, The Cranley is a distinctive boutique hotel hidden away on a quiet street just minutes from the city centre. Composed of three historic buildings completed in 1869, the four-storey establishment is a pleasure one would not expect to find within walking distance of such landmarks as Hyde Park, Harrods, and the Victoria and Albert Museum. Yet there they are, and The Cranley's proximity to major underground stations makes for easy access from both Heathrow and Gatwick airports, as well as attractions elsewhere in the city

Once inside, the crisp white townhouse façade gives way to marvellously decorated spaces complete with antique mahogany furnishings, brass fittings, and period oil paintings. The hotel's antique collection was curated by renowned expert and media critic, Jonty Hearnden. Classically English, the traditional decorating scheme is enhanced by the use of Regency colours—specifically Beddington Blue, Bone, and Cream—in lustrous Farrow and Ball paints. The charming lobby area is especially suited to lounging, with an ornate fireplace, comfortable easy chairs and sofas, and a view out onto street-

THIS PAGE (FROM TOP): Enjoy a slow breakfast or afternoon tea on a balcony overlooking the city; the exquisite four-poster beds are fitted with embroidered headboards and Irish linens.

OPPOSITE (FROM LEFT): Regency colours enhance the traditional feel; The Cranley boasts ornately designed classic English décor.

level through a number of floor-to-ceiling windows, framed by magnificent silk curtains from Pierre Frey of Paris. This Victorian-style elegance is consistent throughout the property, continuing through all 39 of the guestrooms and suites.

The highlight of each room is indubitably the handcrafted Bellestrata bed. At a cost of approximately £10,000 each, these masterpieces of comfort are paired with goose-down pillows and finished with fine Egyptian linens and handwoven Welsh wools to provide sleep indulgence of the highest order. Make no mistake, however—these restful rooms are rooted firmly in the present with a full array of modern technologies and amenities. An LCD television, dual-line telephones, modem ports, and high-speed Internet access are standard in every room. Complimentary wireless Internet is also present in all public areas.

The Standard Double Room sleeps two on a queen-sized half-tester canopied bed, and has a lovely limestone bathroom with traditional Victorian fittings. For the business-minded, the 17-sq-m (180-sq-ft) space includes an antique mahogany writing desk with easy access to power and telecommunication sockets. Executive Twin rooms have two separate Beaudesert beds with handmade mattresses, and at 26 sq m (275 sq ft), are large enough to accommodate an extra table, ideal for in-room breakfasts. The spacious Four-Poster Rooms are so named for their king-sized four-poster beds with Irish linen and embroidered headboards.

The Junior Suite enjoys a private garden area in addition to a separate sitting room, and is excellent for entertaining. The best views in the house, however, belong to the top-floor Penthouse Suite with its oversized windows and private terrace overlooking rooftops all the way to the London Eye. Whether one enjoys the view from within the large living room, or out above Kensington, it's difficult to feel anything but privileged. That sense is present throughout The Cranley: an overwhelming notion of personal fortune. After all, how many get to go from their doorsteps to the heart of one of the world's great cities in mere minutes?

rooms
37 rooms · 2 suites

food
in-room private dining only

drink
lobby bar

features
complimentary wireless Internet access · laundry and dry cleaning · limousine service · personal shopping assistance · room service

nearby
Buckingham Palace · Harrods · Hyde Park · Kensington Palace · Knightsbridge · National Science Museum · Natural History Museum · Royal Albert Hall · Serpentine Gallery · Victoria and Albert Museum

contact
10 Bina Gardens, South Kensington London SW5 0LA, United Kingdom · telephone: +44.020.7373 0123 · facsimile: +44.020.7373 9497 · email: reception@thecranley.com · website: cranley.steinhotels.com

the gore hotel

THIS PAGE: With fittings such as antique mirrors, heavy drapes and beds carved from oak, The Gore's rooms are pure opulence.

OPPOSITE (FROM LEFT): The restaurant's long opening hours lets diners enjoy a full meal even after watching a late theatre show; pieces of period art and photos grace the walls of the hotel.

Bearing the address One Ninety Queen's Gate, this elegant Victorian townhouse hotel has stood between the desirable neighbourhoods of Kensington and Knightsbridge since it was built in 1892. Its secluded yet superb location on a tree-lined avenue in central London, coupled with an acclaimed bar and bistro, has led to its rise as an extremely popular destination with locals, business travellers, and holidaymakers. All points of interest in the city centre are easily accessible, with many just a short walk away, Harrods and all of Knightsbridge's shopping included. Also close by are the Royal Albert Hall, the West End's theatres, and the national museums of South Kensington, making The Gore Hotel an integral part of London's cultural scene and a highly individual hotel experience.

Recently refurbished in 2006 at a cost of £3 million, the interiors have been fully restored to focus on the building's original features. Artefacts and art pieces of character which have been collected over the past hundred years now take their place alongside

unobtrusive modern comforts. In the main hall and stairway, the walls are adorned with hundreds of paintings and photographs, while refined colours and materials provide a setting that is classic English luxury.

Each of the hotel's 50 bedrooms have been individually designed with personalities of their own, and they continue the hotel's signature look with antique furniture and period artwork. While all rooms, from the aptly named Wonderful Doubles to the more spacious Luxury Doubles, offer warmth and style in equal amounts with chandeliers, statues, and gilt mirrors, it is the collection of 10 Deluxe Rooms that really shines.

These unique creations have no equal in the city of London; some might even call their distinctiveness bordering on eccentricity. Regardless, one thing cannot be denied. They are incredible accommodations suited to the most discerning of tastes. In addition to the softness of pure Egyptian cotton sheets and standard amenities such as minibars, DVD players, and flat-screen televisions, some rooms come with something else that money can't buy: history. A number of these Deluxe Rooms have been named and designed after the preferences of famous celebrities who once spent the night.

The Judy Garland room played host to the star on more than one occasion, with the hotel fondly considering her something of a former resident. The room's centrepiece is the star's own magnificent gilt wood bed, left in

The Gore's care. Dame Nellie Melba's room is an opulent affair, as oversized as the soprano's presence. The décor scheme includes two leopard-print armchairs and a bed lined with pleated silk. Guests may admire themselves in the mirror-lined bathroom while soaking in a deep double bath guarded by bronze statues of David and Venus.

Excellent food is also synonymous with the Gore name, served in the lively Bistro One Ninety. Traditional afternoon tea and British favourites are the draw here, and they are complemented by a well-rounded wine list sourced from around the world. A favourite of theatregoers, the bar and bistro stay open till late, which is just one more example of the hospitality and kind service that has made The Gore a London institution.

rooms
50

food
Bistro One Ninety: informal all-day dining

drink
Bar 190

features
concierge • wireless Internet access • business centre • private event rooms

nearby
Royal Albert Hall • Kensington Palace • Hyde Park • V&A Museum • Harrods • Knightsbridge

contact
190 Queen's Gate
London SW7 5EX, United Kingdom •
telephone: +44.020.7584 6601 •
facsimile: +44.020.7589 8127 •
email: concierge@gorehotel.com •
website: www.gorehotel.com

jumeirah lowndes hotel

It is a given that one will find the world's trendiest brands, and the people who love them, in London's fashionable Knightsbridge district. The houses of Gucci, Chanel, Hermès, Christian Dior, and countless others have carved out enviable positions for themselves in the trifecta of glamorous shopping that is Knightsbridge, Sloane Street, and Chelsea.

The exclusive area is also highly sought after as a residential and holiday destination, as its central location makes it suitable both as a starting point for those who are seeing London for the first time, and for those who retreat to it several times a year. Such definitive sights as Hyde Park, the Royal Albert Hall, Harrods, the West End theatre district, Buckingham Palace, and the Tate Gallery are only a short walk or cab ride away.

Nestled in the prime of Knightsbridge, in famous Belgravia Village, is the charming Jumeirah Lowndes Hotel. A five-star boutique hotel, it has become famous in a short time for being one of the very best of its kind in the Kensington and Chelsea borough. Its

situation on Lowndes Square, a verdant patch of serenity in the middle of town, and stylish, modern interiors make it a perfect venue for leisure and business needs.

With 75 guestrooms and 12 suites behind a stately, pillared façade, the Jumeirah Lowndes Hotel provides all the services of a larger hotel with the charm and manner of a private establishment. Rooms are designed to transmit the beauty of nature with décor that features prints and colour palettes inspired by the changing of seasons, whilst offering the paragon of comfort with touches like sheets of pure Egyptian cotton, marble bathrooms, and Temple Spa bath amenities.

Each room is equipped with everything one could need, including a minibar, large LCD TV with satellite channels, wireless Internet, coffee and tea facilities, and even a high-fidelity clock radio with iPod dock. Business-minded guests will find two separate phone lines, data ports, large working desks, and even in-room espresso machines for the ultimate in convenience. With every need anticipated and cared for, little remains but rest and relaxation.

The standard Guest Room offers superb comfort and luxury for discerning travellers with a choice of king-sized or twin bed configurations. Ranging from 14–17 sq m (151–183 sq ft), they are suitable for two adult occupants and open out to views of either Lowndes Square or the Halkin Arcade courtyard. Those in town for longer stretches

THIS PAGE: *Decorated in warm, bright tones, Mimosa Bar & Restaurant brings a touch of Mediterranean chic with its food and designer cocktails.*

OPPOSITE (FROM LEFT): *The rooms feature luxurious touches like pure Egyptian cotton sheets; relieve fatigue and jet lag with soothing therapies offered at the Peak Health Club & Spa.*

beds. Fully furnished to make their occupants feel at home, their well-placed windows let in lots of natural light in the morning and they are particularly enchanting to return to after a long day out in town.

Also designed for three adults, but with more accommodating floor plans, are the Executive Suites at 40–47 sq m (431–506 sq ft). The separate lounge areas are equipped with extra-large double sofa beds and easily double up as impromptu venues for informal business meetings. Some Executive Suites offer balconies, and all are proud to have excellently designed interiors, luxurious en-suite marble bathrooms, and king- or twin-sized beds that are just right for falling into. But the jewel of the suite-only sixth floor is undoubtably the Luxury Suite, the Jumeirah Lowndes Hotel's finest creation. This close-to-apartment-sized, 48-sq-m (517-sq-ft) retreat has the largest living, dining, and sleeping areas in the house, and even boasts two private en-suite bathrooms. The suite is perfect for accommodating up to four adults, and unforgettably romantic for just two.

Guests can enjoy full use of the Peak Health Club & Spa, located on the 9th floor of adjacent sister hotel, the Jumeirah Carlton Tower. It features an airy modern gymnasium with all-glass outward-facing windows that give visitors a panoramic view of the city beyond as they work. A team of personal trainers help with any necessary fitness assessments, whether it includes the use of

of time may want to do some stretching out of their own in the very spacious 23-sq-m (248-sq-ft) Deluxe Rooms. If you may be doing a spot of entertaining, or would just like to spend some time people-watching, choose an Executive Deluxe Room and enjoy a private balcony overlooking the Square.

Three superlative suite options exist to serve the needs of families, larger groups, and those who are simply accustomed to having things a cut above the ordinary. The smallest of them are the Junior Suites, which range from approximately 24–37 sq m (258–398 sq ft) in size, and are still extraordinarily spacious as rooms go. They sleep three adults and feature inviting open-plan lounge areas with sofa the gym, aerobics studio, or the beautiful 20-m (66-ft) indoor pool. The spa also offers a host of beauty treatments and therapies aimed at rejuvenating both mind and body. The menu includes Swedish, therapeutic, sports, and deep muscle massages.

While anyone can tell you that London's dining scene has now become one of the most vibrant in the world, with even pub fare going gourmet, the Jumeirah Lowndes Hotel's Mimosa Bar & Restaurant is one of the city's best kept secrets. Exuding a new brand of Mediterranean chic, the bar matches glamour with flavour in every one of its signature drinks. Try the Grand Mimosa Champagne cocktail, the fabulous Mimosa Peace Martini, or perhaps even the exotic Bloody Mimosa with tomato and clam juice.

The restaurant serves modern European food, and as with the bar, everything on the menu has been kissed with the essence of the Mediterranean. Morning coffees, afternoon meals and cocktails can be enjoyed in a lively, continental fashion out on an al fresco terrace overlooking Lowndes Square. Key dishes include juicy scallops with lime and salsa, and chicken breasts smothered in an aromatic pesto and served with tomatoes and Taleggio polenta.

With its up-to-the-minute sense of style, it might be easy for a wandering shopper to mistake the Jumeirah Lowndes Hotel's lobby for just another designer outpost in the heart of Knightsbridge. But there is more here than meets the eye—an establishment with a wholly unique identity—that's just waiting to be discovered.

rooms
75 rooms · 12 suites

food
Mimosa Bar & Restaurant: modern European

drink
Mimosa Bar & Restaurant

features
The Peak Health Club & Spa · event and meeting room · hair salon · horse riding · limousine service · complimentary wireless Internet access in the lobby

nearby
Cadogan Hall · London Underground stations · Royal Court theatre · V&A museum · history and science museums· shopping

contact
21 Lowndes Street, Knightsbridge London SW1X 9ES, United Kingdom · telephone: +44.020.7823 1234 · facsimile: +44.020.7235 1154 · email: jlhinfo@jumeirah.com · website: www.jumeirahlowndeshotel.com

the royal park

THIS PAGE: The luxurious four-poster beds are handmade and come with fine linen sheets.

OPPOSITE (FROM LEFT): Savour a fine Continental breakfast in bed; bathrooms match bedrooms for luxury, with their marble fittings and lush amenities; The Royal Park comprises three historic Georgian-era buildings.

On a quiet, tree-lined street in Central London lies an elegant townhouse hotel. Mere steps away from the bustle and flow of city traffic, The Royal Park occupies three Grade II-listed Georgian-era buildings. The exclusive hotel resides in privileged seclusion on Westbourne Terrace, west of Piccadilly, and north of Hyde Park. Notable attractions such as Buckingham Palace and Green Park are nearby, with the Paddington station of the London Underground only 300 m (984 ft) from the front door.

Built over 165 years ago, the ivory-white townhouses project an air of sophistication that carries well into the inner reaches of its rooms and lobby. Public spaces have been renewed with conservation-quality paint in the Regency hues of Berrington Blue, Bone, Cream, and Ointment Pink and adorned with details such as antique chandeliers, fireplaces, and period oils. The upholstery on the solid dark wood furnishings is a mix of buttoned leather and lush fabrics that set the tone for a refined stay in the lap of luxury. Fine touches such as handwoven curtains complete the atmosphere of classic chic.

Once guests arrive at the Royal Park Hotel, they are welcomed by the hotel's young and dynamic team. Staff are pleased to attend to guests' every need, from check-ins and showing guests to their rooms to making sure guests enjoy a relaxing and comfortable stay. Two elevators allow convenient access to the 48 rooms and suites. High-speed Internet access comes standard, as do flat-screen LCD televisions, and dual-line telephones with voicemail, while DVD players are available on request. These are in addition to the large electronic safes, well-stocked minibars, personal climate controls, and professional hairdryers that well-travelled guests will expect.

The spacious Standard Double Rooms feature handmade Bellastrata beds in a queen size, dressed with Italian freda linen. Their rich mahogany furniture include an armchair, antique working desk, and a dining table. Views

rooms
48 rooms and suites

food
breakfasts served in lounge • in-room dining

drink
lounge bar

features
meeting rooms • 24-hour room service • concierge • high-speed Internet access

nearby
Hyde Park • Buckingham Palace • Piccadilly Circus • Harrods • Green Park • Paddington station • Oxford Street • Westfield Shopping Centre • shops

contact
3 Westbourne Terrace
Lancaster Gate, Hyde Park
London W2 3UL, United Kingdom •
telephone: +44.020.7479 6600 •
facsimile: +44.020.7479 6601 •
email: info@theroyalpark.com •
website: www.theroyalpark.com

from these rooms look out over the rooftops of London, while the larger Executive Double Rooms face the Westbourne Terrace area.

The Four Poster Rooms and Suites offer elegant sophistication and the opportunity to really enjoy a special occasion. The king-sized four-poster beds are an inviting place to relax after a long day out in town. Featuring period furnishings and artwork, the suites are truly lavish from the very moment one steps into the entrance area. The bedroom enjoys a gilded mirror and the elaborate four-poster bed is fitted with silk valences and canopy. The separate sitting rooms are the perfect place for entertaining guests.

The elegant fittings in all the rooms make it easy to enjoy the hotel's 24-hour private in-room dining service and Continental breakfasts

in bed. The bathrooms are made completely from marble; most have large bathtubs, and all offer sensual and refreshing Superior Zen Zone toiletries. After dinner, guests can pour themselves a cognac at the honesty bar and relax in the cool blue sitting room, while business meetings may be conducted in the elegant green room. It may prove difficult to leave the comforts of the hotel, but the well-tended garden at the back of the hotel offers a compelling venue from which to enjoy a fine summer evening with a glass of wine.

Naturally, the quintessentially English property also prides itself on quintessentially fine English hospitality. Its well-connected concierge is happy to make anything possible, and after just a few days, The Royal Park hotel begins to feel like home.

the caesar

THIS PAGE: *Located near the heart of London, the hotel makes an ideal base for exploring the city.*

OPPOSITE (FROM LEFT): *While rooms may appear simple, they are comfortable and welcoming, with a full range of amenities; the hotel features design details such as exposed brickwork.*

Visitors to London often find that the UK's most exciting city provides a more than adequate range of recreational activities, leaving most hotel rooms empty for the duration of the day. A happy problem, to be sure, for the thriving multicultural capital is awash with first-class shopping, dining, and theatrical pursuits, but one that also makes the case for high-quality four-star hotels like The Caesar. Located squarely in the Queens Gardens area in the City of Westminster, the designer hotel offers a peaceful residential district location and a polished sense of style, without an exorbitant pricetag.

Major tourist hubs such as Oxford Street, Hyde Park, Regent Street, and Bond Street are nearby, and easy access to the rest of London is available through the Bayswater and Paddington underground stations. The close proximity of the latter allows those flying in through Heathrow Airport to reach the hotel with a minimum of fuss.

The street-facing view of the building features a beautiful Victorian façade, whose original windows have been replaced by large single panes which afford a glimpse of the hotel's modern interiors. Alongside the bold flourishes of colour, contemporary furnishings, and modern Guitart prints found throughout, an exclusive collection of Roman mosaic art gives the property an extra dash of historic character. In many ways, The Caesar appears more gallery than guesthouse until one lays eyes on its 140 charming bedrooms.

The hotel has seen a recent renovation, and all Standard, Executive, and Deluxe Rooms are comfortable and spacious, with a modern décor scheme which couples light tones and fresh colours with the luxurious feel of dark woods and exposed brick walls. The king-sized or single beds are supplemented with fine

rooms
140 rooms

food
Restaurant XO: international cuisine and breakfast buffets

drink
XO Bar

features
gymnasium • open-air garden • wireless Internet access • laundry and pressing service • disabled access • 24-hour room service • meeting rooms • sauna

nearby
Hyde Park • Marble Arch • Portobello Road • Paddington Station • Oxford Street • Regent Street • Bond Street • Kensington Gardens

contact
26-33 Queens Gardens Hyde Park London W2 3BD, United Kingdom • telephone: +44.020.7262 0022 • facsimile: +44.020.7402 5099 • email: thecaesar@derbyhotels.com • website: www.thecaesar.co.uk

linens and quality pillows for the kind of sleep that a busy day out on the town deserves. All rooms are equipped with wireless Internet access, direct dial telephones with voice mail, and large televisions with pay-per-view and a host of premium satellite channels. Welcome trays with tea and coffee are also provided, in addition to 24-hour room service.

For families or those travelling in groups, The Caesar offers a number of Triple Rooms generous enough to accommodate three full-sized single beds. They come with all the comforts of other standard rooms, including radios, in-room safe boxes, and bathrooms equipped with professional hair dryers. Larger still are the Executive Double Rooms, which are suited to business travellers desiring a mix of privacy and practicality. Fresh fruit, newspapers, and mineral water are delivered to these rooms on a daily basis.

More than just a place to stay, The Caesar is also a dining venue of distinction in the area with its Restaurant and Bar XO. Stylishly appointed, the restaurant serves a menu of fine international cuisine, while the bar is an ideal place to relax with any one of a wide selection of cocktails.

In London, as it is in any city where a high standard of living is taken almost for granted, it is refreshing to discover an establishment that offers all the trappings of a privileged life at good value. The Caesar is one such hotel, offering a complete package that includes the all-important central location.

the landau at the langham, london

THIS PAGE: *Head Chef Andrew Turner specialises in creating dishes which combine classic and contemporary flavours.*

OPPOSITE (FROM LEFT): *The restaurant interior was designed by the renowned David Collins Studio; a vaulted corridor displays the restaurant's selection of wine.*

Named after the style of carriage in which the Prince of Wales rode to The Langham, London hotel's opening in 1865, The Landau enjoyed one of London's most talked-about gourmet debuts when it launched in November 2007. Part of its parent hotel's £70 million designer makeover, no expense has been spared in making the restaurant more than just a venue for exceptional cuisine. Like the original landaus, which were luxurious open carriages that allowed onlookers to catch a glimpse of their occupants' finery, The Landau is a singularly spectacular establishment that is both a place to see and to be seen in.

Designed by the acclaimed David Collins Studio, which also handled the chic Artesian cocktail bar that shares the restaurant's street level entrance, The Landau's interiors employ a high-fashion, ultra-refined look dubbed 'Contemporary Oriental' by its creators. Victorian-era details such as antique brass chandeliers, gilded timber panelling, and embossed leather furniture create a royal atmosphere that is contrasted with the spirituous inclusion of silk Chinoiserie screens. Moving swiftly around the rich interior is a graceful team of staff smartly outfitted in uniforms by Stewart Parvin and tailored by Kashkets, holders of six Royal Warrants.

With the newly completed wine corridor, diners encounter an example of The Landau's fine gastronomy at the same instant as they do its groundbreaking design. Leading them from the entrance hall to the dining room is a long, vaulted limestone corridor lined with some 1,400 bottles suspended and ready for choosing in a series of exquisite glass cabinets.

The Landau's extensive wine list is continually compiled by Master of Wine John Atkinson, and features a number of specialist varieties provided exclusively to him by independent vineyards. Ensuring that every bottle finds its place is resident sommelier Zack Saghir, who has nearly three decades of experience. With a collection as large as the wine corridor's, Saghir is able to work some extremely creative pairings, bringing out the best in the contemporary European cuisine.

Grazing menus are the highlight of The Landau's dining experience, as created by Head Chef Andrew Turner, one of the first in the UK to introduce the concept. His signature touch is a passion for experimentation and fresh seasonal ingredients sourced from the best of British farmers. Much of his fare has roots in traditional European favourites, deconstructed and then reassembled to become new masterpieces. Grazing menus come as meals with between five to seven courses, and may include such favourites as Chef Turner's crispy organic hen's yolk and artichokes and blue-fin tuna with mango and olives.

A visit to The Landau is always a special occasion. Details such as fine chinaware by Vera Wang and designer cloakroom tags by Bill Amberg sweeten the deal, but it is surely the exquisite food and designer ambience that keeps diners coming back time after time.

His signature touch is a passion for experimentation...

rooms
Postillion: private dining room

food
contemporary European

drink
wine and champagne list of over 1,400 bottles

nearby
Oxford Circus • New Bond Street

contact
The Langham, Portland Place
London W1B 1JA, United Kingdom •
telephone: +44.020.7965 0165 •
facsimile: +44.020.7323 2340 •
email: info@thelandau.com •
website: www.thelandau.com

theo randall at the intercontinental london park lane

THIS PAGE (FROM LEFT): **Seating up to 120 diners, the main dining room has a sophisticated décor; rich colours and elegant style characterise the restaurant.**

OPPOSITE (FROM LEFT): **The restaurant's rustic Italian food emphasises the quality of the ingredients; even the bathrooms have been appointed to high standards.**

Following a monumental refurbishment to the tune of £80 million, lasting nearly two years in all, the InterContinental London Park Lane reopened in late 2006 with an all-new ground-floor restaurant. Its name was already well known to followers of London's culinary scene—formerly of the ultra-chic River Cafe, where he worked for 17 years and earned a Michelin star, Head Chef Theo Randall was the driving force behind the eponymous restaurant in the heart of Mayfair.

Seating 120 diners, with an additional 20 at the bar and 24 in a private dining room, the spacious restaurant benefits from a clever interior design which creates a feeling of openness while retaining a mood of intimacy. Rich chocolate walls and flooring anchor the atmosphere in sophistication, with glass and mirrored panels lending brightness to the space. Furnishings are similarly a combination of dark wood tones and cream, set off against crisp white linen. The sleek result is one that puts diners at ease, a look whose simplicity belies the care that has gone into it.

The same can be said for Randall's approach to food. Inspired by years of travel in rural Italy, his cooking is a refreshingly uncomplicated, back-to-basics exercise in teasing out the true nature of the ingredients others take for granted. In his hands, quality produce becomes the base for rustic Italian cuisine that holds the power to surprise even the most jaded of gourmands. Citing a love for the food in establishments such as Da

Cesare in Alba and Al Pompere in Verona, Randall's presentations forgo contemporary fashion in favour of traditional platings which contribute to the relaxed atmosphere.

An emphasis on freshness defines the restaurant's signature flavours. Randall works with a number of small, artisanal producers to obtain organic vegetables and first-class Italian-sourced products such as the extra virgin olive oil used. The nature of his suppliers dictates that the menu is in a continual state of flux with the seasons, a challenge which Randall gamely accepts. This year's spring menu is marked by the appearance of fresh plum tomatoes, borlotti beans from Lamon, Roman artichokes, and a variety of wild herbs.

A typical meal might begin with the Aperitivo Rossini, which makes lovely use of the new season of Italian strawberries, served with prosecco. Antipasti selections include an

...holds the power to surprise even the most jaded of gourmands.

capacity
120 • bar: 20 • private dining: 24

food
traditional Italian

drink
wine list

features
private dining • cookery courses

nearby
Hyde Park • Mayfair • Knightsbridge • Piccadilly • Victoria station

contact
1 Hamilton Place, Park Lane
London W1J 7QY, United Kingdom •
telephone: +44.020.7318 8747 •
email: reservations@theorandall.com •
website: www.theorandall.com

Insalata di Granchio, which is a platter of fresh Devon crab with rocket, fennel, aioli, and bruschetta; and the Cape Sante—Scottish scallops with braised cima di rape, chilli, capers, parsley, and delightful lentils di Castelluccio.

For mains, the Cappelletti di Vitello comes highly recommended, its perfectly cooked pasta bringing out the texture of slow-cooked veal. Also worth mentioning is the chargrilled Aberdeen Angus beef fillet with spinach and salsa verde. Not to be missed is Randall's exquisite Amalfi lemon tart, composed of delicate pastry and deliciously sharp filling. The restaurant's robust wine cellar holds 160 varieties from traditional countries such as France, Italy, as well as New World producers like New Zealand, each one hand-selected to accompany the remarkable cuisine on offer.

artesian at the langham, london

Part of parent hotel The Langham, London's multimillion pound refurbishment programme, the chic Artesian bar was opened in early 2007. The history of the The Langham, London, a Victorian hotel in Marylebone which has the distinction of being Europe's first Grand Hotel in 1865, ensures that the bar is nothing less than an example of glamour and refinement.

Its one-of-a-kind design was conceived by the acclaimed London-based David Collins Studio, known for their work on some of the finest establishments in the city, including J Sheekey in Soho and the Claridge's Bar. Featuring a concept he calls 'Contemporary Orientalism', Collins has blended the hotel's Victorian grandeur with exotic Eastern influences in an eye-catching manner that artfully avoids overwhelming the senses.

The colours and textures used in the décor—cream walls, white marble, and cool, embossed leather couches in a shade of mulberry—have different effects on the space throughout the day, changing moods with the light and heightening the visual effect of the bar's high, moulded ceilings and timber chandeliers. The Anglo-Chinese theme reveals itself most clearly around the room's focal point: an intricately carved bar counter of stained oak and lilac marble that the hotel affectionately calls 'Chinese Chippendale'.

While the décor may suggest Victoriana, the food and drink menus are virtually ahead of their time. London hospitality experts, the Gorgeous Group, contributed their flair for trendspotting to the project, and the result is a bar that makes specialty rums the toast of the town. With two exclusively crafted house spirits from Guyana and Panama, along with over 60 varieties of imported premium rum, the bar signals a revolution in luxury drinking.

Featuring heavily on the menus are classic cocktails revived by the bar's expert mixologists from long-forgotten recipes, retuned to fit seamlessly into the 21st century. For those keen to savour the familiar, the bar also carries a selection of whiskies, vodkas, and champagne. Even the ice is remarkable—the Artesian's high-tech 'energised ice' melts more slowly and retains the potency and flavour of drinks over longer periods.

A menu of gourmet bar food is served until well after dark to accompany nightcaps, and everything on offer has been designed to perfectly complement the cocktail menu. Everything at the Artesian is served on fine china by Wedgwood, with cutlery by Royal designer Robert Welch, and a collection of elegant John Jenkins crystal and glassware.

Embodying the new face of London entertainment, the impossibly romantic, effortlessly fashionable Artesian is on the leading edge of after-hours style in the city. Where most bars cover their walls in dark colours to approximate a sense of intimacy, the light interiors of the Artesian—draped in silk curtains and adorned with handcrafted details—represent a brand of comfort that sophisticated patrons have long sought.

THIS PAGE: The bar's mixologists are masters of their trade.

OPPOSITE (FROM LEFT): Sophisticated and cosy, the Artesian blends aesthetic influences from the Victorian era and the Orient; Artesian serves over 60 varieties of the finest premium rum.

...the Artesian signals a revolution in luxury drinking.

capacity
70 seating · 100 standing

food
light snacks · sharing platters

drink
cocktails · designer rums · other spirits

nearby
Oxford Circus · New Bond Street

contact
The Langham, 1c Portland Place, Regent Street
London W1B 1JA, United Kingdom ·
telephone: +44.020.7636 1000 ·
email: info@artesian-bar.co.uk ·
website: www.artesian-bar.co.uk

thesoutheast

WARWICKSHIRE

NORTHAMPTONSHIRE

CAMBRIDGESHIRE

NORFOLK

SUFFOLK

BEDFORDSHIRE

BUCKINGHAMSHIRE

LUTON

HERTFORDSHIRE

OXFORDSHIRE

ESSEX

SWINDON

The Forbury Hotel <

Reading
WEST BERKSHIRE
READING

GREATER LONDON

SLOUGH
WINDSOR AND
MAIDENHEAD

North
Sea

SOUTHEND-
ON-SEA

THURROCK

WILTSHIRE

WOKING-
HAM
BRACKNELL
FOREST

Epsom

MEDWAY

HAMPSHIRE

SURREY

KENT

SOUTHAMPTON
Southampton

PORTSMOUTH

WEST SUSSEX

EAST SUSSEX

Rye

BRIGHTON
AND HOVE
Brighton

Legend

Airport

Highway

Main Road

Urban Area

Lake

500–1000 m

200–500 m

100–200 m

Hampshire

ISLE OF WIGHT

Ventnor

> The Hambrough
> The Wellington Hotel
> Chewton Glen

Hotel Pelirocco <

Zanzibar International Hotel <
The George in Rye <

0 km   25   50 km

the southeast

the home counties

The Southeast, broadly the area surrounding London— south to the English Channel, east along the Thames Estuary and west up the Thames Valley—is generally known as The Home Counties. And before you ask, there are probably as many explanations of the name as there are counties in the region.

Kent, Surrey, Sussex (East and West), Berkshire, Buckinghamshire, Hertfordshire, Middlesex and Essex absorb London's urban overspill in crowded suburbs before spreading across the leafy 'stockbroker belt' to a countryside of affluent communities and pretty villages clustered around Norman churches.

Along the Southeast coast, one of the most settled seacoasts in Europe, busy ferry and fishing ports alternate with seaside resorts, yacht havens and that surprising oasis of post-modern hip, Brighton.

kent and the kent coast

Called the Garden of England, Kent is a region of rich farms and fruit growing. The cowls—tilted, conical chimneys—of oast houses, where hops were once dried, are still distinctive sights unique to Kent. Between the high chalk ridges of the North and South Downs, the area known as The Weald is a patchwork of small woods, tight ravines and ancient fields.

Considering its place in history and associations with St Augustine, Canterbury is a surprisingly modest, partly-walled city. The 1,000-year-old Cathedral, mother church of Anglicanism, was the destination of Geoffrey Chaucer's pilgrims in his *Canterbury Tales*.

Along the Kent seaside, from the Thames Estuary to Dover, 19th-century resorts display varying degrees of fading gentility, but some areas are on the up-and-up. The curious can stop briefly in the seaside resort of Margate—to see the place artist Tracy Emin famously reviled as 'the town that screwed [her] up'. Further west, the picturesque fishing village of Whitstable has a large artists' community, a high street lined with galleries and shops, and several seafood restaurants on the gourmet pilgrimage route. At the Sportsman, a much-lauded gastropub on the Whitstable-Faversham Road, they serve local rock oysters with hot chorizo, seared ray with cockles and jasmine tea junket for afters.

THIS PAGE: Historic destination of pilgrims ancient and modern is Canterbury Cathedral, not far from St Augustine's abbey.

PAGE 94: Spring poppies bloom profusely on the South Downs.

The rich mix of deciduous trees, unlike anywhere else in England, makes for splendid autumns.

across the downs to the sea

Beyond the commuter belt south of London, Surrey's roads wind across gently undulating hills and through thick woodlands, and are popular with cyclists. The rich mix of deciduous trees, unlike anywhere else in England, makes for splendid autumns draped in intense swathes of crimson, gold and burnt umber.

Box Hill, famed for its exceptional natural beauty, signals the start of the chalk-and-clay Downs. This is English vineyard territory. Denbies, located beside the London Road in Dorking, is the largest English estate vineyard, growing 18 grape varieties on 107 hectares (265 acres). There are various boutique vineyards in Godstone (Quarry Road) and Bolney, West Sussex (Bookers on Foxhole Lane) and Ditchling Common, near Brighton (Ridgeview Wine Estate, Fragbarrow Lane), where long rows of champagne vines are eventually turned into bottles of English sparkling wine—with critically favourable results.

The South Downs rise dramatically from The Weald. A 100-mile-long footpath, the South Downs Way, meanders along the crest, between Victorian Eastbourne and medieval Winchester, dipping and climbing to about 243 m (800 ft).

On a clear day, views can extend right across the Channel and all the way to France—a tranquil and empty space. From this vantage point, it's hard to imagine the busy, stylish world below the downs on either side.

Come off the downs to the north to find great country houses and eccentric fantasies such as Charleston, home of Bloomsbury artists Duncan Grant and Vanessa Bell, near Lewes in East Sussex. Charleston was considered the unofficial country home of the Bloomsbury group, and literary luminaries such as Virginia Woolf and EM Forster were frequent visitors here. Come July, an annual contemporary art auction to raise funds for Charleston features the work of such artists as painter and sculptor Maggi Hambling, punk rocker Patti Smith, prolific cartoonist Quentin Blake, designer Zandra Rhodes and acclaimed textile artist Kaffe Fassett.

Descend from the downs to the south, and a completely different world opens up, along what is arguably the most fashionable stretch of coast in England.

If picturesque Rye, with its preserved-in-aspic collection of medieval, Tudor and Georgian buildings, is a tad too perfect for your tastes, head for the larger—and grittier—Hastings, home of the largest beach-based fishing fleet in the UK. The town owes an enduring place in history due to its role in the Norman conquest of England, and attracts visitors today by dint of its

THIS PAGE (FROM TOP): Oast house cowls are uniquely Kentish; champagne in all but name, sparkling wine from Ridgeview Wine Estate is grown from champagne vines and made using champagne processes.

OPPOSITE: Autumn in East Sussex.

seaside attractions and hosting of various sporting and cultural events. The 70-seat Electric Palace Digital Cinema (39a High Street, Hastings), a hip, independent digital theatre in the Old Town, hosts the 'Shot by the Sea' Hastings Film Festival every July.

Beyond Regency Brighton, Georgian and Victorian seaside resorts and residential communities line up one after another, some chic, some family oriented, all affluent—Shoreham-by-Sea, Worthing, Bognor Regis. Shoreham Airport (off A27 west of Brighton), with its Art Deco terminal, is regularly featured in in film and television, and is well worth a detour for film buffs, having appeared in star-studded vehicles such as *The Da Vinci Code* and the long-running detective series *Agatha Christie's Poirot*.

Further to the west, the Solent, a 80-km- (50-mile-) long, 8 km- (5-mile-) wide stretch of water between the Isle of Wight and the south coast of Hampshire leads to Southampton Water and one of Europe's biggest cruise ship hubs. Serious yachtsman from around the world rate these challenging waters highly. From multi-fingered Chichester harbour, bobbing with sailboats, to the cruise port of Southampton, this deeply indented shore is lined with yacht havens, drawing pleasure craft by the thousands. The most stylish seafarers head for quaint Ventnor, on the Isle of Wight or Marmion Road in Portsmouth's Southsea district—chock-a-block with independent boutiques.

a river runs through it

If you had to pick two English counties to typify the good life, Noel Coward-style, Berkshire and Buckinghamshire are certainly the likeliest candidates. Buckingham is dotted with great houses, once weekend playgrounds for Rothschilds (Waddesdon Manor) and Astors (Cliveden near Maidenhead). Its historic villages conceal urbane sophistication beneath their sleepy façades. Old Amersham may have a High Street lined with ancient coaching inns—The Crown (number 16) and the Kings Arms (number 30) featured in Four Weddings and a Funeral—but it is also home to Chef-Patron Laurie Gear's much lauded cooking at The Artichoke (9 Market Square).

Berkshire is a Royal favourite, home to Windsor Castle—the Queen's weekend bolthole—and Ascot, where some of the most prestigious horse races in the world are held. The incarnation of the Thames that cuts through its centre is narrow and slow, the islet-studded waterway of classic English novels. Kenneth Grahame based the quiet, muted landscape of his children's storybook *The Wind in the Willows* on his time spent in Cookham, a quintessential Thames Valley village complete with cricketing green, eccentric artist (Stanley Spencer) and pub, The Bel & The Dragon (Cookham High Street), most famously favoured by Leslie Charteris' literary creation, Simon Templar, otherwise known as The Saint.

THIS PAGE: *Serious yachtsmen from all over the world rate highly the challenging Solent off the South Hampshire coast.*

OPPOSITE: *Cliveden, where Nancy Astor hosted her notoriously extravagant—and sometimes scandalous—house parties.*

...the good life, Noel Coward-style...

brighton

In the early 19th century, Regency architect John Nash turned the Prince Regent's simple, neoclassical summer retreat into the **Royal Pavilion**, Brighton. Even then, the Indian-style palace, with its domes and towers, fretwork on the outside, its gilt and ormolu, swags and furbelows and wildly exotic Chinese Chippendale interiors, was the very definition of 'over the top'. If the modern vernacular understanding of the word 'camp' had been in current

parlance back then, it would have been used to describe this bizarrely colourful extravaganza of excess.

So it somehow seems rather appropriate that when Brighton was well on its way to becoming just another one of England's growing collection of fading dowager seaside resorts, it was the power of the pink pound that not only rescued it but also turned it into one of the most uniquely entertaining destinations in the southeast of England.

Like its transatlanctic sibling San Francisco, modern Brighton reflects the many and varied tastes of its large, highly affluent, and creative gay community. It has lashings of style, great shopping, a busy club scene, chic wine bars and sophisticated pubs and eateries.

All this is leavened with a healthy sense of irony. Just take the seafront, for example. Facing Brighton's long shingle beach and its iconic Victorian pier, smart little bistros and wine bars

coexist with such cheesy seaside regulars as traditional Brighton rock sellers, vendors of beach inflatables and racks of kitschy 'kiss-me-quick' seaside postcards. The locals wouldn't have it any other way.

Most visitors to Brighton head straight for **The Lanes**, and with good reason. This warren of narrow, winding lanes, hidden courtyards and cul-de-sacs is crammed with high-quality antiques, jewellery and designer fashions, especially along **Brighton Place** and **Meeting House Lane**. Try **Copacabana** (19 Brighton Place) for selected fashion from all over Europe, the Far East and 'Left Coast' San Francisco. **Charley Barley** (17 Meeting House Lane) stocks trendy clobber for the chic under-eight set.

More alternative **North Laine**, nearby has hundreds of shops along **Sydney Street**, **Bond Street**, **Gardner Street** and **Kensington Gardens**. This boho district is characterised by head-spinning, manic variety. Side-by-side with piercing parlours, funky streetwear and flea markets, look for understated Danish designer **Noa Noa** (37 Gardner Street), bespoke tailors **Gresham Blake** (20 Bond Street) and top club fashion shop **Ju-Ju** (24 Gloucester Road).

Stamina is a must for clubbers in Brighton. It has the highest nightclubs-to-area ratio in the UK; 29 in a 4-sq-km (1.5-sq-mile) radius. The hottest venues in the notoriously fickle club scene change faster than the English weather. The best bets are the clubs lined up under the **King Road Arches**, on the beach. The **Honey Club** (214) and **Digital** (187–193) are perennially hip and popular.

Clubs aren't the only parties in Brighton. **Brighton Pride**, a week-long Festival at the end of July, concludes with one of the best parades of its kind this side of San Francisco. The **Brighton Festival**, three weeks in May, runs to more conventional music, art, theatre, dance, family events and outdoor spectacles. And, in a town where any excuse is just cause for a party, the lighting of thousands of arty paper lanterns on the beach for **The Burning of the Clocks** at the winter solstice, is among the best events that visitors can take in.

THIS PAGE (CLOCKWISE FROM TOP): DJ Fatboy Slim hosts a Brighton beach party; The Burning of the Clocks in winter; no visit is complete without one— a colourful stick of Brighton rock; the Lanes—a must-visit in Brighton.
OPPOSITE: The Royal Pavilion, the very definition of 18th-century camp.

playgrounds of the rich + famous

During The Season—that time of the year when England's high society, its royals, glittering celebrity crowd and Europe's beautiful people come out to play—the English Southeast, and particularly to the south and west of London, is where they do it.

The country's most stylish and well-connected people all gather in Surrey, West Sussex, Berkshire and Hampshire for the year's top equine and sailing events. **Royal Ascot** in June, when the Queen and other members of the royal family join the racing fraternity at **Ascot Racecourse**, is just the tip of the iceberg. During the summer months, the Southeast's social calendar is filled with several chic events involving the sporting passions of the rich and famous: horses—jumpers, thoroughbreds, polo ponies—vintage cars and world-class racing yachts.

Played and enjoyed by princes and potentates, the glamorous sport of polo is surprisingly democratic. Anyone with the price of a ticket can watch the game played at some of the Southeast's most exclusive private clubs. In fact, you needn't even buy a ticket to enjoy the most glittering polo event of the summer. The **Cartier International Polo Day**, at **Guards Polo Club** in July, is played in Windsor Great Park—a public park. Find a space along the fence—as hundreds of people do—and you can rubberneck one of the largest and richest polo clubs in Europe (Prince Philip, the Duke of Edinburgh is president) to your heart's content. Of course, if you do buy a ticket to the stands, you get to be a member for the day and to hobnob with international film stars, global billionaires, and 160 of the world's top polo players.

Polo has been played on Lord Cowdray's West Sussex Estate, **Cowdray Park**, since 1910. Known as the home of British Polo, Cowdray hosts the **Veuve Clicquot Gold Cup**. The finals attract an international celebrity crowd and must be booked in advance. But for most matches, even the semi-finals, anyone can buy a ticket on the gate.

Seriously stylish motor sport enthusiasts head for **Goodwood** in July when the Earl of March's West Sussex Estate hosts the **Festival of Speed**, one of the great social and sporting occasions of the motor sport calendar. Historic racecars and performance cars of all classes and eras compete in races and hill climbs on the historic Goodwood course, the first motor racing track built after the Second World War. Star drivers such as Sir Stirling Moss, Jenson Button, Lewis Hamilton, Nigel Mansell and Mika Hakkinen take part. The **Cartier Style et Luxe** auto design competition, judged by international designers and filmmakers, is a highlight.

In early August, the **Solent** around the Isle of Wight turns white with sails as **Cowes Week** gets underway. More than 1,000 sailboats, their crews ranging from Olympians and world-class professionals to weekend sailors, compete in up to 40 races a day. The social scene, a mix of elegant private parties and public entertainments, draws a chic, international crowd of yachtsmen, socialites and regatta fans to the island town of Cowes, facing Southampton Water.

THIS PAGE (FROM TOP): Goodwood track during the annual Festival of Speed; Cowes Week regatta on the Solent.

OPPOSITE (CLOCKWISE FROM TOP): Celebrity polo, Cartier International Polo Day; a classic car tune up at Goodwood; Ladies Day at Royal Ascot—where fabulous millinery is a major focus.

the george in rye

THIS PAGE (FROM LEFT): *Each bedroom features a unique centrepiece; the restaurant serves modern English cuisine with a creative Mediterranean influence.*

OPPOSITE (FROM LEFT): *The hotel's décor is unmistakably English; first opened in 1575, The George in Rye has a history which few other hotels can hope to match.*

The George in Rye hotel began life in 1575 simply as 'The George', and was the first instance of a coaching inn in the small East Sussex town of Rye. Over the years, the hotel was moved once, then expanded to occupy several interconnected buildings, with its large ballroom and public house becoming a central part of Rye's social scene until early in the 20th century, when it fell into neglect.

New owners Alex and Katie Clarke rescued the property in 2004, devising an extensive programme of restoration and refurbishment that saw the inn reopening in late 2006 as The George in Rye hotel. Bringing together their combined years of knowledge and experience in the fields of hospitality consulting and design, the couple's efforts have produced a hotel and restaurant unlike anything else for miles.

As a set dresser on many high-profile film and television productions, Katie Clarke, working with design partner Maria Speake from acclaimed firm Retrouvius, understood the challenges of working with a space that had to be renewed and yet retain its embedded history. Lovingly decorated with a mix of the traditional and contemporary, The George in Rye's interiors recall the best elements of English style by juxtaposing antiques, select artwork, and elegant pieces of local handmade furniture.

Each bedroom is a one-of-a-kind design, partly owing to irregularities in the original structure. Room designs take a direction set by a unique centrepiece, and differ in terms of colour, fabrics, and layout. The bed in Room 19 has an ornate headboard made from an ancient tapestry showing a scene at sea, while Room 8 features a mustard yellow roll-top bathtub in the bedroom area itself.

A look at the Standard Double and Twin rooms will demonstrate the level of care that has gone into ensuring the comfort of guests. The hotel uses superb Vi-Spring beds, and those are complemented with the finest Italian linen by Frette. The en-suite marble bathrooms feature soaking tubs with power showers, Lefroy Brooks fittings, and toiletries by Aveda. All rooms also enjoy high-speed Internet access, flat-screen LCD televisions, and designer clock radios by Tivoli.

Lovingly decorated with a mix of the traditional and contemporary...

rooms
24 rooms

food
The Dining Room: Mediterranean and British

drink
The George Tap

features
ballroom · high-speed Internet access · private dining · DVD library

nearby
Lamb House · Ypres Tower · Camber Sands · nature reserve · churches · vineyards

contact
98 High Street, Rye
East Sussex TN31 7JT, United Kingdom ·
telephone: +44.017.9722 2114 ·
facsimile: +44.017.9722 4065 ·
email: stay@thegeorgeinrye.com ·
website: www.thegeorgeinrye.com

A number of Deluxe Double and Twin rooms offer an upgrade from the Standards with larger floor areas and in some cases, the option of separate walk-in showers beside bathtubs, and gorgeous four-poster beds. The honour of largest rooms goes to a set of Junior Suites, which have king-size, feature, or four-poster beds in the midst of very spacious accommodations. The extra space allows for seating areas with corduroy chaises longue in some, and large bay windows that look out to either the enclosed courtyard garden, or onto the varied rooftops of the town.

Owner and manager Alex Clarke shares a long history with good food—his family background includes sister Sam Clark, who runs the popular London restaurant, Moro—and has worked to ensure The Dining Room lives up to his high standards. All food is made from fresh ingredients provided by the nearby farms around Rye, Sussex and Kent. Head Chef Rod Grossmann was formerly of Moro's kitchen, and has used his experience to good effect, coming up with an innovative menu that features modern English dishes with a sunny Mediterranean touch.

In just a few short years, The George in Rye hotel has given many an all-new incentive to visit Rye, one of England's most unique small towns. In fact, it has the distinction of being the only four-star luxury hotel in 1066 Country, but even that has not stopped its owners from continually innovating their forward-thinking historical hotel.

zanzibar international hotel

THIS PAGE (FROM LEFT): *Spread over two levels, the Morocco suite brings a taste of the exotic; the India suite is resplendent with lush fabrics and designs.*

OPPOSITE (FROM LEFT): *Enjoy a glass of champagne or a sumptuous breakfast in the Grand Salon; the hotel is a creative twist to the usual seaside getaway.*

In the up and coming town of Hastings, a row of tall Victorian terraces is host to an unexpected gem: the Zanzibar International Hotel, a young boutique hotel which infuses a flavour of the exotic into the quintessential British seaside sojourn. With eight suites, each decorated a different theme with inspirations taken from faraway locations around the world, ranging from Morocco to Japan, guests can be immersed in a sumptuous, imaginative environment—all without ever leaving the shores of East Sussex.

A crisp, modern aesthetic runs through the hotel. Walls are painted in white, giving the space a clean, contemporary feel, while leather-upholstered furniture complements the period fittings impeccably. The hotel seamlessly blends the old and the new, with the public areas boasting décor such as fine antique chandeliers, classic candelabra and restored fireplaces. Adding a dash of colour and zest are daring pieces of art and stylish decorative items that the owner has collected on his personal trips around the world.

Zanzibar International Hotel boasts eight distinctive suites, each complete with its own en-suite spa, luxurious linens and all the sophisticated touches needed for a relaxing stay. The largest and most indulgent is the South America suite, with its glorious sea view, a Brazilian hand-carved wooden bed and a free-standing jacuzzi bath large enough for two. Just as stunning is the Antarctica suite, which comes with a mini-sauna and steam room, from which guests can admire the ocean. The white-on-white décor and faux polar bear throw provide a cool counterpoint, giving the room a fresh, airy feel.

Offering a more mystical setting, the Morocco suite is richly accented with sensual fabrics and sequined textures. A simple spiral staircase leads up to the mezzanine floor with a cosy loft bed. Likewise, the India suite is an alluring combination of simple white paired with regal flourishes, dominated by a bespoke design of mirrored tiles.

Spa features are the centrepiece of other suites, such as the deep-soak square bath in the Japan suite or the in-room massage shower and steam cabin in the Bali suite. The subtle Africa suite also has a jacuzzi and looks out over the water. Located on the first floor is the Egypt suite, with a splendid garden view, supplemented by skylight windows in the peaked roof—providing the illusion of a seaside stay under the stars, while ensconced in perfect comfort.

...infuses a flavour of the exotic into the quintessential British seaside sojourn.

The detail and care that has been lavished on the décor also manifests itself in the close attention paid to every facet of hospitality. Guests are welcomed upon arrival as if into a friend's home, with a glass of champagne in the Grand Salon, where they can admire both the seafront views and the hotel's Victorian architecture. Breakfast is made to order, with all ingredients bought from local organic or farm-reared sources. It can be served in the privacy of the guest suites, or in the leisurely opulence of the Grand Salon.

The creative themed suites, in-room spas and touches such as a DVD borrowing library tempt one to stay in all day, but for those wishing to venture further, the hotel is just a short walk along the waterfront from the centre of Hastings. While the hotel has no restaurant, the owner and staff are happy to make recommendations and reservations for guests. A stay at the Zanzibar International Hotel can be about romance or solitude, leisure or a little luxe enjoyment—whatever the splendid view of the sea inspires.

rooms
8 suites

food
breakfast

drink
Champagne Bar

features
taxi hire • concierge • spa baths • massage therapies • DVD library

nearby
waterfront • beach • town centre • shops • restaurants • museums

contact
9 Everfield Place, St Leonards-on-Sea East Sussex TN37 6BY, United Kingdom • telephone: +44.0.1424.460 109 • email: info@zanzibarhotel.co.uk • website: www.zanzibarhotel.co.uk

hotel pelirocco

Brighton is known for being one of the UK's most popular holiday destinations. With its seaside location, entertainment facilities, vibrant nightlife and restaurant scene, the city sees an average of 8 million tourists each year. Not surprisingly, some of them aren't interested in having the same experience. Those on the lookout for something fun and frivolous often head for the Hotel Pelirocco, Brighton's naughtiest, artiest, most fabulous rock 'n roll establishment.

Featuring 19 unique bedrooms, each one designed, painted and decorated by a well-known artist, musician, or pop culture entity, there's one for every imaginable fantasy. Motown fans will love 'Soul Supreme', a shimmering love song to a bygone era in the form of a double room swathed in shiny gold with dark purple undertones. A timeline of important milestones in the genre is painted across the walls, and there's even a gold microphone to accompany the selection of classic records by the vintage 1960s turntable. Party animals will appreciate 'The Ocean Room', a bedroom disguised as a chic bar after the VIP room at Brighton's club of the same name. Bathed in a luminous white glow, it has a mock bar and lounge seats for everyone who's ever felt at home in a nightspot.

Extremely popular with couples, and occasionally groups of three or even more, the hotel offers a number of rooms with romantic themes aimed at playful adults. 'Absolut Love', in association with the vodka brand, joins such saucy names as 'The Pin-Up Parlour', dedicated to UK sex siren Diana Dors, and 'Betty's Boudoir', after 1950s bombshell Betty Page.

In 2006, the hotel jumped into bed with Durex to create the most luxurious and thoroughly decadent room in the kingdom. The result is the Durex Play Room, pure sexiness from floor to mirrored ceiling. It

THIS PAGE (FROM LEFT): The Playstation Bar serves traditional English fry-up breakfasts and cocktails; all the rooms in Hotel Pelirocco feature a playful sense of style.

OPPOSITE (FROM LEFT): Dedicated to sex symbol Diana Dors, the Pin-Up Parlour is gloriously kitschy; some bathrooms are large enough for two or even more.

...Brighton's naughtiest, artiest, most fabulous rock 'n roll establishment.

rooms
19 rooms

food
The PlayStation Bar: English breakfasts

drink
The PlayStation Bar

features
PlayStation game consoles • network gaming • Durex Play Time adult room service • wireless high-speed Internet access • conference room

nearby
beach • Brighton town centre • clubs • restaurants • shopping

contact
10 Regency Square
Brighton BN1 2FG, United Kingdom •
telephone: +44.12.7332 7055 •
facsimile: +44.12.7373 3845 •
email: info@hotelpelirocco.co.uk •
website: www.hotelpelirocco.co.uk

features a 2-m (8-ft) circular bed, a pole for private dances, a stylish lounge area, and a huge bath tub that might just accommodate four. Another result of the pairing is a very special room service menu called 'Durex Play Time'. The service offers a selection of stylish vibrators and lubricants that can be delivered to any room at a moment's notice. To provide even more entertainment, a Sony PlayStation console is installed in every room.

While commercials for the PlayStation gaming machines have always claimed some incredible abilities, cooking has hitherto not been on their list of features. Now, however,

one may enjoy full English breakfasts every morning at The PlayStation Bar. For guests who prefer sleeping in, it becomes a charming place to relax and enjoy a cocktail and cult movie in the afternoon.

It's easy to be overwhelmed by the seemingly anarchic noise and energy at the Hotel Pelirocco. Art, music, and glorious excess pours from its every crevice, and the hallways display an ever-changing gallery of paintings and photographs donated by Brighton's hottest creative talents. With such a vibrant atmosphere, every stopover is guaranteed to be strikingly special.

the forbury hotel

Lying at the very spot where the River Thames meets the River Kennet, Reading was once a quiet county town which enjoyed importance as a river port. Today, it is a place where the most cutting edge of technology rests alongside tranquil country haunts such as Mapledurham House. One can enjoy a brisk morning of fly-fishing or playing polo on the Royal Berkshire polo grounds, then head to The Oracle, a large shopping centre whose opening launched Reading into the UK's top 10 retail destinations, for lunch or a spot of shopping in the afternoon. One thing for certain is that all of these enticing activities would mean nothing without an equally enticing base from which to begin, and The Forbury Hotel more than fits the bill.

Built on the site where the Berkshire Shire Hall used to stand, the £6 million townhouse hotel offers a collection of just 23 guestrooms amidst incredible design details that make it one of the most unique and charismatic

properties in the UK. Combining elements from a remarkable list of artists and designers, the hotel's stylish interiors were coordinated by Nicholas Hollinshead, who makes the bold claim that minimalism is not a word in his dictionary. Indeed, every step taken through the building reveals ever more intricate details in spaces of increasing character. Rooms feature animal statuettes contributed by Claire Norrington and paintings by a number of preeminent modern artists such as Paul Ambille. Impressionist landscapes by Isabelle de Ganay and nudes by Alain Bonnefoit find themselves proudly on display.

The lobby and reception lounge showcases a handsome pewter and leather desk in the same space as a Chesney fireplace by Kelly Hoppen. Throughout the halls, the restored original marble flooring and hand-painted chinoiserie walls with touches of silver gilding go hand-in-hand towards creating a rich and evocative atmosphere. Even the aural experience has been custom designed, with thousands of hours of mood music expertly selected by Rob Wood, ex-editor of *Jockey Slut* magazine. Looking beneath their feet, guests will discover lavish rugs with designs by Diane von Furstenberg, Bill Amberg, and world-renowned British designer Lulu Guinness.

With such an abundance of original thought and visual creativity, one easily expects the experience of the guestrooms to exceed the already high standards set by the hotel's public spaces. Catching a glimpse of

the awe-inspiring chandelier in the stairway on the way up, with the piece in question hanging the full height of the hotel and composed of some 84,000 glass beads, will confirm that those instincts were correct.

Each room is an individual creation fashioned from seven exquisite templates, varying in theme, colour palette, and choice of materials. One thing they all have in common: comfort and top-notch amenities. All beds are by Hypnos, royally appointed producers of some of the world's most comfortable mattresses, and are covered with French long-combed cotton satin sheets and duvets bearing the hotel's embroidered mark. A set of four large duck-down pillows on every bed provides the necessary accompaniment

for a good night's rest. All other furniture is crafted from English cross-sawn oak by the King's Road designer William Yeoward, and completed with fabrics from Osborne and Little, Nina Campbell, Designer's Guild, Cole and Son, Kenzo, and Paul Smith.

The Forbury Hotel is wired for the future with the very latest and best in modern communications and business tools. When the time comes to unwind, guests will appreciate the inclusion of Bang and Olufsen audio-visual systems in every room, complete with large televisions and CD/DVD players. Instead of a simple kettle, personal espresso machines are provided, each capable of

brewing a perfect cup from the four provided blends of coffee. If one should overindulge, a long soak in one of the double-ended baths should reverse the effects of caffeine. Add cool stone walls, an ice bucket at the end of the bath, and a lighting system that goes from bright to romantically subdued at the press of a button, and the results are intimately relaxing. Every room also includes a special welcome bag with tealights, a wooden massager, slippers, herbal balm, and even a rubber bath duck amongst other surprises.

Food culture is a central part of the hotel's charm, and the Cerise Restaurant & Bar is one of the best in the sophisticated Forbury Square area. Located on the lower ground floor with a stylish street-side entrance complete with water features, the restaurant is an exceptional dining experience helmed by Head Chef Michael Lecouteur. As much effort goes into the sourcing of ingredients for the kitchen as into the actual cooking. Michael's ingredients are sourced from far and wide from the best in the business, including Flying Fish of Cornwall, and Aubrey Allen, National Catering Butcher of the Year 2007.

International tapas are served in Cerise every evening, and the house mojito recipe was obtained directly from one visit to Cuba. The restaurant is proud to practice weekly food tastings for its staff. Through these, every member is given a chance to develop an awareness of the ingredients, processes, and the best pairings of wine and spirits to serve

rooms
23 rooms • 16 apartments • 1 penthouse

food
Cerise Restaurant & Bar: European fine dining •
Eden: fine dining with seasonal produce

drink
Cerise Restaurant & Bar

features
30-seater cinema • Cellar dining room • Library •
childcare services • event planning team • valet
parking • concierge • penthouse function room

nearby
Forbury Gardens • Reading train station • The
Oracle Shopping Centre • golf • fishing • horse
riding • rowing • theme parks • clay pigeon
shooting • polo

contact
26, The Forbury, Reading
Berkshire RG1 3EJ, United Kingdom •
telephone: +44.118.958 1234 •
email: reservations@theforburyhotel.co.uk •
website: www.theforburyhotel.co.uk

with the ever changing menus. The difference this makes to the diner is extraordinary. Newly opened at the hotel is Eden, a fine dining restaurant with a menu inspired by the best seasonal produce available in the British Isles.

The Forbury Hotel employs a team of dedicated event planners, and provides a number of venue options for private events. One of them is a fully equipped cinema that seats 30, and also screens films throughout the week for the enjoyment of all guests. The Library is more intimate, and will please those looking to host smaller parties with friends. The Cellar Dining Room provides the perfect venue for business meetings or private dinners. Stylish yet functional, it comes with a boardroom-style table and luxury chairs.

The hotel is also home to Reading's most luxurious apartments. A mere 50 paces from the hotel, they are truly a home away from home. The 16 fabulous two-bedded apartments mirror the artistic style and sheer elegance of their sister hotel. Perched on top is a brand new penthouse which offers stunning views of the Reading skyline. With oversized windows and a balcony area, the penthouse doubles as a trendy place to stay and to host a business meeting with a difference, with a generous boardroom that accommodates up to 20.

The Forbury Hotel's team conceived of a warm, personal boutique hotel from the very beginning. Their philosophy is embodied in their motto, "We stay with you", and indeed, one soon feels like a guest in a very special home.

the hambrough

The Isle of Wight, just off the south coast of Great Britain, has traditionally been a resort destination loved for its diverse natural environments and seaside views, accompanied by stays at quaint, rustic accommodations. As the very first modern five-star luxury hotel on the island, The Hambrough hotel introduces a side that few have ever seen, and opens up a series of new possibilities for anyone seeking a very special getaway.

Located on the southern edge of the island, in the popular health resort town of Ventnor, The Hambrough hotel is flanked by views of Ventnor Bay and the dramatic cliff face of St Boniface Down. In the midst of this spectacular territory, the hotel has chosen to place a sensitive emphasis on classic style and modern designer comforts, a move certain to be appreciated by discerning guests. The exclusive boutique hotel offers just seven rooms, including two Studio Suites. All are decorated in a warm, minimalist scheme that communicates a sense of serenity to match the view of nature provided by the large picture windows and balconies.

Neatly positioned to enjoy the best view of St Boniface Down is the superbly appointed Deluxe Room. Like all of the other rooms at The Hambrough, it comes with its own Illy espresso machine to provide any moment of the day with its perfect companion. Other standard features found in the Deluxe Room are a flat-screen television, CD/DVD players, luxuriously soft 100 per cent wool carpeting,

and a large en-suite bathroom. The latter comes complete with underfloor heating, a separate shower stall, and fine toiletries from the Molton Brown collection.

The larger Executive Double rooms are unique in having two distinctive views each, from both sides of the property. The front half of the rooms get a 90° slice of the seaward scene, while the rear areas overlook St Boniface Down. The extra floor space allows a relaxing lounge area, complete with sofa, armchairs, and a window from which sunlight and the sea breeze are allowed to drift in. The lounges in the Luxury Rooms have just one view, but what a view it is: encompassing a 180° sweep of the coastline from the horizon to St Catherine's Point, they neatly capture the spirit of the seaside resort. Those same vistas

THIS PAGE (FROM LEFT): Enjoy modern British cuisine at the restaurant; sip at a cocktail on the outdoor terrace while watching sun set.

OPPOSITE (FROM LEFT): In keeping with its atmosphere of exclusivity, the hotel only has seven rooms; with its exquisite food, it's easy to see why the restaurant has been awarded two AA Rosettes.

rooms
7 rooms

food
restaurant: modern British

drink
bar

features
wireless Internet access • personal espresso machines • Garden Room: private event & meeting space • room service

nearby
castles • beach • restaurants • shops • cycling • horse riding • windsurfing

contact
Hambrough Road, Ventnor
Isle of Wight PO38 1SQ, United Kingdom •
telephone: +44.019.8385 6333 •
email: info@thehambrough.com •
website: www.thehambrough.com

are available from the highlights of the two Studio Suites: large private balconies which extend from spacious lounge areas equipped with LCD televisions and a library of films to choose from on a rainy day.

A stay at The Hambrough hotel is far from ordinary under any circumstances, but a series of occasion-specific packages offered by the hotel promise to make any special day one to remember. Everything and anything—from a night of romance, complete with champagne, a bed covered in rose petals, and luxurious bubble baths, to an extravagant birthday celebration with a cake, flowers, and personalised card waiting behind the closed doors of the room—can be arranged.

Any event or meeting can also be elevated with a meal from the hotel's restaurant, made exclusively from fresh, seasonal ingredients available at the daily market. The restaurant holds two prestigious AA Rosettes, and one only needs to dine there once to understand why. It offers a varied menu of modern British lunches and dinners, which can be enjoyed in the restaurant proper, or in the privacy of guests' own rooms.

At this hotel, the guest experience is limited only by the imagination. Incorporating fine dining, an air of laid-back sophistication, and considerable indulgence, the slower pace of life on the Isle of Wight has found an ideal match in The Hambrough hotel.

the wellington hotel

THIS PAGE (FROM LEFT): *The hotel occupies a gorgeous, carefully refurbished Victorian building; at the restaurant, savour fresh seafood caught at Ventnor Bay.*

OPPOSITE (FROM LEFT): *Rooms enjoy floor-to-ceiling windows, and some have a private balcony; the hotel is perfectly placed to enjoy views of the pristine sea.*

A Victorian building in the town of Ventnor, overlooking the English Channel from its spot on the Isle of Wight's southern coast, The Wellington Hotel effortlessly delivers the kind of holiday experience which, along with other surrounding properties, has made the island the hotly sought-after resort it is today.

Its period façade harks back to the region's busiest years, when it experienced a surge in popularity following Queen Victoria's establishment of Osbourne House as her summer residence. Fully restored following a meticulous refurbishment of the entire property, the island's history can be read on the very contours of the hotel's anatomy. Within, striking feature walls made of natural stone remain intact alongside elegant pieces of furniture and smooth, polished wooden floors. The interior design scheme respectfully echoes the building's heritage through the use of simple, quality finishings. Many of the original components that defined Victorian-era architecture, such as ornate fireplaces and ornamental mouldings, have been retained.

From the hotel's sprawling front deck, the full extent of St Boniface Down's cascading slopes and natural beauty may be observed suspended over pristine Ventnor Bay. The entire building is oriented to enjoy a fully sea-facing view, with virtually every room in the property affording guests an unforgettable vista. Each of the 28 accommodations are furnished to the highest standards in neutral hues, providing a serene backdrop from which to enjoy the panoramic views and large, airy floor-to-ceiling windows. Rooms in the Super Deluxe category feature private balconies with loungers overlooking the dramatic drop-off below, and are suited to romantic private dining opportunities or evening drinks.

Much of the local terrain teems with wildlife, doubtlessly encouraged by the Isle of Wight's advantageous microclimate which maintains higher temperatures and more clement weather over that of the mainland throughout the entire year. Those tempted to venture directly into the inviting waters will find the beach only a five-minute walk away,

rooms
28 rooms

food
restaurant: cross-continental and seafood

drink
Wellington bar

features
outdoor terraces • wireless Internet access

nearby
beach • restaurants • shops • cycling • horse riding • watersports • town centre

contact
Belgrave Road, Ventnor
Isle of Wight PO38 1JH, United Kingdom •
telephone: +44.019.8385 6600 •
facsimile: +44.019.8685 6611 •
email: enquiries@thewellingtonhotel.net •
website: www.thewellingtonhotel.net

through the hotel's terraced gardens. From the outlying portions of the bay, one may watch fishermen at work, or travel further along the coastal path to the sheltered waters of Steephill Cove. Pleasures of a more man-made nature are also situated close by, with the hotel built at equal elevation to the shops and restaurants of Ventnor town centre.

For fine dining, however, there is little need to leave the property, for meals at The Wellington Hotel's restaurant and dining room are perhaps some of the best to be found in the area. Much of the food served consists of time-honoured favourites made with freshly caught local seafood such as Ventnor Bay Crab and lobster. Remaining ingredients are sourced from nearby counties, and are always served in season. Standout options from the menu include a Dorset Downs Saddle of Lamb, prime steaks and meats, and a superb array of desserts.

With its excellent cuisine, ideal location and beautiful architecture, The Wellington Hotel is an easy choice for anyone wishing to see the best of the Isle of Wight. Embodying all the attributes which have made the isle a popular destination, its value is as strong for repeat visitors as it is for first-timers.

chewton glen

Situated on 52 hectares (130 acres) of lush gardens, meticulously manicured lawns, and a natural parkland teeming with wildlife, Chewton Glen is an independently owned and operated luxury resort on the south coast of England. Near the town of New Milton in Hampshire, the hotel is flanked on both sides by highly diverse landscapes. To the north is the New Forest National Park, one of the largest expanses of green pasture and ancient forestation in England, remaining virtually untouched over the past 900 years. To the south of the hotel lies the coastal beach and sea, only a 10-minute walk from the front door of the manor. Between the unlimited possibilities for adventure and exploration offered by these remarkable regions, the Chewton Glen stands as a five-star haven of indulgence and restoration.

A member of the distinguished Relais & Chateaux group since 1981, one of only 25 in the country, Chewton Glen has long been a favourite of industry professionals and discerning travellers in the know. A long list of

accolades includes nods from *Condé Nast Traveller* magazine's Annual Readers' Choice Awards ('2nd Best Hotel in the World' in 2007), *Meetings & Incentive Travel Magazine* ('Best UK Hotel' in 2007 and 2008), and *Travel + Leisure Magazine* ('Number One Country Hotel in England' in 2006). Also widely known for its award-winning Marryat restaurant and spa, Chewton Glen has held three AA Rosettes continuously since 1993, while the World Travel Awards named it 'England's Leading Spa Resort' in 2006.

Housed in an 18th-century building that has been incrementally renewed over the years, Chewton Glen's appearance remains flawless. The very latest improvement was a £400,000 remodelling of the mansion's three public lounges. Created by interior designer Anita Rosato, who has overseen much of the property's recent development, the new spaces retain all the spirit and classic appeal of the original décor, while displaying richer fabrics, bright colours, and fine furnishings. Every conceivable modern convenience makes an appearance at the hotel, but the owners have thankfully taken pains to ensure that its all-important charm is never supplanted by contemporary trifles.

The look of the 58 rooms and suites is also defined by a reverent appreciation of the past, with each one featuring a well-coordinated collection of antique furniture paired with new materials and carpeting to produce a style that is as timeless as it is fashionable.

The layout and content of the rooms vary, so each one has a unique character. However, all rooms enjoy such luxuries as a well-stocked minibar, complimentary wireless Internet access, in-room safes, and trouser presses. Should the entertainment provided by the large televisions and satellite channels be insufficient, DVD players are also standard, with a library of films available for borrowing at the reception. Fully marble, the en-suite bathrooms are generously sized and stocked with soft robes and quality toiletries. Double basins are a standard feature provided for hassle-free convenience.

THIS PAGE: Set in the midst of lush greenery, Chewton Glen is the epitome of country relaxation.
OPPOSITE: Natural light floods the pool during the day, and the blue sky painted on the ceiling adds to the sunny atmosphere.

Room types are divided up into Bronze, Silver, and Gold, although any one of these is sure to please all but the most demanding of guests. For those, a selection of exquisite suites guarantees satisfaction. Bronze Rooms top out at around 42 sq m (452 sq ft), with traditional styling and views of the parkland. Some have their own balconies and bathrooms with walk-in showers. Silver Rooms are larger at around 46 sq m (495 sq ft), and are available in a range of designs that vary as distinctly as from a country house to a city apartment. Gold Rooms offer the best mix of luxury and value, and are very large at 60 sq m (646 sq ft), including a lounge with sofas and armchairs.

The view from the balconies and terraces of these rooms overlooks the croquet lawn and golf course. Inside, their epic bathrooms have a soaking tub and two walk-in showers each.

Suite accommodations range from the smaller Junior Suites at 60 sq m (646 sq ft) to the grand Marryat Suite, which covers 83 sq m (893 sq ft) of area with the most opulent furnishings and amenities. The latter boasts CD sound systems by Bang & Olufsen, huge flat-screen televisions, and wood panelling in the main bathroom. If one needs to entertain, the unusually large sitting room opens out onto a balcony terrace spacious enough to host a cocktail reception. A number of Duplex

THIS PAGE (FROM LEFT): With its simple yet satisfying fare, there's no question that Marryat deserves all the accolades it has earned; suites come with sitting areas, ideal for entertaining guests.

OPPOSITE (FROM LEFT): The outdoor terrace offers al fresco dining; in the winter months, warm up in front of the open fireplaces.

Suites are more suited to those with families, and provide two bedrooms, a living area, and bathrooms spread over two levels. Private gardens with high walls allow parents and children to enjoy their exceptional vacations with complete peace of mind.

Having been voted the UK's Favourite Spa Retreat, it is not surprising that peace is the operative word at the Chewton Glen Spa. Focused on bringing together the attributes of the hotel's spectacular location with the very best in natural skincare and beauty treatments, the spa offers a full menu of renewing therapies drawn from around the world. Molton Brown Body Treatments are at the heart of many of the spa's massage programmes, while another well-known name with 35 years of experience, Linda Meredith, has developed products for facials that are not available anywhere else but in the 10 deluxe treatment rooms here. At the heart of the spa is a Roman-inspired 17-m (56-ft) ozone-treated pool with tall columns and a painted ceiling reminiscent of the blue sky. An outdoor pool is also available, but the main attraction here is surely the high-tech hydrotherapy pool which administers six different treatments to help relieve stress and improve blood circulation.

Light, healthy meals are available from the spa's pool bar and lounge, but for more substantial fare, the award-winning Marryat restaurant has no equal. Executive Chef Luke Matthews has 15 years of experience in the kitchen of the Marryat alone, during which

time he has honed his craft to perfection with the use of wholesome, organic ingredients from local suppliers. They are often credited by name on the last page of the menu, which is peppered with British classics and seasonal ingredients cooked in the purest way possible. The exquisite yet uncomplicated flavours are testament to Chef Matthews' delicate touch.

Combining luxury hotel, spa, and country club, the Chewton Glen is a self-contained destination on England's beautiful south coast. Find the strength to venture out from the marvellous facilities and one will discover spectacular natural environments well worth exploring, but at the end of a long day, returning to the comfortable folds of the hotel is the greatest possible privilege.

rooms
35 rooms · 23 suites

food
Marryat: fine dining · Pool Bar: light buffets

drink
Lounge bar

features
spa · pools · 9-hole golf course · 4 tennis courts · croquet · gym and fitness facilities · landscaped gardens

nearby
beach · New Forest National Park · Isle of Wight · fishing · horse-riding · sailing · hiking

contact
New Milton
Hampshire BH25 6QS, United Kingdom · telephone: +44.014.2527 5341 · facsimile: +44.014.2527 2310 · email: reservations@chewtonglen.com · website: www.chewtonglen.com

thesouthwest

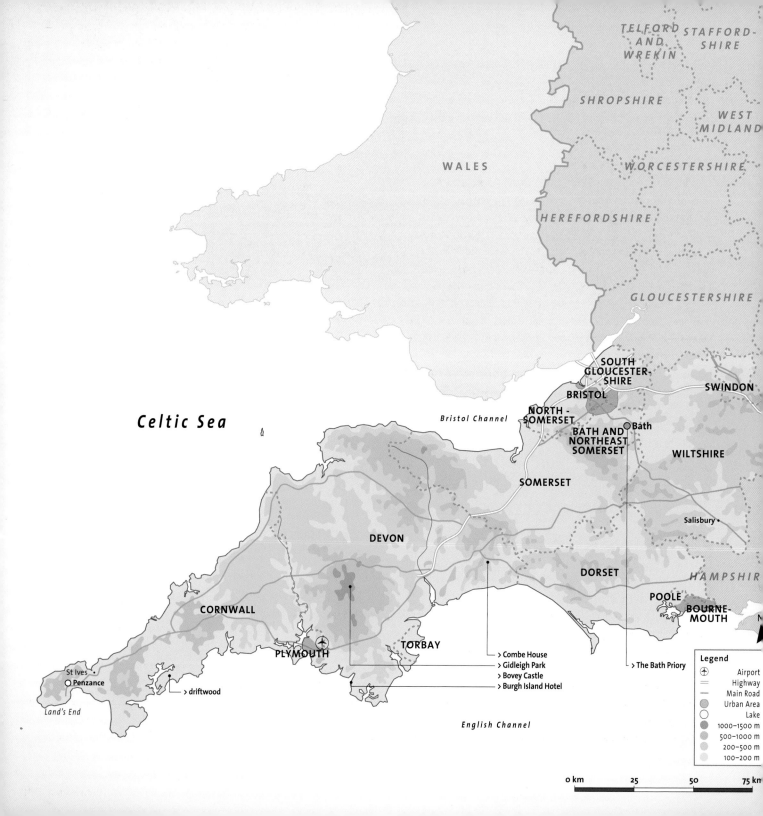

TELFORD
AND
WREKIN

STAFFORD-
SHIRE

SHROPSHIRE

WEST
MIDLAND

WORCESTERSHIRE

WALES

HEREFORDSHIRE

GLOUCESTERSHIRE

Celtic Sea

Bristol Channel

SOUTH
GLOUCESTER-
SHIRE

BRISTOL

SWINDON

NORTH-
SOMERSET

BATH AND
NORTHEAST
SOMERSET

○ Bath

WILTSHIRE

SOMERSET

DEVON

Salisbury •

DORSET

HAMPSHIR

POOLE

BOURNE-
MOUTH

CORNWALL

TORBAY

> Combe House
> Gidleigh Park
> Bovey Castle
> Burgh Island Hotel

> The Bath Priory

PLYMOUTH

St Ives •
○ Penzance

> driftwood

Land's End

English Channel

Legend

⊕ Airport
═ Highway
── Main Road
⬤ Urban Area
○ Lake
■ 1000–1500 m
■ 500–1000 m
■ 200–500 m
■ 100–200 m

o km   25   50   75 km

the southwest

scintillating southwest

The chic pleasures of the Southwest are among England's best-kept secrets. Long a holiday favourite of families and surfers, the southwestern counties of Somerset, Dorset, Devon and Cornwall attract some of the country's wealthiest and most stylish celebrities. Madonna and Guy Ritchie, BBC TV host and film critic Jonathan Ross, Oasis guitarist and sometime-vocalist Noel Gallagher and former football player and sports commentator Jamie Redknapp all have homes in Dorset. In Cornwall, American Singer Tori Amos has a recording studio in Bude, and Jean Shrimpton, one of the original 1960s supermodels and populariser of the mini-skirt, quietly runs a small hotel in Penzance.

Most are drawn by the region's undeniable natural beauty. From an imaginary diagonal line between Bristol and Southampton, this long peninsula narrows to Land's End in Cornwall. Separated from Wales by the Bristol Channel and the River Severn and washed on the south by the English Channel and the Atlantic Ocean, its undisturbed and protected landscapes are surrounded by hundreds of miles of deeply indented coastline, golden beaches, cliffs and coves.

During the Second World War, parts of rural Somerset were so deserted that the army built decoy towns on open land to trick Axis bombers. It's still quiet and lightly populated, the rustic idyll only interrupted by few towns. One of these is the elegant spa city of Bath. Since pre-Roman times, the fashionable have 'taken the waters' here. Today, Bath, with its Georgian crescents and promenades, is also packed with opportunities for dining and shopping.

a land where legends thrive

Hip visitors head for Glastonbury, where the legendary connections with King Arthur, and the Holy Grail, have been nearly overshadowed by one of the biggest and wildest pop music and performing arts festivals in Europe. Every year, the Glastonbury Festival features a staggering, international array of top contemporary acts. Once a mud bath for students and New Age travellers, this Woodstock for the modern age now attracts such hip and fashionable celebrities as Kate Moss, Gwyneth Paltrow, Stella McCartney, Keira Knightley and Sienna Miller.

Dorset has been inspiring writers for generations. This is Thomas Hardy country, the coasts, fields and farms serving as the model for his fictionalised Wessex. Robert Louis Stevenson, PD James and John le Carre all lived and wrote in Dorset. Jane Austen set *Persuasion* against the Lyme Regis seascape. Later, one of the most memorable scenes in John Fowles' *The French Lieutenant's Woman* is set on The Cobb, Lyme Regis's atmospheric harbour wall.

THIS PAGE (FROM TOP): The Royal Crescent in Bath dates from the 18th century, and is often considered one of the greatest Georgian terraces in England; Amy Winehouse headlining at Glastonbury Festival.

PAGE 124: The woodlands of Exmoor in their brilliant palette of autumn colours.

The county boasts beauty, style and wealth. From the fossil-strewn cliffs and beaches of its Jurassic Coast, England's only natural UNESCO World Heritage Site, 44 per cent of Dorset is designated an Area of Outstanding Natural Beauty. It's one of the sunniest places in England and one of the richest. Sandbanks, an exclusive enclave on Poole Harbour, has some of the most valuable real estate in the world, outstripping Singapore, New York and Paris. On the main street—a scant kilometre known as Millionaire's Row—square footage costs more than twice that of New York's Fifth Avenue. On some days, just contemplating the value of yachts in Poole Harbour (second to Sydney as the world's largest natural harbour) can take your breath away.

Devon, the land of cream teas and thatched cob cottages, of Lorna Doone and the heather-covered wilds of Dartmoor and Exmoor, offers more than cosy clichés. The south coast has a distinct Mediterranean air—which may be why people call the area around Torquay, Brixham and Paignton the English Riviera. Café- and shop-lined quays front villages crowded with pastel-coloured houses that march helter skelter up crisscrossing lanes.

Devon shophounds head for the Castle and Cathedral Quarters of Exeter for independent fashion and jewellery designers, quays strung with craft workshops and colourful street markets. Try Sidewell Street Market for a good rummage of vintage and new clothing and handbags. Toot Garook (19 Queen Street) offers three floors of contemporary design goodies, and the resident goldsmith at Silver Lion (12 Gandy Street) produces exclusive pieces set with unusual gems.

cornwall: exoticism in the southwest

From west of the River Tamar to Land's End, Cornwall is a land of wild moors, and strange, mysterious stories. Echoes of Cornish, a Celtic language, closer to Breton than Welsh or Gaelic, can be heard in Cornwall's unusual place names: Tintagel, Mevagissey, Porthqwarra, Polzeath, Penzance. On its beaches or in the boat havens of Falmouth and Fowey, it's easy to forget Cornwall's history of piracy and smuggling. Cornish 'wreckers' were known to draw unsuspecting ships onto the rocks with false lights in the night. Daphne du Maurier based her novel *Jamaica Inn* on the real smugglers' hostelry of the same name. The inn, at the centre of desolate Bodmin Moor still attracts the curious with the largest collection of smugglers' artefacts in Britain.

Cornwall is the only part of England where palm trees are common. The exceptionally mild climate fosters dozens of particularly exotic gardens. The Lost Gardens of Heligan near St Austell is a jungle of subtropical plants. The waterside gardens at Trelissick, overlooking the Fal estuary, have spectacular views. At Boconnoc, visitors walk through a rare surviving medieval deer park. And the 10-hectare (25-acre) Trebah Garden in Falmouth, follows a tumbling stream down a ravine with waterfalls, ponds full of carp and exotic water plants.

THIS PAGE: *Colour and character mark sunny towns of the Southwest such as Bideford.*

OPPOSITE: *Golitha Falls on the River Fowey in Cornwall's mysterious Bodmin Moor.*

...a tumbling stream down a ravine with waterfalls, ponds full of carp and exotic water plants.

refined resorts of the southwest

The English were slightly late to the spa party, leaving all that indulgent messing about with steams, creams and jets of hot water to their more decadent European cousins.

One exception was **Bath** in Somerset, where Romans, and Celts before them, enjoyed the natural hot mineral springs that bubbled out of the ground. The original springs, in restored pools and baths, were in use until declared unsafe in the 1970s.

Of course, now that the English have embraced spa culture with a vengeance and luxurious spas have cropped up all over the country, it was only a matter of time before Bath's historic spa became a feature of this fashionable resort once again. The new **Thermae Bath Spa** opened in 2006, in a glass-and-steel building designed by Sir Nicholas Grimshaw. Among its several therapeutic treats is an open-air, rooftop pool, fed by the natural hot springs, where visitors can relax and watch the sunset over the spires of Bath.

Retail therapy is another fine form of indulgence in Bath where independent designer boutiques are thick on the ground. Make your way toward **The Upper Town**—**Bartlett Street**, **George Street** and **Margaret's Buildings**—to start your hunt among its delicious little shops tucked into Georgian townhouses. On the way,

try **Kimberley** (Trim Street) for well-edited designer collections, and **The Dressing Room** (7 Quiet Street) for international lingerie brands and nightwear. **Prey** (3 York Buildings, George Street) is a wonderfully eclectic 'micro-department store' that specialises in fashion, jewellery and diverse other beautiful objects.

Since the 19th century, artists have been inspired by West Cornwall. Whistler painted in St. Ives in the

1880s; earlier in the century, JMW Turner visited **Newlyn** and **Penzance**. Two highly distinctive schools of art developed, the **St Ives School** and the **Newlyn School**, and artists continue to thrive in the area today.

The St Ives School spawned some of the great painters and sculptors of British modernism. Sculptor Barbara Hepworth spent most of her life there, working with a circle of artists which included her husband, painter Ben Nicholson and sculptor Naum Gabo. Their work, along with other modernist and contemporary art is beautifully showcased at the **Tate St Ives** on Porthmeor Beach. Nearby, at the **Hepworth Museum and Sculpture Garden** located on Barnoon Hill, visitors can explore the artist's workshop and studio.

Take a walk along the beach road and through the lanes, lined with old fisherman's cottages, with names like Virgin Street, Teetotal Street and Salubrious Terrace, to the Mariner's Church in Norway Square. There, artists still working in the St Ives tradition show their work through the **St Ives Society of Artists'** galleries housed in the main body of the church and the crypt.

Don't overlook Penzance, where The Newlyn School flourished around in the 19th and 20th centuries. The **Newlyn Gallery** (New Road, Newlyn) and the **Exchange** in Penzance (Princes Street), have recently given the contemporary art scene there a much-needed shot in the arm. When they opened, in 2007, *The Times* of London reported, 'Galleries have been sprouting like mushrooms in the shadow of The Exchange...'

THIS PAGE (CLOCKWISE FROM TOP LEFT): Locally inspired contemporary art is on exhibition at The Tate St Ives; sculpture by Barbara Hepworth; the historic Roman baths at Bath.

OPPOSITE: Bath's new multi-million-pound Thermae Bath Spa is a hot draw for locals and visitors alike.

dining out in the southwest

The Southwest is justifiably known as one of the best areas in England, outside of London and the Home Counties, in which to eat out. Fresh seafood from local fishing fleets and farms devoted to heritage breeds and organic local produce ensure a steady supply of the kind of top-quality ingredients that lure in the very best chefs and keep them here. Devon and Cornwall, in particular, are noted for producing some of the best cheeses, creams and boutique farmed meats to be found in Britain.

Added to that is this region's longstanding popularity for holidays and long weekends and thus it's not surprising that there are more than enough excellent restaurants in the Southwest to satisfy even the most demanding gourmet. This is just a small selection.

Stephen Shore's Restaurant, the **Moody Goose**, survived a move from Bath, Somerset, where it had been winning critical plaudits for nine years, to a country setting in nearby Midsomer Norton, with its Michelin stars and AA rosettes intact. The kitchen is tiny—Shore runs it with just one other chef—and an emphasis is placed on modern British cooking. Local small game—wood pigeon, quail, rabbit—regularly makes an appearance on the menu.

The **Horn of Plenty** in Tavistock, Devon, a restaurant with rooms, has been going strong for decades. Go for an early summer dinner to enjoy the spectacular views from the dining room. Goats' cheese gnocchi or the truly exceptional Devonshire lamb with wild mushrooms might be on the menu for the evening.

Michael Caines, executive chef at **Gidleigh Park** in Devon, is considered to be one of England's most talented chefs, which probably accounts for the two Michelin stars the hotel's restaurant has already garnered. Cuisine is modern European, with seasonal à la carte menus and tasting menus that change weekly—think ravioli of Brixham crab with lemongrass and ginger, John Dory with crushed olive potatoes and banana parfait that looks like a work of modernist architecture. If you're not staying at the hotel, go for lunch to enjoy a walk in Gidleigh Park's beautiful grounds.

English seafood guru Rick Stein is probably responsible for starting Cornwall's great gourmet revolution. His small empire of restaurants based in Padstow includes **The Seafood Restaurant** (fish and shellfish), **St Petroc's Bistro** (hearty, peasant-inspired European fare), **Rick Stein's Café** (traditional English caff) and **Stein's Fish & Chips** (first class take on the humble chippie).

Fifteen, on Watergate Bay, is the brainchild of Jamie 'The Naked Chef' Oliver, one of the country's most celebrated—and internationally recognisable—young chefs. Annually, Oliver offers up to 20 disadvantaged young people the chance to spend a year as apprentice chefs—a process featured on Oliver's TV programme. The cooking that results is remarkable, and the views of surfer's paradise Watergate Bay spectacular.

And one young man to watch is Nathan Outlaw, now presiding over his eponymous **Restaurant Nathan Outlaw**, at the Marina Villa in Fowey. Outlaw's fans, and his Michelin star, have followed him across Cornwall, with daily converts to the cause. The restaurant opened in 2007 and by 2008 he had once again won the coveted accolade—for the third time. Outlaw's simple menu descriptions— Ling with razor clams and shallots, bay and bacon; Pork Belly with curry and apple, fried eggs and cress— belie a high level of sophistication and humour. This restaurant is tipped as a rising star and a definite stop on any Cornish foodie tour.

THIS PAGE (CLOCKWISE FROM TOP RIGHT):
Elegant minimalism sets off the gorgeous food at Fifteen Cornwall; chocolate tart from Horn of Plenty; Rick Stein's Seafood Restaurant; traditional pasties get the gourmet treatment at Rick Stein's Patisserie.

OPPOSITE (FROM TOP): There is no lack of great dining options in Cornwall; figs and rocket from Nathan Outlaw; picture-perfect Padstow Harbour.

the bath priory

THIS PAGE (FROM LEFT): Enjoy a cool morning walk in the gardens; the city of Bath has long been renowned for its excellent spas, and the hotel's is no exception.

OPPOSITE (FROM LEFT): Most rooms in the hotel display motifs of the flowers they are named after; the hotel's restaurant serves light and fresh seasonal food.

One of the most charming cities in the UK, enjoying the countryside air of Somerset and blessed with many examples of classical Georgian architecture, Bath is the historic jewel of the southwest. Declared a UNESCO World Heritage Site in 1987, its popularity stems from attractions such as Bath Abbey and the Royal Crescent, as well as the Roman Baths and recently opened Thermae Bath Spa, the UK's only naturally heated springs.

Not far from all the city centre's activity, barely a five-minute ride in a taxicab and just past Royal Victoria Park, is a luxury country hotel of great character and distinction. The Bath Priory occupies a row of 19th-century Gothic houses built from the distinctive amber-coloured stone that is indigenous to the region, sheltered by 2 hectares (4 acres) of award-winning English country-style gardens. Magnificent ash and cedar trees, over 150 years old, share space with fragrant flower beds throughout the picturesque grounds. A Victorian Kitchen Garden grows fresh organic herbs and produce to supply the hotel's restaurant, which has held the coveted distinction of a Michelin star for nine consecutive years.

Mirroring the tranquillity of its natural surroundings, The Bath Priory's 31 guestrooms are decorated in calm, neutral tones, and have large windows that let in lots of sunlight and provide fantastic views of the front courtyard and landscape gardens. Each one features a unique design furnished with rare antiques and objets d'art, and carries the name of a flower—often a room's wallpaper will bear a motif symbolising its name. The Carnation suite has a large four-poster bed, separate dressing room, and a scenic garden view, while Heather and Lilac have extravagant marble bathrooms and delightful little balconies that overlook the greenery to the south. Behind the classic décor, a recent renovation has equipped many of the bedrooms with the latest in technological accoutrements: Bang & Olufsen televisions, satellite channels, and ISDN lines.

Central to The Bath Priory experience is an understanding of nature's importance, and this is reflected in the hotel restaurant. Head Chef Chris Horridge works exclusively from seasonal crops, many from the hotel's own gardens, which are tended by Chelsea Medal-winner Jane Moore. The light and elegant

...there are no moments here that are not utterly beautiful.

rooms
31 rooms

food
restaurant: modern British

drink
extensive wine selection

features
Garden Spa · landscape gardens · fitness centre · 2 temperature-controlled pools · private dining space · meeting facilities · ISDN Internet access

nearby
Bath Abbey · Bath city centre · Bath Race Course · Dyrham House · Roman Baths · The Royal Crescent · Royal Victoria Park · Thermae Bath Spa · theatre · golf course

contact
Weston Road
Bath BA1 2XT, United Kingdom
telephone: +44.012.2533 1922 ·
facsimile: +44.012.2544 8276 ·
email: mail@thebathpriory.co.uk ·
website: www.thebathpriory.co.uk

meals are inspired by the surrounding country environment. Knowing this, it's no wonder that the airy 64-seat restaurant has been awarded the prestigious Michelin star and AA Rosette for years running.

Of course, being in the heart of Bath, the hotel shares an extraordinary dedication to the spa arts. The spa at The Bath Priory offers a full menu of manicures, beauty treatments and massage therapies, as well as the use of a solarium. At the luxurious Garden Spa facility, guests have access to an air-conditioned gym, indoor and outdoor pools, a sauna, steam room, and back spa.

Staff at the hotel are dedicated to ensuring that guests enjoy a relaxing vacation. With its excellent location and setting, the personable Bath Priory Hotel, Restaurant & Spa is the perfect frame for observing the passing of seasons. Splendid in summertime and intimate in the winter, there are no moments here that are not utterly beautiful.

combe house

THIS PAGE: *Wild pheasants and Arabian horses freely roam the park surrounding Combe House, adding to the peaceful feeling of a country landscape.*

OPPOSITE: *The historic Linen Suite maintains details such as the original wooden drying rack, which stretches across almost the whole of the sitting room.*

Old enough to have been mentioned in the *Domesday Book*, yet fresh enough to be named Country House of the Year by the 2007 *Good Hotel Guide*, Combe House combines historic charm with generous hospitality. With over 1,400 hectares (3,500 acres) of idyllic countryside and a babbling brook at its doorstep, yet only accommodating up to 32 guests overnight, this cosy country retreat is an attractive getaway all year round.

Approached on a long, winding drive through meadows and parkland, Combe House sits on gentle Gittisham Hill, offering exquisite views of the unabashedly romantic landscape. Beyond the front door of broad oak, the Great Hall awaits. Maintained in 16th-century style, it displays carved wooden panelling, fine antique furniture and looming sandstone fireplaces. Dramatic arrangements of fresh flowers add a final bright touch to the traditionally Old World ambience.

Today, Combe House's Elizabethan and Jacobean characters take centre stage. Gables, finials and transom windows, accentuated by wall hangings and antique family portraits, bespeak the serenity of a bygone age.

While all amenities are in step with modern standards, the house has been restored with a profound respect for its history, limiting its anachronistic elements. 15 individually designed and decorated bedrooms are spread over the former servants' and masters' quarters, all handsomely styled and enjoying lovely views of the gardens. Each room features its own highlights, from oak-panelled bathrooms and four-poster beds to mullioned windows, striking artwork and hand-painted designs.

The larger and more spectacular rooms lie at the front of the house, in the wing formerly occupied by the masters of the house. Draped in elegant silks, linens and carpets, these master bedrooms and suites luxuriate in the opulence of the past. They also have generous sitting areas with armchairs or sofas, perfect for unwinding with a good book.

The humbly named Linen Suite used to be a Victorian laundry, now transformed into a crisp, comfortable abode. Lime-washed walls daubed in tones of linen white create a soothing retreat, complemented by pale wool carpets, soft cotton linens and Devon lambswool throws. Modern furnishings in the sitting and bedroom areas are complemented by hand-painted pieces.

At the same time, the suite's history has been creatively memorialised. Its main highlight is a round copper bathtub, a startling 2 m (6 ft) in diameter. In the bedroom, commissioned artwork offers a contemporary reinterpretation

The meals and special occasions of Combe House have become legendary. In 2008, the restaurant earned a Michelin Rising Star for the second year in succession, apt recognition for its exquisite culinary creations. Helmed by two Master Chefs, the restaurant's menus are composed of only fresh seasonal ingredients from West Country farmers and fishermen. Most vegetables are picked from the estate's own gardens, and all preserves are made on the premises.

Dining in the Panel Room is a visual treat. Dignified portraits glimmer from every wall, vividly brought to life in winter when the fireplaces are in use. For a more intimate dining experience with a touch of history, parties may choose to dine in the restored Georgian Kitchen, where a wood-fired stove, cast-iron cooking range and copper pots and pans take pride of place, visible by the light of candles and Tilley lamps.

The old spaces of Combe House also house a number of ancient underground cellars, yielding ideal conditions for the laying down of fine wines. The wine list is both

THIS PAGE (FROM LEFT): Tall windows and bright flower displays give the rooms a sense of airy space; the Linen Suite also features a large copper bathtub, a nod to its days as a Victorian laundry.

OPPOSITE (FROM LEFT): Suites boast rich furnishings and antiques; savour exquisite British cuisine prepared by their expert chefs.

of the laundry with a vibrant burst of colour, while overhead in the sitting room, the original drying rack has been suspended intact. There are also books about the lives of Victorian laundry maids for guests to browse.

For couples who desire a more secluded location, the Combe Thatch Cottage is tucked away in the woods. It is pet-friendly, so guests may enjoy the private walled garden with their dogs. The exterior of the original cottage has been preserved, while the interiors have been enlivened with fine contemporary furnishings in soft white and stone. A sojourn here can be topped off with a romantic soak in a another copper bath and a stroll through Gittisham—a charming thatched village from a bygone era.

...it is the warmth and care of the owners and staff that set a stay at Combe House apart...

rooms
15 rooms and suites · 1 thatched cottage with private walled garden

food
local produce by two master chefs of Great Britain with a Michelin rising star

drink
bar · exciting wine list

features
landscaped gardens · meeting facilities · exclusive use for weddings · social and corporate special events · breakfast, coffee, lunch and dinner all year round

nearby
Southwest Coastal Path · Dartmoor National Park · Cathedral City of Exeter · Honiton with tea shops and galleries · National Trust Historic Houses and Gardens

contact
Gittisham, Honiton, near Exeter Devon EX14 3AD, United Kingdom · telephone: +44.014.0454 0400 · email: stay@thishotel.com · website: www.thishotel.com

impressive and exciting. The entire property is also available for guests to exclusively host a wedding or any other special occasion. The grounds can accommodate up to 100 guests, or 150 with a marquee.

Above all, it is the warmth and care of the owners and staff that set a stay at Combe House apart from other country havens. Ken and Ruth Hunt, who own the property, are happy to chat, recommend memorable landmarks out in the parkland, or entice guests to try the unique Victorian-style bath, which uses rain water heated by a log fire. Tea and home-made biscuits are served in the manor's Great Hall, where ample sofas in an informal atmosphere provide private reading nooks or an ideal location for enjoying idle conversation with friends.

Guests interested in exploring Devon may relish a tramp through the countryside, with the medieval village of Gittisham just a ten minute walk away. Today it is still dotted with cob and thatch cottages, and boasts a Norman church in its midst. Honiton is known for its antiques and pottery collections, and nearby, the South West Coastal Path and the rugged spaces of Dartmoor beckon.

Back at Combe House, the freely roaming wild pheasants and Arabian horses and the splendid, carefully tended gardens set it in a romantic class of its own. Small wonder, then, that it has been awarded Small Hotel of the Year 2008 for South West Tourism. Harking back to a glorious past, Combe House has all the hallmarks of a gracious homestay in a manor house, set in peace and tranquillity.

gidleigh park

Set in a sprawling green valley in the Devon countryside, surrounded by the unspoiled natural beauty of Dartmoor National Park—the largest region of open land in the south of England—Gidleigh Park had always been one of the country's finest hotel retreats. With its exquisite location on the banks of the North Teign River inviting long, drawn-out walks to nowhere in particular, and an incredible two-Michelin-star restaurant to return to in the evenings, its charms were outnumbered only by the number of devotees who reappeared year after year for a slice of the unhurried country life.

So when new owners Andrew and Christina Brownsword closed Gidleigh Park's doors in the January of 2006 for an 11-month refurbishment, ruminations were heard from all corners of the country as to what improvements their plans for the property could bring. The answers were revealed in 2007 when the 14-bedroom establishment reopened with 24 bedrooms, each one completely remodelled to the highest standards. Sensitive to the charms of the old Gidleigh Park, the couple have retained much of the hotel's original spirit while making changes in a number of key areas to better receive guests of the 21st century. Throughout the hotel, modern conveniences are discreetly integrated, although one is more likely to notice the rare antiques and art pieces curated by the Brownswords in association with interior designer Carole Roberts.

Throughout these changes, the property has retained its classic black and white Tudor-style exterior, while all guestrooms and public areas have been completely refurbished. Aiming to have the interiors perfectly reflect the period in which the original manor was constructed, the refurbishment has taken cues from the 'Arts and Crafts Movement' of the late 19th century. Using all-new and carefully selected contemporary pieces of furniture, the original wood panelling and decorative details can now be seen in their best light—wholly modern, yet faithful to Gidleigh Park's history.

While serving at Gidleigh Park in 1999, Executive Chef Michael Caines, MBE became one of the youngest chefs ever to receive two Michelin stars. Food at the restaurant is as fantastic as it ever was, if not better, and it continues to draw guests and diners eager to discover what has been called 'some of the best dining in the UK' by The Times. Featuring modern European cuisine with more than a few sparks of inventiveness, the seasonal Tasting Menus are an essential part of any visit. All ingredients passing through the kitchen represent the finest local produce available, and the various fresh breads, scones, and marmalades available are homemade on the premises. Gourmet aficionados know a good wine goes a long way towards rounding

THIS PAGE: Every room in Gidleigh Park is an individual creation, so guests feel almost as if they are staying at a private house.

OPPOSITE: The gorgeous countryside around Gidleigh Park shows different facets of beauty as the seasons change.

off a perfect meal, and the newly built cellar which stores approximately 7,000 bottles sees to it that no glass ever stands dry.

To preserve the privacy of guests and the exclusivity of its location, the hotel offers just 24 bedrooms. Each one is a unique creation featuring a distinctive blend of luxurious fabrics, carefully selected furniture, and colour schemes individually imagined to best suit their particular room. The end result is a room which feels almost like a private house out in the country. Unlike most country houses, however, they come with ultra-modern comforts such as high-definition TVs and wireless Internet access. All rooms have large en-suite marble bathrooms that are magnificent beyond expectations, with lush details such as L'Occitane toiletries and thick cotton robes and towels.

Deluxe rooms offer views of the valley and gardens, and two have their own private balconies. One very special Deluxe room even has a hot tub on its roof, allowing guests to enjoy views of their surroundings while they soak. Master rooms are generally the largest of the rooms, and they offer stunning marble bathrooms as well as a number of elegant finishing touches.

Families and small groups with a taste for the country lifestyle may find the Pavilion best suits their needs. A stand-alone thatched cottage in the grounds, overlooking the croquet lawns and the fields beyond, it offers two bedrooms with en suite bathrooms, an open-plan lounge which also serves as a kitchen and diner, and a covered verandah. Guests with dogs are also welcome to include their companions in their stays at the Pavilion.

THIS PAGE (FROM LEFT): The luxurious marble bathrooms come with decadent L'Occitane toiletries; unlike most country hotels, all rooms at Gidleigh Park have a range of modern amenities.

OPPOSITE (FROM LEFT): Private balconies allow guests to enjoy the country's tranquil beauty; the hotel's two-Michelin-star restaurant is not to be missed.

rooms
24 rooms

food
restaurant: modern European

drink
honesty bar and pantry

features
18-hole putting course • bowling green • croquet • guided walks • heated and lit dog kennels • in-room spa treatments • landscaped gardens • room service • tennis court

nearby
Castle Drogo • Drizzlecombe complex • archery • canoeing • fishing • four-wheel-drive tours • golfing • horse riding • mountain biking • rock climbing

contact
Chagford
Devon TQ13 8HH, United Kingdom •
telephone: +44.016.4743 2367 •
facsimile: +44.016.4743 2574 •
email: gidleighpark@gidleigh.co.uk •
website: www.gidleigh.com

The latest additions to accommodations at Gidleigh Park are also the finest. Two incredible Spa Suites offer the most indulgent escapes possible with integrated wellness facilities. Dartmeet, the largest in the house, has a bathroom of almost equal size to the bedroom, complete with a huge tub topped with blue Lapaz marble, a sauna, steam room, double walk-in showers, heated bench, and French doors that open out to the bathroom's very own balcony. A night at Dartmeet includes dinner by Executive Chef Michael Caines, making for a truly romantic occasion.

Despite all the emphasis on indoor luxury, there can be no question that the one thing that has kept visitors returning to Gidleigh Park over the years is what appears outside of its windows. The splendid gardens, woodlands, and landscaped terraces add up to no fewer than 22 hectares (54 acres), and are beautiful all year round. Seen in springtime, the fields are thick with bluebells and wild orchids, while summer brings about thick clusters of fragrant roses and lavender. Between autumn and winter, the majestic trees—a combination of ash, birch, oak, and beech—shower down golden leaves before standing in stark contrast to a rolling landscape of snow. No matter when one chooses to visit Gidleigh Park, the fresh air and sweeping views have a restorative quality that goes beyond mere pleasure.

bovey castle

Tucked in the sprawling expanse of Dartmoor National Park, Bovey Castle offers the full experience of a modern country stay. While the Tudor-style architecture and exquisite period furnishings effortlessly evoke the languor of a bygone era, Bovey Castle offers plenty of new conveniences and diverse leisure pursuits to pamper the discerning traveller.

The castle was originally commissioned by Lord Hambledon and financed by his father, the business magnate W H Smith. Completed in 1906, the building subsequently became a railway hotel before slowly falling into decline. It was only in 2004 that Bovey Castle reopened in full magnificence, including a new wing that was constructed in the style of the original castle. The new wing houses a spa, clubhouse and additional guest suites. The vast parklands, formal gardens and rivers within the estate are also thriving once more, with the luxuriant Victorian-style gardens especially enhancing the historic feel.

Arriving at Bovey Castle is a moment to be savoured, from the wrought iron-gated entrance wending up a gently rising hill to the forecourt decorated with flower-bedecked stone troughs. Stepping inside is akin to entering a grand country home. Impressive oak-panelled halls and drawing rooms with large open fireplaces lead to garden terraces offering sweeping views of the grounds.

Bovey Castle has 63 stunning bedrooms and suites, each one dressed to the nines in true 1920s style. While the view outside speaks for itself, the little touches inside have not been forgotten. Guests can select the bedding or pillows of their choice, and the ritzy black-and-white bathrooms are well-stocked with Elemis toiletries. Other touches include Bang & Olufsen televisions, wireless Internet access and even a CD with 1920s jazz tunes to get the mood right.

The finest suite in Bovey Castle is the Easdon, located at the top of the ornate wooden staircase. Sumptuously adorned in red and gold, the room retains many original features such as a carved marble fireplace and a wall of traditional lattice windows, framed in crewel fabric. French doors open out onto a private balcony overlooking the moors, the perfect nook for a quiet evening drink.

For more privacy, Bovey Castle also has 14 guest lodges in its gardens. Constructed from granite, with slate roofs, they are spacious and airy, with oak-beamed cathedral-style ceilings and outdoor dining areas on the terrace or

One of the most popular activities is the daily falconry display, which takes place after breakfast on the castle terrace outside the dining room. Guests who wish to learn more about falconry can request for personal walks and rides with the castle's renowned falconer, and may even handle the hawks themselves.

Other activities run from archery and wine tasting to the more energetic demands of rock climbing and mountain biking. Couples may also enjoy a romantic interlude in a hot-air balloon. Children have their own dedicated activities during the school holidays, with a playbarn equipped with the latest electronic games and the Bovey Rangers, a supervised club with a number of indoor and outdoor activities tailored for 7- to 14-year-olds.

The castle grounds are also home to a championship golf course that was designed in 1926 by famous British golf course designer J F Abercromby. Now fully restored, the par-70

balcony. Each lodge is large enough to house three bedrooms and some have an additional architectural curiosity: a minstrels' gallery.

The most secluded hide-away on the grounds is the Rose Cottage, which overlooks the golf course. The two-bedroom refuge has its own private garden and a kitchen that is well-provisioned by the hotel. Ideal for couples, guests here can relax in total privacy, with only nature and each other for company.

Apart from the gorgeous country views, Bovey Castle also makes the most of its location in the heart of Dartmoor National Park, surrounded by 110 hectares (272 acres) of unspoiled English nature. The castle hosts a plethora of outdoor activities which allow guests a deeper appreciation of nature or a taste of traditional English pastimes.

THIS PAGE (FROM LEFT): Rooms pair 1920s design influences with a full range of modern amenities; located in the exquisite gardens, the private lodges are ideal for longer stays or large groups.

OPPOSITE (FROM LEFT): The Victorian gardens are beautifully kept; enjoy a swim in the spa's pool or soak in the relaxing jacuzzi.

rooms
63 rooms and suites • 14 lodges • 1 cottage

food
The Mulberry: fine dining • Castle Bistro: casual • The Edwardian Dining Room: classic English •

drink
Oak Bar

features
meeting rooms • hot-air balloon rides • spa • archery • cycling • falconry

nearby
Dartmoor National Park

contact
North Bovey, Dartmoor National Park Devon TQ13 8RE, United Kingdom • telephone: +44.0.1647.445 000 • facsimile: +44.0.1647.445 020 • email: booking@boveycastle.com • website: www.boveycastle.com

course still earns accolades today, having been named one of the top 100 golf courses in the UK by *Golf Monthly*. Winding through the estate and along the Bovey and Bowden Rivers, the challenging course attracts both amateur and professional players.

Another key hotel attraction is the spa, set in a new wing that blends harmoniously with the stonework and architectural features of the original castle. It has a full suite of saunas, steam rooms, hydrotherapy rooms, treatment rooms and a gymnasium. From the orangery, the Art Deco pool opens out to the sun terrace and an outdoor plunge pool which overlooks the dramatic English moors.

No grand country stay would be complete without a splendid repast, and Bovey Castle has a trio of restaurants to fill that need, all serving only the freshest local produce. The Edwardian Dining Room pays homage to the house's Art Deco history, with hand-painted silk chinoiserie wall coverings setting the stage for a memorable meal. The Mulberry Restaurant puts a contemporary spin on its menu, while the informal Bistro serves meals throughout the day in a casual atmosphere.

While it may be barely a century old, Bovey Castle has acquired a full measure of dignity and sophistication as it brings a luxury castle experience to the modern visitor. Whether guests are drawn by the appeal of England's largest national park, the castle's 1920s ambience or the promise of pure indulgence, there is the right balance of old and new, past glory and present grandeur to make a stay here unlike any other.

burgh island hotel

THIS PAGE: *The hotel is located on Burgh Island, which enjoys mild weather and excellent scenery.*

OPPOSITE: *Have a refreshing drink while soaking up warm rays of sunlight in the outdoor terrace.*

For many travellers, the idea of a secluded island resort that enjoys a comfortably warm climate is not one that occurs when English holidays are discussed. Yet off the south coast of Devon, near the quiet seaside village of Bigbury on Sea, is a place that most readily fits that description. Although only 200 m (656 ft) from the mainland, the island is located in a differentiated atmospheric zone known as the 'English Riviera', where local temperatures are often several degrees higher than in other parts of England. The clement weather is especially enjoyable in the fall, but visit in summer and one will discover cool sea breezes and much flora and fauna to appreciate.

A survey of the bay will reveal scores of aquatic wildlife, from exotic dolphins and seals, to more familiar human surfers nearer the golden beaches. Largely undeveloped, the idyllic island harbours unspoiled swathes of greenery which follow the hand of nature, creating homes for untamed bird populations

and families of wild rabbits and badgers on the slopes. Comfortably nestled on the shoreline of this paradisal scene are two buildings that make coming away to this hidden location even more of a pleasure, offering five-star boutique accommodations, fine dining, and a comfortable community atmosphere: the unique Art Deco-style Burgh Island Hotel and a charming public house named The Pilchard Inn.

Retreats at the hotel begin in one of two extraordinary ways. Arrive early enough to witness the ebbing of the tide, and a sandbar slowly emerges from beneath the water, so guests may enjoy a slow stroll to the island or travel in one of the hotel's landrovers. Arrive at high tide, however, and a chance to board an unusual vehicle presents itself. Dubbed the 'Sea Tractor', this custom hydraulic transport is a major attraction of the Burgh Island Hotel, and the only one of its kind in the world. Consisting of a raised carriage platform atop a set of tractor wheels, it traverses the strait by driving on the sea bed whilst keeping passengers safely above water level. The historic icon has been popular with locals, tourists, and guests of the hotel since it was first designed in 1969 by the esteemed scientist Robert Jackson CBE, reputedly in exchange for a case of champagne.

Established in 1929, the hotel has seen its share of historical events and famous visitors. Surviving the Second World War, it was remodelled as a series of apartment-style

THIS PAGE (FROM LEFT): *Enjoy a pre-dinner cocktail or two under the bar's gorgeous glass ceiling; Agatha Christie herself stayed at the Beach House suite while penning two of her mysteries.*

OPPOSITE (FROM LEFT): *Rooms enjoy unique Art Deco-style interiors; the restaurant serves fine food made from fresh local produce.*

accommodations before being returned to an accurate image of its 1930s heyday as an Art Deco hotel. At one point, it even enjoyed infamy as a smuggler's den. Past guests have included pop supergroup the Beatles, pioneer female aviator Amy Johnson, mystery novelist Agatha Christie and the talented writer and musician Noel Coward, who famously arrived intending to stay for three days, but ended up remaining for three weeks instead. The hotel served as the inspiration for a number of Madam Christie's most famous works, including the seminal whodunnit *And Then There Were None* and *Evil Under the Sun*.

Many of the hotel's 24 guestrooms have been named after famous visitors from the past. Each one is a masterpiece of Art Deco interior design and creativity, and no two rooms are alike because they draw inspiration from a range of entirely different sources.

The Noel Coward suite is clean and simple with a spectacular view and charming furniture. A number of musical references can be found around the room in the form of an antique radio and unique artwork celebrating his tastes. In contrast, the Avon suite was once a stopping point for the actress Clara Bow, and despite being named for the nearby Avon River, it is unmistakably dedicated to the beautiful 'It' girl whose picture hangs above the bed. Full of feminine touches, soft fabrics and mirrored surfaces, the room has a light and airy energy. Guests of the Avon also enjoy a private balcony and access to a large sun

deck shared with the Josephine Baker suite. Named for the famous singer and entertainer, the Baker bedroom features dark, velvety bedsheets and audacious zebra-print cushions. Despite appearances, all of the period rooms offer modern conveniences, including wireless Internet access and spa-grade REN toiletries.

Fans of Agatha Christie may opt to stay in the Beach House suite, the place where the authoress wrote her two novels set on the island. Recently rebuilt, the beachfront property is a picture of luxurious isolation. The bedroom area is built on supports directly over the beach, and at high tide, residents can literally watch waves beneath their feet.

rooms
24 rooms and suites

food
seafood

drink
The Pilchard Inn: adjacent pub

features
spa • gym • Mermaid Pool: seawater rock pool •
billiard room • study and TV room • wireless
Internet access • fresh flower arrangements •
Sea Tractor rides • tennis court • helipad •
walking routes • croquet • sauna • laptop hire

nearby
Bigbury on Sea • Avon river • fishing • beaches

contact
Bigbury-on-Sea
South Devon TQ7 4BG, United Kingdom •
telephone: +44.015.4881 0514 •
facsimile: +44.015.4881 0243 •
email: reception@burghisland.com •
website: www.burghisland.com

As one might expect from a lodge built on the boundaries between man and nature, meals at the hotel are prepared strictly from local produce. Chef Conor Heneghan creates a new menu every morning, with select herbs and vegetables straight from the island's own kitchen gardens and all cuts of meat from no further than 32 km (20 miles) away to ensure optimum quality. In addition to the exquisite food, the restaurant at Burgh Island Hotel offers an unmatchably classy dinner experience. The hotel assures guests that it is impossible to be overdressed for a meal at the opulent Ball Room, and it's right. Guests are encouraged to show off their finest formal wear, from elegant suits to elaborate evening dresses. To top it all off, a band comes in every Wednesday and Saturday night, so guests may dance to toe-tapping swing classics well into the wee hours of the morning. Those wishing for a more casual meal may also choose to dine in The Captain's Cabin or The Pilchard Inn.

Unlike a typical English holiday destination in every way, Burgh Island Hotel represents a welcome change from the usual countryside and urban landscapes. More than all that, the unorthodox Burgh Island Hotel goes out of its way to provide the comforts, pleasures and luxuries that one might expect to see from a world-class island resort.

driftwood

THIS PAGE: Rooms are an eclectic mix of sophisticated and cosy, with marine-inspired designs.

OPPOSITE (FROM LEFT): The classic deck chairs are ideal for lounging; the soothing sounds of the nearby sea and the comfortable beds ensure that all guests leave driftwood well-rested.

Traditionally, the tourism industry in Cornwall has been driven by British visitors, but England's southernmost county is receiving ever more international attention by the year. This is due in part to its favourable position on the tip of the peninsula, bounded by the English Channel and Celtic Sea, which guarantees mild weather all year round—perfectly complementing the miles of clean, sandy beaches and unspoiled greenery.

Situated in a prime position to enjoy Cornwall's natural scenery is driftwood, an exquisite beach house that affords its guests all the pleasures of a privileged seaside retreat. The property boasts incredible views of the sea from almost all of its rooms, and a two-room cabin is set in marvellous seclusion on a cliff overlooking Gerrans Bay. Surrounded by 3 hectares (7 acres) of coastal splendour with access to a private beach and cove, it is a

place where distractions simply cease to exist, replaced by the quiet, lulling sounds of the waves. The driftwood also features a sheltered garden terrace and sunbathing areas with classic deck chairs modelled after those once found on British steamships. These, and just about any spot on the grounds, are ideal for enjoying a few evening drinks or a perhaps a romantic private picnic.

All accommodations at driftwood echo the marine setting, and are furnished in a manner that is at once sophisticated and homey. Rooms are decorated in light colours that are occasionally livened up with aquatic blue or grounded earth tones. Glass jars filled with seashells and sand sit alongside cosy collections of books, magazines, and even board games, and every room is equipped with a television and access to a video library.

The surrounding area is lovely throughout all four seasons, with even the coldest winters being milder and sunnier than elsewhere on the mainland, and so one rarely feels the urge to leave driftwood's tranquil atmosphere. However, many unique places of interest lie only a short drive away. From the 14th-century church of St Just-in-Roseland, the gardens of Trelissick and Heligan, the Tate Gallery in St Ives, to the futuristic conservatories of the Eden Project, there is much to be discovered in the Cornish countryside.

Dedicated to serving only the best, food at the driftwood restaurant is sourced from local suppliers. Under the mastery of their

head chef, the restaurant has been honoured with three prestigious AA Rosettes—and rightfully so. For the very best that the sea-facing establishment has to offer, try its superb tasting menu, with inventive courses prepared from the freshest seafood, locally reared meats, and seasonal vegetables.

What driftwood offers goes beyond the mere provision of features and recreational activities, although it does offer a bar, children's games room, and drawing room for the enjoyment of all. Instead, the real draw of the hotel is how everything, from the gracious staff to the easy-going lack of rules, leaves guests free to discover what is most relaxing for themselves.

rooms
15 rooms

food
seafood

drink
hotel bar

features
private beach · children's games room · living room · drawing room · tv room with videos · wireless Internet access

nearby
St Mawes · Portscatho village · St Just-in-Roseland church · Eden Project · Falmouth Maritime Museum · gardens · golf · horse riding · tennis · surfing · fishing

contact
Rosevine, near Portscatho South Cornwall TR2 5EW, United Kingdom · telephone: +44.018.7258 0644 · facsimile: +44.018.7258 0801 · email: info@driftwoodhotel.co.uk · website: www.driftwoodhotel.co.uk

thewestmidlands

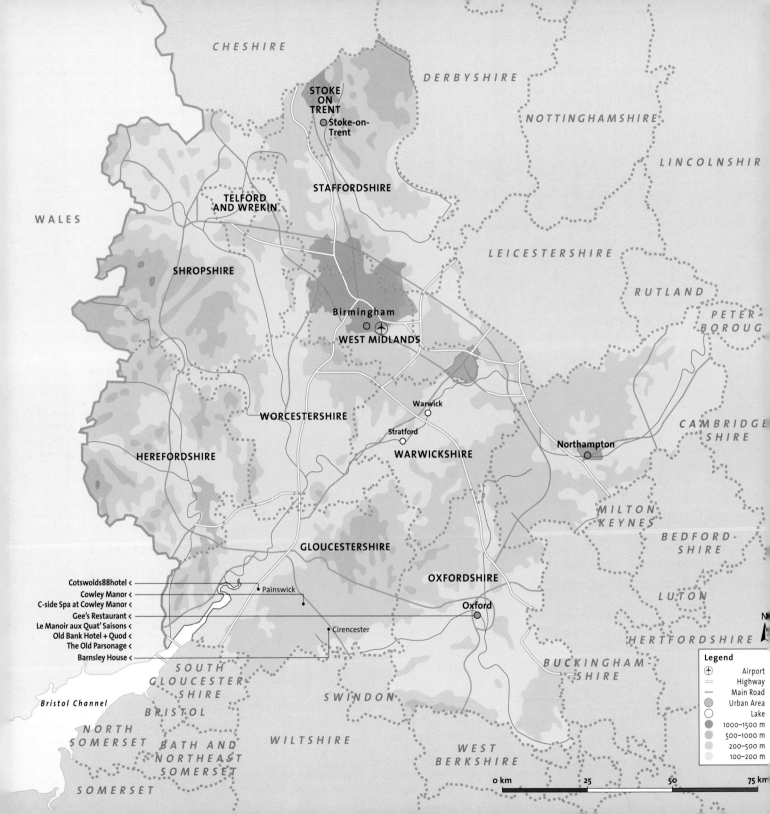

CHESHIRE

DERBYSHIRE

STOKE
ON
TRENT

○ Stoke-on-
Trent

NOTTINGHAMSHIRE

LINCOLNSHIR

STAFFORDSHIRE

TELFORD
AND WREKIN

WALES

LEICESTERSHIRE

SHROPSHIRE

RUTLAND

PETER-
BOROUG

Birmingham
○
WEST MIDLANDS ✈

WORCESTERSHIRE

Warwick
○

CAMBRIDGE
SHIRE

Stratford
○

HEREFORDSHIRE

WARWICKSHIRE

Northampton
●

MILTON
KEYNES

BEDFORD-
SHIRE

GLOUCESTERSHIRE

OXFORDSHIRE

LUTON

Cotswolds88hotel ‹
Cowley Manor ‹
C-side Spa at Cowley Manor ‹
Gee's Restaurant ‹
Le Manoir aux Quat' Saisons ‹
Old Bank Hotel + Quod ‹
The Old Parsonage ‹
Barnsley House ‹

• Painswick

• Cirencester

Oxford
●

HERTFORDSHIRE

N

BUCKINGHAM-
SHIRE

SOUTH
GLOUCESTER
SHIRE

BRISTOL

SWINDON

Bristol Channel

NORTH
SOMERSET

BATH AND
NORTHEAST
SOMERSET

WILTSHIRE

WEST
BERKSHIRE

SOMERSET

Legend
✈   Airport
    Highway
    Main Road
○   Urban Area
○   Lake
    1000–1500 m
    500–1000 m
    200–500 m
    100–200 m

0 km   25   50   75 km

the west midlands

the heart of england

Shakespeare's birthplace, the dreaming spires of Oxford and the crucible of the Industrial Revolution are all part of the 'Heart of England'. From golden stonebuilt cottages of the Cotswolds and quaint thatched hamlets of Oxfordshire to diverse urban districts of Birmingham, Derby and Stoke-on-Trent, this is where you'll find some of England's most familiar landscapes.

the beginning

Stonehenge rises up out of Salisbury Plain in Wiltshire like the first Englishman's claim to the landscape. It stands in the middle of a concentration of prehistoric structures—Avebury's stone circle and avenues of standing stones, the foreboding and mysterious Silbury Hill, the Rollright Stones in Oxfordshire—that give this area a primal Britishness. Local pubs such as the 400-year-old Red Lion in Avebury are long on character, but more into grub than gastronomy. Cap a day out with a meal in Howard's House, a restaurant with rooms in the bizarrely named village of Teffont Evias. Open for dinner, they'll serve you a set lunch with enough advance warning.

oxford

Oxford is not your garden variety college town. The students and faculty of the England's oldest university are sophisticated and affluent, as is the city they dominate. In a part of England where ethnic eateries are, frankly, less than wonderful, cosmopolites are well-served by Thai and Indian restaurants. One doesn't expect a carved oak staircase and 400-year-old oak panelling in a Thai restaurant but that's what you'll find at Chiang Mai Kitchen, located down Kemp Hall Passage off High Street. In good weather, it is hard to better the ambience of Aziz Pandesia, with its terrace on the river beside Folly Bridge. The Turf Tavern (Bath Place), one of Oxford's oldest (and coolest) pubs, is located just off New College Lane. Liz Taylor and Richard Burton canoodled there during the early days of their romance.

THIS PAGE (FROM TOP): Stonehenge cuts a grand profile at dawn; a panoramic aerial view of Oxford's Radcliffe Camera.
PAGE 154: Topiary at Hidcote Manor in Gloucestershire.

If the shopping bug strikes, head for Oxford Covered Market (between Market and High Streets) for food stalls and designer boutiques. The Garden (99-100 Covered Market) is decked out in dried flowers and herbs.

the cotswolds

The range of hills that forms a ridge across Oxfordshire, Gloucestershire and Warwickshire, rolls through some of the loveliest countryside, grandest country estates—both Princess Anne and Prince Charles live here—and

picturesque villages in England. Here are meadows covered with wild flowers in spring, a painterly scattering of livestock in summer; here are hamlets of low-built houses so deeply covered in thatch they seem to grow out of the earth. Towns have names reminiscent of an episode of *The Avengers* or *Miss Marple*—Chipping Camden, Lower Slaughter, Upper Swell, and surrounding Stratford-upon-Avon, a host of scattered villages associated with Shakespeare.

Chic travellers worried about overdosing on the bucolic and the historic need only head for the Regency spa town of Cheltenham, scene of the famous and very social jump-racing festival. There's great boutique shopping, along the Promenade in the Montpellier Quarter—international designers at Cousins of Cheltenham (10/11 Montpellier Walk) and Silks (11 The Courtyard). Tucked in among the shops of 'The Suffolks' is one of the country's best restaurants. At Le Champignon Sauvage (24-26 Suffolk Road), owner and one-time National Chef of the Year David Everitt-Matthias holds two Michelin stars, four AA Rosettes and several other awards.

the cradle of industry

Ironbridge, spanning the Severn near Telford in Shropshire, was a wonder of its age. In the 18th century, travellers came from all over to see the world's first cast-iron bridge, made possible by the first large-scale production of cast-iron here—one of the triggers of the Industrial Revolution. Looking at the delicately beautiful metal lace span, England's first UNESCO World Heritage site, it's hard to imagine that from this quiet stretch of the Severn, close to the Welsh border, in the middle of rich Shropshire farmland, spread the 'dark Satanic mills' of William Blake's *Jerusalem*.

From 18th- to mid-20th-century, the Midlands were at the heart of English manufacturing. Networks of canals were built to carry products and raw materials around the country. Today the region's heavy industries have morphed into technology and service businesses. Its international trade connections have fueled a retail explosion, and you will find amazing shops in unexpected places—a specialist Japanese cookery shop, Setonaikai, in the Tudor town of Shrewsbury; a jewel box of vintage clothes and accessories, The Looking Glass, in the Shropshire market town of Bridgnorth. Along restored waterways, now highways for pleasure craft, lock keepers' houses and warehouses have become scenic pubs, like the Shroppie Fly on the Shropshire Union Canal in Audlem, or Boat Inn on the Oxford Canal in Kidlington.

The Staffordshire 'Potteries', the six separate towns that make up Stoke-on-Trent, are an exception. There, traditionally skilled craftsmen keep fine china and ceramics manufacture alive and well, and also explore ceramics as a contemporary fine arts medium. While history of ceramics is explored at the Potteries Museum & Art Gallery, Wedgewood, Spode and several other manufacturers have exhibitions of classic and contemporary ceramic art.

THIS PAGE (FROM TOP): *Attention to the very tiniest details at the Royal Shakespeare Company; at Oxford, even the gargoyles appear to be earnest scholars.*

OPPOSITE: *Jumpers take a hurdle at Cheltenham, one of the top jump racecourses in England.*

...*Cheltenham, scene of the famous and very social jump-racing festival.*

heritage + culture in the heart of england

Shakespeare was born, educated, raised a family, died and was buried in the heart of England. With a little time out for London of course, the greatest playwright in the English language, spent most of his life in and around **Stratford-upon-Avon**. Unlike other English villages that have only recently been recognised by England's preservationists, Shakespeare's fame helped to preserve the chocolate-boxy prettiness of Stratford for hundreds of years. Dickens was a visitor; the greatest actors of the 18th and 19th centuries came to see the houses.

But like some gorgeous women who can cruise through life on looks alone—as long as they hold up— Shakespeare's birthplace can come as a disappointment to the discerning traveller who lingers for too long. Stratford's Shakespearean heritage is, nevertheless, one of the country's greatest treasures and some things shouldn't be missed.

Remember to steer clear of peak periods such as school holidays, stay and dine elsewhere in the region, then book tickets for a **Royal Shakespeare Company** production—it's always an unforgettable experience. In its own theatre complex (part of which is undergoing renovations until 2010) beside the **River Avon**, the RSC stages Shakespeare extensively, and also works by his contemporaries, modern classics and specially commissioned plays in iconoclastic, imaginative, eye-opening styles. The best directors working in British theatre cast British actors at the top of their game or rising fast, as well as the cream of the country's character actors. In 2008, for example, the RSC production of Hamlet featured David Tennant, he of *Dr Who* fame, and Patrick Stewart.

Arrive slightly earlier in the day to take in one or two of the so-called Shakespeare houses. These pieces of history are surprisingly entertaining and well-presented, with guides in each house explaining a different aspect of Tudor or Elizabethan life. The ones most worth visiting are **Shakespeare's Birthplace** (Henley Street), **Mary Arden's** (his mother, at Station Road, Wilmcote), **Anne Hathaway's Cottage** (Cottage Lane, Shottery) and **Hall's Croft** (marital home of Shakespeare's daughter, Old Town, Stratford-upon-Avon). The gift shops stock souvenirs relevant to and designed for the specific property.

After the theatre, drop in at the **Dirty Duck** (Waterside) for a drink or a late supper. The food is nothing special but half the cast turns up at this 15th-century watering hole so the people-watching is great.

Stately homes, castles, literary and industrial areas, historic and prehistoric sites are all thick on the ground in this particular part of England. Staying in the same general area, those of a romantic inclination may want to consider the speculated illicit romance of Queen Elizabeth I and Robert Dudley, the Earl of Leicester on a visit to **Kenilworth Castle** in Warwickshire. The castle now lies in ruins, but the gatehouse where Dudley is said to have courted Elizabeth has been restored and maintained. Part of the exhibit is a copy of a letter Dudley wrote to Elizabeth before he died. When the Virgin Queen died, 15 years later, it was found in a casket by her bedside, the words 'His Last Letter' written on it in the Queen's own hand.

Return to the 21st century at the privately-owned **Machado Gallery** in Barford, Warwick, about 13 km (8 miles) from Stratford, where colourful contemporary painting and ceramics are exhibited in a comfortable, oak-beamed, period house and its garden.

THIS PAGE: Kenilworth Castle, where Dudley, Earl of Leicester is said to have courted Queen Elizabeth I.

OPPOSITE (CLOCKWISE FROM TOP): The Royal Shakespeare Theatre on River Avon; David Tennant, most famous for his film and TV roles, in the anticipated 2008 RSC production of Hamlet; Shakespeare's classroom, preserved down to each authentic detail.

glitter + glam

If you've ever dreamed of owning a competition-standard Ferrari creation or whizzing around a bona fide Formula 1 racetrack in head-spinning style, the ultimate driving experience can be had at **Silverstone**, home of the **British Formula 1 Grand Prix**. In between professional races at this glamorous Northampton racing circuit, visitors can spend their day learning the ropes on professional race car driving and then follow in the hallowed tyre tracks of Lewis Hamilton, Mika Hakkinen, Michael Schumacher and the like by steering a Ferrari, a Lotus, a Silverstone single-seater or another high-performance vehicle around the hairpin bends and daredevil corners of this world-famous racetrack.

High-profile events such as the Formula 1 races bring the tides of glitterati from the colourful and hectic worlds of sports, media, show business and European high society to the English Midlands. And wherever they go, it's pretty much guaranteed that indulgent A-lister luxury shopping is sure to follow close behind them.

A hundred and five km (65 miles) away, the once-unlikely candidate of **Birmingham** is fast turning into the glamourous shopping capital of the region. Shoppers here spend more on retail and fashion than in any other British city. And at the Birmingham **Harvey Nichols**, in the new, canalside shopping centre **The Mailbox**, the average customer's per capita spend is considerably higher than at any of the company's other outlets in the whole country—even those in retail hotspots Leeds and London.

The real revelation in this born again shopping city, however, is the historic **Jewellery Quarter**, where a compact little district that has been quietly harbouring generations of goldsmiths, die casters and various other metalworkers for the past 300 years has only just recently emerged as the hottest destination to visit for those seeking contemporary designer jewellery in England.

The artisans and craftspeople who settled in the **Hockley** area of Birmingham once made the die-cast, mass-produced pen nibs and 'toys'— actually badges and little charms of metals, stones and enamels—in the area's factories. When the factories closed, small workshops remained concentrating specialist skills in the area. Today, the factories are filling up with trendy new flats for the young professionals moving into the area.

Out of the 400 jewellery-related businesses located in the Quarter, 100 of them are small retailers and jewellery designers and makers. They spread out in all directions from a point of origin roughly placed at the clock tower in the centre of the district, on **Warstone Lane** and **Vyse Street**. Here, in a shop such as SP Green & Co. Ltd (34 Warstone Lane), it is entirely possible to spend up to tens of thousands of pounds on a custom-made rope of brilliant-cut diamonds (that will sell in a London jeweller's for twice the price) or to pop across the street to **Artfull Expression** (23-24 Warstone Lane) and commission a young designer to create an original and personalised work in the precious metals and gems of your choice.

But of course, not all chic and glamorous shopping will necessarily involve spending the equivalent price of an SUV on accessories. And even celebrities like a bargain every now and then (what constitutes a bargain to them is, however, open to debate). In this vein, it's no surprise then that personalities such as Princess Anne, celebrity super-couple Victoria and David Beckham, Dame Helen Mirren, Ivana Trump, and *The Weakest Link* dominatrix Anne Robinson have all been spotted snapping up armfuls of bargains at **Bicester Village**.

Hordes of well-dressed—and, needless to say, well-heeled—savvy shoppers from all over Europe and the Far East regularly trawl this huge 'village' of chic designer outlets, 16 km (10 miles) from Oxford, to stock up on their discounted Diors, Ralph Laurens (typically—a £7,000 coat reduced to £3,000), and Salvatore Ferragamos, their Pringle knitwear and their brightly coloured Mulberry leathers. Up in these rarefied heights of retail, even the most seasoned of bargain-hunters will be impressed.

THIS PAGE (CLOCKWISE FROM TOP RIGHT): Elegant shopping in Birmingham; polished escalators take shoppers into the glamorous Mailbox; Bicester Village boasts a slew of deeply discounted luxury brands; Bicester's small-town ambience.

OPPOSITE: *Formula 1 drivers line up at Silverstone, the world-famous home of Britain's Grand Prix.*

le manoir aux quat' saisons

THIS PAGE (FROM LEFT): *Twin bathtubs let couples take a romantic bath right next to each other; fresh vegetables and herbs are picked right from the garden to supply the hotel's restaurant.*

OPPOSITE (FROM LEFT): *Some rooms even have their own fireplace; the restaurant's food is made solely from organic ingredients.*

A legendary presence on the map of fine British hotels and restaurants since opening in 1984, Le Manoir aux Quat' Saisons is the culmination of a lifelong dream for one of the world's most recognised and highly acclaimed chefs, Raymond Blanc (OBE). Starting his career in the 1970s and quickly becoming one of the youngest chefs to earn a Michelin star, Blanc envisioned an English countryside hotel set amidst beautiful surroundings that would work in perfect harmony with a fine dining restaurant. The experience would result in a unique destination that offered guests perfection as only he could imagine.

Named after his first restaurant, Les Quat' Saisons in Summertown, Oxford, the hotel succeeds in delivering the experience Blanc imagined by simple virtue of the staff's unrelenting passion for pleasing customers. As with the lushly landscaped gardens that surround the property, everything about the restaurant, guestrooms and service seems to work together in natural harmony.

Even so, the restaurant is undoubtedly the main attraction for most visitors. It is the only country house hotel in the UK to earn two Michelin stars for 23 consecutive years. Descriptions of the modern French cuisine often spiral into the realm of hyperbole, but given the quality and inventiveness of the menu, it is not hard to see why.

Under the direction of Blanc's hand-picked protégé Gary Jones, a Michelin-starred chef in his own right, the kitchen brigade of 50-odd chefs and assistants turn fresh, seasonal ingredients into colourful gourmet creations.

rooms
18 rooms · 14 suites

food
modern French

drink
wine list

features
Raymond Blanc Cookery School · in-room spa treatments · Japanese tea garden · private dining

nearby
Cotswolds · Oxford · gardens · theatre · golf · shooting · fishing · horse riding · shops

contact
Church Road, Great Milton
Oxford, OX44 7PD, United Kingdom ·
telephone: +44.018.4427 8881 ·
facsimile: +44.018.4427 8847 ·
website: www.manoir.com

The hotel's own vegetable garden provides the restaurant with over 90 types of fresh vegetables and 70 types of herbs for much of the year, adding a dimension of taste that few others can offer. The 10-course Menu Découverte offers the ultimate indulgence— a journey of culinary discovery from the minds of Blanc and Jones, with highlights such as new season soft poached gull's egg, white asparagus and bacon.

If the food is a sublime reinvention of the past, then the setting is a perfect fit. Over 400 years of history lies in the walls of the enchanting manor. In the 16th century it played host to monks; today it welcomes guests from all the world over into 32 exquisite, individually designed rooms and suites. Referred to by names rather than numbers, each one is a blend of traditional and contemporary design, some with more of one direction than the other. Lavande is the name given to the largest suite in the original building, and its bright interiors feature a silk velvet sofa in striking purple on solid oak flooring. Its sitting room has an open fireplace and views of the gardens. Lalique uses glass, marble, and mirrored surfaces to create a modern look. Designed by Emily Todhunter, the spacious suite overlooks the quiet inner courtyard of the manor.

It would take many repeat visits to explore the hidden pleasures of each room, from the Deluxe and Superior bedrooms to the romantic split-level Dovecote loft. Many of the restaurant's fans however, seem more than happy to do just that.

old bank hotel + quod

A conveniently situated contemporary hotel in the prime of Oxford's High Street area, the Old Bank Hotel has succeeded in making a name for itself in a town best known for its academic and natural environments. From its place in the middle of the High, as the street is known, the hotel enjoys proximity to the main university and other colleges, Radcliffe Square, Oriel Square, and Merton Street.

Popular attractions such as the Modern Art Oxford, the Ashmolean museum, and the Sheldonian Theatre are just minutes away on foot. Those preferring to commune with nature will find the Christ Church meadow and river similarly accessible. Renowned for its quiet, picturesque beauty, the High connects visitors to miles of lovely gardens and countless hours of shopping and culture in the heart of Oxford.

The history of the hotel's grand stone building dates back to before the 18th century, when it took on the beautiful Georgian façade that still greets guests today. Together with its main hall, the building was used as a branch of the Barclays bank for many years, explaining the name. Upon its opening in 1999, it was the area's first new hotel development in over 130 years. Boasting a forward-thinking design philosophy which honours and builds upon the past with modern conveniences and technologies, the Old Bank Hotel is a truly refined boutique hotel that also sets itself apart through the use of bold, powerful art.

It possesses a collection worthy of a large gallery or museum, dominated by striking modern paintings and photography hung to great effect throughout the public areas and guest rooms. Culled from the owner's private collection spanning 35 years, the mix includes young and established artists alike, with contributions from Stanley Spencer, Michael Ayrton, and Henrietta Dubrey. One project

THIS PAGE (FROM LEFT): *Guestrooms are appointed in understated and elegant modern style; an extensive collection of art and photographs adorn the walls of the reception area.*

OPPOSITE: *As its name suggests, the Old Bank Hotel occupies a building which once housed a branch of Barclays Bank.*

specially commissioned for the hotel is Paddy Summerfield's 'Handheld' collection of black and white Oxford photographs.

The hotel's 42 guestrooms and suites are all decorated along the same lines, with elements of the contemporary meeting the classic. Sizes range from the warm and intimate to the shockingly spacious, with sleek grey furnishings between cream-toned walls. Note the luxurious linens and velvet-edged bedcovers which do justice to the heavenly spring mattresses beneath. Likewise, only the best was considered for the Old Bank

Hotel's en-suite marble bathrooms: exclusive Miller Harris toiletries, comfortable cotton bathrobes, and power showers.

Views from each room vary, but those overlooking the High Street offer the most excitement, without the disturbance of noise, thanks to soundproofed windows and walls. From high above street level, the suites have clear, unobstructed views to the dreaming spires and beyond. In-room entertainment consists of cable television channels, and CD sound systems with DVD players on request. All the expected amenities are provided, from coffee and tea facilities, to safes, and even an ironing board and iron. Executive workspaces include generous writing desks made of oak, complimentary Internet access, and dual-line telephones with voicemail.

The Old Bank Hotel does not have a spa on the premises, but has engaged the services of a leading health and beauty company to provide guests with in-room beauty and massage treatments. Using exclusive products from Jessica® and Aromatherapy Associates, guests are treated to a range of therapies which combine pure essential oils with Eastern and Western massage techniques, facial scrubs, and foot reflexology to renew dull skin and tired bodies in the comfort and privacy of their own rooms.

On the ground floor, the former banking hall has been converted into the Quod Brasserie and Bar, which opens out to the street through the building's main entrance. The most capacious restaurant in town, Quod Brasserie is also the busiest, having achieved that rare combination of success that is both sizable and sustainable. The leather décor, stone floors and high ceilings no doubt play a part. Under the tasteful direction of owner Jeremy Mogford, the restaurant enjoys an up-to-the-minute design paired with a large collection of British art by names such as Sandra Blow and Gary Hume. Outside, a terraced dining area is superb for eating and drinking in fine summer weather, and perhaps even the occasional barbecue. Such is the buzz about the place that even guests of the hotel are advised to make advance reservations. Should seats be unavailable, however, the bar is always open for those waiting, and serves an extensive selection of cocktails and fine wines.

The food is inspired by modern British and Italian favourites, and like the environment that it is served in, strives to be as simple and uncomplicated while reaching for the highest standards of quality. Wherever possible, the kitchen sources for ingredients from nearby

THIS PAGE: *The outdoor terrace is an inviting venue for a slow meal or drinks in the summer.*

OPPOSITE (FROM LEFT): *Take a seat at the Quod Bar and enjoy a cool cocktail or glass of fine wine; with its varied menu of British and Italian favourites, it's easy to see why Quod Brasserie is so popular amongst the locals.*

rooms
42 rooms and suites

food
Quod Brasserie: modern British and Italian

drink
Quod Bar

features
in-room spa treatments • high-speed Internet access • dry cleaning • complimentary parking • 3 meeting rooms • concierge

nearby
Oxford University • Bodleian Library • gardens • museums • shopping • theatre

contact
Old Bank Hotel
92-94 High Street
Oxford OX1 4BN, United Kingdom •
telephone: +44.018.6579 9599 •
email: info@oldbank-hotel.co.uk •
website: www. oldbank-hotel.co.uk •

Quod Brasserie
telephone: +44.018.6520 2505 •
email: info@quod-restaurant.co.uk •
website: www.quod.co.uk

farms and suppliers, and the menus are a constant reflection of the best that each season has to offer. Fresh seafood is regularly flown in from Jersey while local beef and Pol Dorset lamb come from the owner, Jeremy Mogford's, Oxfordshire farm. The blackboard specials change twice daily, but servers are so well-acquainted with the cuisine that one need only ask them for a word of advice.

Open for breakfast, lunch, tea and dinner, the restaurant serves a wide range of à la carte items, from a wonderful smoked haddock and poached egg offering at breakfast, to soups, pizzas, steaks, and risottos throughout the rest of the day. On weekdays, the Quod Brasserie is popular for its two-course set lunches which offer outstanding value, and it

is in the afternoons here that one can observe a lively and diverse cross-section of Oxford society. On weekends, the restaurant's Sunday lunches are an institution all their own amongst the town's families, and one can expect a convivial atmosphere to accompany the traditional roast meats and Yorkshire puddings. Turn up for dinner, and live jazz performances from local veterans will provide the perfect backdrop to enjoy the end of a weekend over drinks.

Without a shortage of style on display, both in the memorably appointed hotel and the adjoining Quod Brasserie, the Old Bank Hotel is an easy recommendation for anyone desiring an experience that goes well beyond the stodgy and predictable.

the old parsonage

THIS PAGE (FROM LEFT): *The rooms
juxtapose antique furnishings
with contemporary aesthetics;
enjoy classic British food in a
cosy and intimate dining room.*

OPPOSITE (FROM LEFT): *Lounge with a
cup of hot tea and a book in
front of the roaring fireplace;
guests may dine at the heated
outdoor area all year round.*

In the midst of Oxford's often busy downtown area, surrounded by the city's world-famous university, shops, and museums is a charming hotel that at first brush seems like it came from another time and place. That's because the Old Parsonage Hotel, as its name clearly suggests, is housed in a building with over 400 years of history, built from solid stone walls clad over the sides with spring colours courtesy of climbing wisteria vines. The front door is a heavy, ancient thing carved from oak, and once inside, the scene that greets visitors is quintessentially British.

The library lounge area and adjoined restaurant are cosy, alternately painted in warm, inviting colours and lavishly panelled in dark wood. Scores of framed paintings and portraits adorn the walls, and the furnishings are tasteful and refined, with chairs and couches in buttoned leather and patterned upholstery. In winter, the building's original fireplaces keep the place warm while summer invites guests to venture onto the outdoor terraces for a weekend barbecue.

The hotel's marvellous location on the grounds of St Giles Church puts it within minutes of Oxford's key addresses. Museum lovers will appreciate the Ashmoleon and Pitt Rivers being a short walk down the street, while the picturesque lanes and many restaurants, cafés, and bars that line Jericho and Little Clarendon Street have something for everyone. The Old Parsonage Hotel has a number of bicycles, and even a small punt at the nearby Cherwell Boathouse, which lies completely at the disposal of hotel guests. Tours of the colleges and surrounding regions can be arranged through the concierge.

In all, 30 guestrooms and junior suites are available, individually decorated in a fashion that blends the crisp colours and clean lines of modern interior design with elements of classic comfort. Antique furniture sits on soft, deep-pile patterned carpeting, while large windows provide plenty of sunlight and floral touches lend the living areas a cheerful disposition. Room sizes and features vary, with some having special significance. Fans of Oscar Wilde can choose Room 26, where the writer was known to stay on occasion during his time at Oxford. Guests seeking privacy will like Room 31, a loft in the older part of the building, accessible through a private staircase. All accommodations are equipped with large televisions, minibars, and Internet access.

Dining at the Old Parsonage Hotel's restaurant also reveals the philosophy that makes the establishment a local favourite: rustic charm paired with the best of modern practices. Chef Nick Seckington and his team serve a selection of classic British favourites, renewed with creative contemporary touches. Other special creations are rotated daily, with dishes which often make use of wild game and freshly caught seafood. All ingredients are dictated by the season and sourced from local farms and suppliers, with the majority of the high-quality meat coming from a nearby affiliated Oxfordshire farm. A heated outdoor dining area is available, and the full menu is also served in the restaurant's intimate bar section which features live jazz on weekends.

When it comes to location, convenience is often central to a traveller's desire, but that isn't all a hotel should offer. The greatest hotels embody the characteristics of their individual locales, and in this, the Old Parsonage Hotel succeeds admirably, offering a stay which counts as a destination in itself.

rooms
30 rooms and suites

food
modern British

drink
pub

features
in-room spa treatments • high-speed Internet access • private roof terrace • church garden • complimentary use of bicycles and punt

nearby
university colleges • Ashmolean museum • Jericho • shopping • theatre • gardens

contact
1 Banbury Road
Oxford OX2 6NN, United Kingdom •
telephone: +44.018.6531 0210 •
email: reception@oldparsonage-hotel.co.uk •
website: www.oldparsonage-hotel.co.uk

barnsley house

The picturesque image of a quiet English country house and garden is a national institution. Since Rosemary Verey began her work on the Barnsley House grounds in the 1950s, the property has won international acclaim as the finest example of an English garden anywhere. Every year, tourists and gardening enthusiasts from all over the world make their way to Gloucestershire to observe Barnsley's flowering majesty.

Built in 1697 by Brereton Bouchier, the squire of Barnsley, the grounds were acquired by the Verey family in 1939, which marked the beginning of its transformation into a place of tranquillity. Recently, the property has undergone a transformation of a different kind, one that has retained all of its charm and now allows for even greater appreciation by visitors. In July of 2003, Barnsley House was reinvented as a boutique hotel dedicated to luxury living and absolute relaxation.

In addition to the splendid main gardens—enchanting as ever with their winding walks, knot gardens, manicured lawns and sunlit meadows—new developments have created 18 guestrooms and a fully equipped spa. Built from natural stone and English hardwoods, the spa's six treatment rooms and facilities perfectly match the peaceful surroundings. Similarly, it is impossible not to be at ease when walking through the new Spa Garden. It features a reflecting pond with waterfalls, stone sculptures and terraces for lounging. After a day of indulgence, the restaurant at Barnsley House has a menu that adapts daily to make use of fresh local ingredients,

THIS PAGE (FROM TOP): *The restaurant serves vegetables gathered straight from the gardens; the Deluxe Garden Rooms offer views of the sculpted grounds.*

OPPOSITE (FROM LEFT): *Originally built in 1697, Barnsley House is a piece of history in its own right; the spa offers a relaxing treat.*

rooms
8 rooms • 10 suites

food
restaurant: modern European with an Italian influence

drink
bar

features
landscaped gardens • spa • tennis court • meeting room • private cinema • dvd library • high-speed Internet access • chauffeur service • helicopter charter service

nearby
Cotswold village • peace and quiet • golf • hot-air balloon rides • river rowing • clay shooting • horse riding • croquet • flying

contact
Barnsley, Cirencester
Gloucestershire GL7 5EE, United Kingdom •
telephone: +44.12.8574 0000 •
facsimile: +44.12.8574 0925 •
email: info@barnsleyhouse.com •
website: www.barnsleyhouse.com

including vegetables straight from the hotel gardens. Just across the road is sister property The Village Pub, which offers mouth-watering gastro pub food and genuine local ales.

Rooms vary widely, some offering a place from which to enjoy the surroundings, while others offer the privacy of their own gardens. All rooms come with complete entertainment systems and high-speed Internet access, as well as complimentary champagne and fresh orange juice. For the best view of the gardens, stay in one of the three Deluxe Garden Rooms. Situated in the main house, they offer sweeping views of the main garden. Even more indulgence can be had at the two Garden Suites or two Deluxe Garden Suites. The Garden Suites are either on the first floor, offering a panoramic outlook, or in a private cottage within the garden itself. The cottage has its own garden, hot tub, and wood-burning stove for an independent experience. The Deluxe Garden Suites go two steps further with private entrances and exclusive features such as personal terraces, gardens, or a conservatory. They are the largest of all, with separate living, dining, and sleeping areas. Throw a dinner party with a difference, or just spend some quality time with a loved one.

Over the last half-century, Barnsley House has grown in popularity and repute as one of England's most loved botanical sites. Today, it stands ready to deliver a five-star holiday experience far from the madding crowd, nestled safely in the heart of the Cotswolds countryside.

cowley manor

THIS PAGE: *A gorgeous crystal feature catches the light.*

OPPOSITE (FROM LEFT): *The large bathrooms are all unique and come with luxurious amenities; the heated outdoor pool may be enjoyed all year round; home-style British classics are served at the hotel's restaurant.*

Often called the 'Heart of England', the Cotswolds is a historic English area of stunning natural beauty. Deep within it lies the magnificent Cowley Manor and its lush expanse of private gardens. Spanning over 22 hectares (55 acres) in total area, the Cowley grounds contain a veritable ecosystem of natural features. While leisurely exploring the gardens, guests may find features such as a Victorian cascade, four large reflecting lakes, and a small river. Completing the picturesque aesthetic of the countryside terrain is an original medieval church.

Built in 1885, the main building itself resonates with timeless beauty, a piece of architectural brilliance inspired by the Italianate style and designed to fuse a formal classical outlook with the kind of eye-pleasing tranquillity that one expects from a pastoral landmark set amidst rolling hills. One of the first hotels in the UK to combine traditional architecture and contemporary elements, the award-winning Cowley Manor juxtaposes large spaces of stately grandeur with a modern feel and a quirky sense of style. One is as likely to rest on a trendy green designer couch as a cowhide chair, and the atmosphere in areas such as the main living room of the house are absolutely relaxed.

Upping the exclusive nature of a stay at Cowley Manor is the fact that there are only 30 rooms on offer, each filled with fine handcrafted furnishings and fabrics designed by some of the UK's best up-and-coming designers. No two rooms are built alike, however, most rooms offer an unrestricted view of the surroundings, and the windows allow guests to enjoy lots of natural light during the day. A signature feature of every Cowley guestroom is a lavishly outfitted bathroom that defies conventions—some bathrooms even match the size of their bedrooms. Every imaginable amenity is

...the main building itself resonates with timeless beauty...

provided: separate rain showers, deep soaking bathtubs, and toiletries from the hotel's award-winning C-Side Spa.

Half of Cowley Manor's rooms are housed in the main building, while the other half occupies the refurbished Stable Block. The five choices of room class are named in an exceedingly straightforward manner: Good, Better, Great, Exceptional, and Best. All rooms include every modern amenity one could desire, such as flat-screen televisions, iPod docking stations, and a library of music and movies. Only one room has the honour of being called 'Best', and it more than lives up to its name. With a four-poster bed, a bathtub big enough for two, and a private terrace overlooking a vista of lakes and woodlands, it's the perfect choice for a romantic escape.

The hotel's staff provides an exceptional level of service with a 'no ego' service attitude, so guests enjoy luxury accommodations with

all the warmth of home. Room service lets those inclined to dine in full view of the land do so from the privacy of their rooms, but the hotel's restaurant provides a good reason not to stay cloistered for long. Occupying the manor's antique wood-panelled ballroom, the restaurant offers spectacular views down to the lakes, and serves modern British food created from fresh, seasonal produce. Old favourites such as Gloucestershire old-spot bangers and mash are examples of the uncomplicated yet wholly satisfying fare.

The hotel is happy to host large parties, and has numerous facilities for private dinner functions and special events. With Cowley Manor, enjoying the spirit of the country in comfort and grace is both easy and rewarding.

rooms
30 rooms

food
restaurant: modern British • private dining rooms

drink
hotel bar

features
private gardens • walking trails • indoor and outdoor pools • C-Side Spa • wedding and event venue • billiard room • medieval church

nearby
Cheltenham • Oxford

contact
Cowley, near Cheltenham
Gloucestershire GL53 9NL, United Kingdom •
telephone: +44.012.4287 0900 •
facsimile: +44.012.4287 0901 •
email: stay@cowleymanor.com •
website: www.cowleymanor.com

cotswolds88hotel

THIS PAGE: The hotel creatively blends a number of design styles, with personal touches such as custom wallpaper.

OPPOSITE (FROM LEFT): All rooms are decorated with a unique theme; the building's exterior suggests a traditional country hotel, but the interiors are wholly modern.

A well-kept secret known only to a select few, the Cotswolds88hotel may be hidden out of sight in Painswick village, but its guestbook is routinely filled in by the who's who of London society and discerning design-savvy fans. An avenue of yew trees leads up to the property, set amidst rolling hills and surrounded by picturesque gardens. The 18th-century building appears to be the epitome of a traditional countryside hotel, yet explore its interiors and what emerges is another picture entirely.

A new hotel concept by interior designer Marchella De Angelis, the Cotswolds88hotel features some of the funkiest, most inventive interiors in the UK. Marchella's beliefs and eclectic interests influence the psychedelic design philosophy, incorporating Feng Shui, spirituality, kitsch, and avant garde art. The sumptuously refurbished rooms are set apart by their own unique themes and custom wallpaper from De Angelis & Garner, an artware brand that Marchella founded with the

rooms
18 rooms

food
organic international

drink
bar and living room lounge

features
spa • boardroom • high-speed Internet access • helipad

nearby
St Mary's church • Rococo Gardens • golf • horse riding • fishing • balloon rides • shooting

contact
Kemps Lane, Painswick
Gloucestershire GL6 6YB, United Kingdom •
telephone: +44.014.5281 3688 •
facsimile: +44.014.5281 4059 •
email: reservations@cotswolds88hotel.com •
website: www.cotswolds88hotel.com

renowned photographer and singer, Kate Garner. In addition to Garner's artistic input, the hotel also displays many pieces of original work by photo artist David Hiscock. Focusing on the splendour of the grounds and building exterior, Hiscock has assembled a document of the Cotswolds in his signature abstract style, a perfect fit for the hotel's eccentric vibe.

Four classes of guest accommodations are offered, ranging from the 'Room with a View', 'Detmar Room', and 'Palladian Room' to the all-out luxurious '88 Suite'. In addition to their unforgettable décor, they come with all the amenities one expects to find in much larger hotels. Large en-suite bathrooms are equipped with either jacuzzi baths or power showers for a soothing end to every day. For ultimate pampering, a menu of holistic spa treatments is available to be enjoyed in the privacy of any bedroom, or at the hotel's fully equipped 'treatment pod'. A specially commissioned fragrance unique to the hotel accompanies every spa therapy, putting the senses into a state of relaxation.

The hotel's ground floor restaurant is also a reflection of the balance between luxury and Zen-like simplicity, with most of the menu created from organic ingredients. A small but stylish bar serves drinks throughout the evening, and the Living Room lounge area is open exclusively for guest use. During the summer, the restaurant opens out onto the garden terrace, making it a wonderful venue for private parties and even weddings.

Few country hotels boast the posh lounge ethos that the Cotswolds88hotel effortlessly carries on its multi-faceted back. As time goes on, this secret getaway is unlikely to stay out of the spotlight, but that doesn't necessarily mean that its standards will change. Proud to cater for the voguish set, expect this corner of the Cotswolds to stay precious a while longer.

gee's restaurant

Quite simply the most popular fine dining location in North Oxford, Gee's Restaurant has been an favourite in the academic town for over two decades. Over the years, countless holidaymakers, students, visiting parents, and gourmands have sought out this 85-seat restaurant for its flawless service, charming setting, and of course, exemplary food.

Located on Banbury Road, within walking distance of the Old Bank and Old Parsonage hotels (also owned by restaurant proprietor Jeremy Mogford), the establishment is housed in a beautiful glass conservatory that was formerly a greengrocer and florist. The front of the Victorian structure faces the street, giving diners a view of the lovely tree-lined avenue to accompany the spacious interiors. Lit up at night, the conservatory is one of the most distinctive sights in Oxford. All the original features of the structure have been preserved, honouring the history of the neighbourhood whilst creating a space that is airy and receptive to natural light. Fittingly, the streamlined décor is matched with a collection of artwork by acclaimed Young British Artist Gary Hume, renowned for his restrained and thoughtful imagery.

A large, covered outdoor terrace provides an additional 40 seats for dining, and is heated so diners need not fear discomfort when the weather turns cool. The al fresco environment is well suited to casual weekday lunches and midday cocktails, and comes to life every Sunday evening with live jazz performances.

Talented chefs have always been a part of the public's attraction to Gee's Restaurant; since 1984 the kitchen has been a proving ground for some of the best in the business, and the current team is no exception. Head Chef Mark Bristow has created offerings which are both sophisticated and heartfelt. It is modern British cuisine defined by Italian and pan-European influences. The kitchen uses only seasonal ingredients, selected for freshness and quality from a variety of local

...one of the most distinctive sights in Oxford.

capacity
85 indoors · 40 outdoors

food
modern British and European

drink
bar and wine list

features
live jazz · outdoor terrace · child-friendly ·
wheelchair access · available for private hire

nearby
university colleges · Ashmolean museum ·
Jericho · shopping · theatre · gardens

contact
61 Banbury Road
Oxford OX2 6PE, United Kingdom ·
telephone: +44.018.6555 3540 ·
email: info@gees-restaurant.co.uk ·
website: www.gees-restaurant.co.uk

suppliers to ensure that the daily specials continually reflect the state and character of the Oxfordshire landscape.

Line-caught seafood and fresh shellfish are flown in twice weekly from Jersey, while top-quality meats come direct from a nearby Mogford-owned farm—its Aberdeen Angus beef and Pol Dorset lamb are fixtures on the menu, which has a wide range of items sure to appeal to any kind of taste. Depending on when one arrives, it holds such delights as Seared Scallops with Cauliflower Puree and Pancetta, Roast Rib of 'Rofford Farm' Beef with Fondant Potatoes and Thyme Jus, and foie Gras Terrine. The dessert selections are equally impressive, especially the heavenly pairing of Treacle Tart with Jersey Cream.

The food is even more extraordinary when paired with the fine wines recommended by resident Wine Manager Joe Rorke. The cellar holds approximately 50 varietals from classic and 'New World' producing countries at any one time, all of them carefully chosen to complement the kitchen's seasonal output. An advanced preservation system, Le Verre de Vin, allows most wines to be served by the glass and then sealed in perfect condition. Wines may also be enjoyed from the bar area, in addition to classic cocktails and spirits.

A unique contemporary restaurant with a long history, Gee's Restaurant skilfully takes all the parts necessary for a superlative dining experience in central Oxford, and combines them to form something even greater.

c-side spa at cowley manor

THIS PAGE: With the indoor and outdoor pools, guests may swim whenever they wish.

OPPOSITE (FROM LEFT): The gorgeous Cowley Manor is home to award-winning C-side Spa; the beautiful countryside scenery provides a visual treat as one indulges in refreshing spa therapies.

Sharing the same incredible location in the Cotswolds as its parent hotel, the award-winning C-Side Spa at Cowley Manor brings together the best of modern therapeutic practices and some of the most picturesque English countryside views. Set in 22 hectares (55 acres) of beautifully kept private gardens complete with waterfalls, lakes, and winding paths, the secluded facility is an ideal place for leaving the cares of the world behind, and surrendering oneself to a relaxing spa escape.

Built entirely below ground level, the whole complex seamlessly blends into the landscape, resulting in an airy and tranquil environment. Enter the spa proper, and one will discover a fresh, clean quality to the stylish interior design. Minimalist lines meet floor-to-ceiling glass windows that allow natural light to flood in, complementing the naturally cool limestone and dark slate walls and creating an intimate space well-suited to relaxation. The spa's highly trained team of professional masseuses and therapists are renowned for their skill and their warm, friendly manner. So unique is this haven of restorative pleasures that it was named one of the 'Best Hotel Spas in the UK' by *Condé Nast Traveller* magazine in 2006. Certainly, there are few spas which may boast of a location in the midst of such natural beauty.

rooms
4 treatment rooms

features
massages • holistic therapies • yoga • wraps •
facials • treatment rooms • indoor and outdoor
pools • state-of-the-art gymnasium • sauna •
steam room

nearby
Cowley Manor • bar and restaurant •
landscaped gardens

contact
Cowley Manor, near Cheltenham
Gloucestershire GL53 9NL, United Kingdom •
telephone: +44.012.4287 0902 •
facsimile: +44.012.4287 0901 •
email: relax@cowleymanor.com •
website: www.cowleymanor.com

In addition to its inviting treatment rooms, the spa is equipped with indoor and outdoor pools, a steam room, a gym and a sauna. Everything necessary for an afternoon of health, well-being, or just pure, indulgent renewal can be found here in one place. All products used are from a range developed specially for the C-Side Spa, and the spa's exclusive treatment menu was designed and developed by the renowned aromatherapist Michelle Roques. Her expertise allowed the creation of regimes that consider the body in its totality, bringing together multiple disciplines, so all effects are felt as a whole.

As a result, the soothing treatments rebalance muscles rather than wearing them down. Combined with essential oils and fundamentals of aromatherapy, the results are worlds away from usual spa therapies. Cloud 9, the signature C-Side massage, involves Qi energy techniques, reflexology, acupressure, and aromatherapy combined with precious ingredients to completely rejuvenate tired bodies. The treatment includes a full body massage, cleansing of the face and as an extra treat, a heavenly scalp massage. Full body wraps are also available to nourish or detoxify dehydrated skin, incorporating sea salt, sandlewood, a hydrating honey mask and deeply detoxifying grapefruit and lavender.

Facial treatments feature a custom skincare system built upon all-natural active ingredients. Applied in three phases—cleansing, massage, and moisturising—they make up a holistic programme for skin renewal. The popular Contour treatment lifts and tones skin with a stimulating lavender gel containing extracts of grapefruit, juniper, and aloe. After a soothing accupressure massage, an exquisite masque of neroli, frankincense, rose and manuka honey completes the indulgent skin therapy.

theeast

North Sea

SOUTH YORKSHIRE

NORTH LINCOLNSHIRE

NORTH EAST LINCOLNSHIRE

DERBYSHIRE

NOTTINGHAMSHIRE

Lincoln

LINCOLNSHIRE

STAFFORD-SHIRE

DERBY

○ Nottingham

LEICESTERSHIRE

RUTLAND

○ Leicester

PETERBOROUGH

> Strattons Hotel + Restaurant

> Tuddenham Mill
> Broad House Hotel

• Swaffham

• Wroxham

NORFOLK

○ Norwich

WARWICKSHIRE

NORTHAMPTONSHIRE

• Ely

CAMBRIDGESHIRE

• Newmarket

SUFFOLK

Cambridge

MILTON KEYNES

HERTFORDSHIRE

• Tuddenham

BUCKING-HAM-SHIRE

LUTON

HERTFORDSHIRE

OXFORDSHIRE

ESSEX

○ Colchester

WEST BERKSHIRE

GREATER LONDON

N

THURROCK SOUTHEND-ON-SEA

Legend

⊕ Airport
Highway
Main Road
Urban Area
Lake
Below Sea Level
500–1000 m
200–500 m
100–200 m

0 km   25   50 km

the east

waiting to be discovered

From a train window, East Anglia looks flat and featureless, a landscape of endless pastures and farmland, occasionally interrupted by a small wood, stretching to a distant horizon. But it would be wrong to underestimate the attractions of the East of England, shaped by man and nature, into a uniquely fascinating region. This area has given rise to one of the world's greatest universities and several of England's loveliest cathedrals. It is the home of English flat-racing and thoroughbred breeding at Newmarket, and a literary centre that has produced some of England's most outstanding modern writers.

Between the head of the Black River Estuary at Maldon—where luxurious natural sea salt is collected—and The Wash, a great bite out of the coast at the mouth of the Great Ouse, East Anglia pushes out into the North Sea. A common Fenland landscape carries on across Lincolnshire, carrying with it a common regional culture.

The East of England was overlooked during England's great motorway building era, in the 1950s and 60s. While the network extended west and southwest of London, and the north/south routes traversed the west side of the country, the eastern counties of Essex, Suffolk, Norfolk, Cambridgeshire and Lincolnshire were left virtually untouched. By the time anyone took notice, the era of motorway network expansion had ground to a halt. As a result, there are fewer of the sprawling motorway developments—big industrial parks, enormous shopping malls, row after row of commuter-belt bedroom communities that are found elsewhere. Nature, older customs and older styles of architecture give a distinct and eccentric character.

british holdouts

The wide, flat sands and navigable rivers of East Anglia were open invitations to the Vikings, Romans, Danes and Normans who washed up on its shores. But historically, invaders have always been challenged by fierce resistance or doggedly stubborn locals.

East Anglia was the homeground of the Iceni, ferocious Celtic fighters who pressed the Romans all the way to London (which they razed) led by their legendary queen, Boadicea. Later, the strongest resistance to William the Conqueror came from the East, where the Anglo Saxons rose up in the Fens and held out for years in the Isle of Ely—now the site of Ely Cathedral.

One of Anglo Saxon history's most important sites, the Sutton Hoo burial, was discovered in Woodbridge, Suffolk in the 20th century. The treasures, undisturbed for 1,300 years, were part of the rare ship burial—the only others are in Scandinavia—of a powerful king. They included a bronze helmet; a gold belt buckle, the gold and jewelled frame of a purse and the greatest hoard of Eastern Mediterranean silver found in Northern Europe, all within remnants of a Viking ship.

THIS PAGE: Ely Cathedral, one of England's loveliest and tallest, is called 'The Ship of the Fens'.

PAGE 182: The little beach huts of Suffolk are a frequent subject of visitors' photographs.

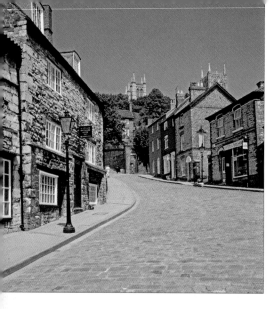

Though most of the treasures are kept in the British Museum in London, a selection, as well as new finds and British Museum replicas, are exhibited at Sutton Hoo itself. Even more impressive for history buffs is the life-sized reconstruction of the burial chamber found within the 'sand shadow' of a 27-m- (90-ft-) long Viking boat.

islands of style

The East of England might well be called the nation's empty quarter. Cities and towns don't bump up against each other as they do in the conurbations of most other regions. Here they're 'islands' separated by East Anglia's three unusual natural landscapes—the watery Norfolk Broads, the Fenlands and the Brecklands. From the university town of Cambridge to the empty golden sands of Cromer—home of tasty crab—they are each distinctive and occasionally eccentric.

Furthest east, where the sunrise first touches Britain, the coastal city of Great Yarmouth is a bustling family resort. In international collecting circles, Lowestoft is synonymous with the rare antique porcelains made here until the late 18th century. The Lowestoft factory has recently been revived and its recreated heritage patterns are sold at its factory shop (Battery Green Road). Further south, Colchester is England's oldest recorded town and home to splendid native oysters that grace the best tables in Britain between September and Easter. Norwich, the unofficial capital of the region, is a university town with a 900-year-old cathedral and a huge open market.

Pushing the northern boundary of the Fenlands—ancient, reclaimed marshes—the small city of Lincoln has a bijoux cathedral and a sparkling annual Christmas market in the public square beneath it. And besides its association with Robin Hood, Nottingham, in the northwest of this region, was a center of Victorian lace-making. Its Lace Quarter, where 19th-century lace-making machines still operate (now linked to computer technology) has, lately, become a centre of luxury residential redevelopment and lifestyle shopping. Native son, designer Paul Smith, has a flagship store in a five-floor, Grade II listed building on Low Pavement.

THIS PAGE (FROM TOP): Steeply cobbled streets wend upward to Lincoln Cathedral's medieval precincts; denizens of a North Sea beach along the coast of Lincolnshire.

OPPOSITE: Wildlife is plentiful in the haunting stretches of the Norfolk Broads waterways.

the norfolk broads

Britain's largest, nationally protected wetland is a network of shallow lakes and waterways in the northeast of East Anglia. A landscape like no other, the waterworld of the Norfolk Broads is a source of reeds for thatched roofs, playground for sailing enthusiasts and an important wildlife habitat. Once thought to be natural features, the Broads were man-made, caused by the flooding of ancient peat excavations. Above the reed beds, keep a sharp eye for the sails of windmills as well as the gaff-rigged sails of traditional Norfolk yachts and wherries. These distinctive boats, evolved from ancient Viking craft, can be hired at the Southgate Yacht Station in Horning.

A landscape like no other, the waterworld of the Norfolk Broads...

east anglia

creative norwich

Almost 1,000 years ago, the people of fashion would bypass Norwich as a matter of rote. At the time England's second-largest city, it had no cathedral or anything to capture the attention of visitors—at least not compared to the country's only miraculous shrine, at **Walsingham**, on the nearby coast.

Today, those making a beeline for Norwich, one of the continent's best-preserved Medieval cities, are literary, art and media enthusiasts rather than religious pilgrims. True, the 900-year-old **cathedral** just beside the **River Wensum**, is one of England's most awe-inspiring places, but it the city's modern creativity spark that draws visitors to its streets now. Off the beaten path, maybe, but Norwich is certainly no countryside backwater.

The creative writing programme at the **University of East Anglia** has produced dozens of best-selling authors and media personalities—Booker and Whitbread Prize winning authors like **Ian McEwan** and **Kazuo Ishiguro**. The university's **Sainsbury Centre for Visual Arts** is a spacious modern galler, that holds several nationally important collections. **The Norwich Arts Centre** is a small but exciting venue for a range of modern art and also includes theatre, film, music, dance and 'live lit'. And, in the centre of Norwich, not far from its huge **open market**, its **Norman castle** (now a museum and art gallery) and medieval lanes, the nationally recognised **Norwich School of Art and Design** is the base for **Aurora**, an annual, juried animation festival that attracts professionals, students and critics from all over the world.

As befits an arty, European destination, Norwich has loads of independent coffee houses, such as **Caley's Cocoa Café** in the city's old **Guild Hall**, as well as restaurants for the serious gourmet such as **Tatlers** (21 Tombland) and **By Appointment** (25-29 St George Street).

Norwich is also a top shopping destination with branches of all the UK's high-street shops and many of its top department stores. More adventurous fashion shoppers head straight for the changing array of independent boutiques in medieval **Norwich Lanes**. Don't miss the spectacular art nouveau interiors of the **Royal Arcade**, situated between **Gentleman's Walk** and **White Lion Street**, stopping at **Marr's** (6) for French and Italian leathers and the **Colman's Mustard Shop** (15) for Art Deco mustard pots. And, just outside the city centre, **The Grapevine** (109 Unthank Road) hosts exhibits theat feature the work of contemporary local artists and ceramicists.

royal style

The Queen's private Norfolk retreat, **Sandringham**, sets a tone of discreet, private wealth in the western reaches of Norfolk. Small Georgian towns like **Swaffham**, with its Saturday market, seem modest—but don't be fooled. The local boutique sells designer dresses for thousands of pounds, and the friendly butcher regularly carries plucked and trussed pheasants from nearby estates.

In fact, this quiet area is laced with surprising pockets of luxury goods, theatre, arts and fine dining. A few miles from Swaffham, the tiny estate village of **Westacre** has its own resident theatre company, **The Westacre River Studios and Summer Theatre**, with Stephen Fry as patron. A mile further, **Castle Acre** has a Bailey Gate, a Norman castle and a ruined Cluniac Priory. Its one main street also has an excellent 16th-century pub—**The Ostrich**—and a marvellous little local convenience store that sells focaccia with rosemary and sun-dried tomatoes next to the tins of baked beans.

THIS PAGE (FROM TOP): Purveyors of the traditional English yellow mustard, Colman's also sells arty mustard pots; Sandringham House, country home of the British Royal Family in Norfolk.
OPPOSITE: The Royal Arcade in Norwich has gorgeous art nouveau interiors.

cambridge

Cambridge University, which is celebrating its 800th anniversary in 2009, was established in what was already a wealthy town with several large religious institutions when a group of scholars, fleeing the wrath of a group of irate Oxford townsfolk, decided to settle there. No one is quite sure what the root issue of the dispute was about, but quite a few will maintain that the Cambridge migrants may have ended up with the better deal after all.

Cambridge is a lovely place, no doubt about it. Though its population is about 120,000, it still retains the ambience of a bustling market town with signs of its medieval past, in its dwellings, its public buildings and its churches everywhere. At least 11 of the medieval parish churches still stand; the oldest, **St Benedict's**, is close to 1,000 years old.

Many of the university's colleges are lined up against the **River Cam**, along a walk known as **The Backs**, reached through the colleges—for a nominal fee. Another way to enjoy views of these splendid, and for the most part gothic, buildings is to go punting on the Cam. Be warned— attempting to pole your way down the river without tipping the punt over is not as easy as it looks and may turn out to be a fairly damp affair, but 'chauffeured' punts are always available for hire.

Those lucky enough to be in or near Cambridge during the holiday season can and definitely should try to attend **A Service of Nine Lessons and Carols**, at **King's College Chapel**, 3.00 pm on Christmas Eve. It's open to anyone who's willing to queue up for places from before 9.00 am, and is well worth the (too) early start. The famous service, broadcast around the world live by the British Broadcasting Corporation, always includes a new, specially commissioned carol by a contemporary composer.

Away from the hallowed ivory towers and pastoral scenes of the university precincts, Cambridge is modern, sophisticated and dynamic with loads of shopping, numerous great restaurants and lively club and music scenes. There are several malls and shopping districts. Trendies can head for the new **Grand Arcade** to check out the latest pieces from the Kate Moss collection at **Topshop** or pick up choice Italian condiments at **Carluccio's Deli**. Down on **Magdalene Street**, one of the city's oldest, glass artist David Mitchell and the artists he represents show at **Café Jello** (13) and craftsman Ian Stevens (28) sells his surprisingly affordable collection of various handmade handbags, folios, briefcases and a wide selection of bespoke leathers.

At the two-Michelin-starred **Midsummer House** (Midsummer Common), you can dine on French Mediterranean cuisine with a light modern twist, on a shaded terrace overlooking the River Cam. The very popular **Restaurant 22** (22 Chesterton Road) is known for its short but exquisitely engineered menus that change every month and always include at least one imaginative choice for vegetarians.

Moving north of Cambridge, **Ely Cathedral** rises above the low-lying Fenlands. Until the fens were drained, Ely was an island—The Isle of Eels—

and its cathedral, which can be seen for miles around, is still known by the deeply evocative name The Ship of the Fens. **The Stained Glass Museum**, housed in the Cathedral, exhibits its namesake art, sourced from the 13th to the late 20th century.

If overdosing on architecture and history and is a concern (frequently a legitimate issue for short-term visitors to England!), not to worry. One can simply head east of Cambridge for **Newmarket**—famed horse country—for a little taste of prestigious sporting action. The town, with its two magnificent racecourses, is the acknowledged home of British flat racing and thoroughbred breeding. After a day (or before a night) at the races, take an informative tour behind the scenes at **The Jockey Club's National Stud**, England's most prestigious stud farm.

THIS PAGE (FROM TOP): Newmarket is the traditional epicentre of England's thoroughbred racing and breeding; idyllic punting on the River Cam; the grandstand at Newmarket— home of English flat racing.
OPPOSITE: The instantly recognisable King's College Chapel, Cambridge.

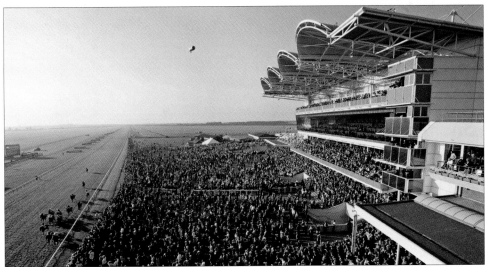

strattons hotel + restaurant

Norfolk's reputation for quiet, rural living has won it many fans amongst those who are tired of the rat race and wish to leave the intensity and commercialism of big cities for the tranquillity of countryside retreats. The small market town of Swaffham strikes an ideal balance between the pastoral and the overdeveloped, and enjoys a place in history as a stopping point for travellers going south from the coast. With its roots in the medieval period, the town today features a large central church, examples of beautiful Georgian and Victorian architecture, and a lively agricultural community that turns out excellent examples of local British produce.

Out of true love for this unique locale, the owners Les and Vanessa Scott founded Strattons Hotel & Restaurant in 1990, running the exclusive 14-room boutique hotel as an independent family business. Located in a large 'Palladian Villa' at the end of a narrow lane, the house consists of a structure with two wings that were added at an early point in its history, which can be traced back over 300 years. Informed by a deep respect for the natural environment and the authenticity of the guest experience, the pair conscientiously operate the hotel as an eco-friendly entity that contributes as much as it receives from the land and the local suppliers who share it.

Visitors to the neighbourhood will not be at a loss to see why, as Swaffham resides in the middle of the Brecklands, a 958-sq-km (370-sq-mile) expanse of natural landscape and wildlife that stretches between Norfolk and Suffolk. The remains of earlier settlements from the time when Swaffham served as a place of rest for pilgrims linger on in the area to the north, now filled with the abandoned ruins of villages, churches, and castles. These beautiful areas, which were mostly used for arable farming at one point, are easily accessible from the hotel's doorstep and are perennially popular with bird-watchers, nature lovers, and anyone inclined to enjoy a quiet walk or bicycle excursion.

Despite its perfect integration with the landscape and rustic, peaceful exterior, the interiors of Strattons Hotel & Restaurant are surprisingly colourful. The first hint comes as one walks up to the front door—standing outside on the lawn is a gigantic abstract figure of a stag, wrought from recycled iron by local sculptress Rachael Long. Perhaps more than any single object at the hotel, it signifies the hotel's two standout traits: ecological responsibility and the daring use of art. Both owners met at an art college in the 1970s, and their creative inspirations can be found all throughout the hotel. Like any true work of art, the process is continuous, and the work can never claim to be finished. Since its opening, the building has been on what the Scotts call a 'rolling maintenance programme', and they have insisted that all improvements and restoration be carried out in the traditional fashion by carefully chosen artisans who respect the original materials and techniques required.

Conservation in the name of repair is one thing, but don't be surprised to learn that the rooms are never finished, either. All of the

suite dedicated to indulgence, and features an Eastern-inspired lounge area with a Buddhist statue and a roll-top soaking tub within the bedroom itself. One of the newest rooms, Linen, gets its name from the large travatine marble bathroom which was once a linen closet. The lavish bedroom features a damask-padded wall, and is equalled in size by a tremendous decked balcony.

Part creators and part curators, Les and Vanessa are literally the hotel's resident artists, and have created a cool contemporary style that manages to fuse a wide range of eclectic pieces, from sculptures, to mosaics, to pieces of antique furniture. In ordinary hands it might be a noisy bit of overindulgence, but here the overall effect is deeply luxurious, and everything appears to belong exactly where it lies. Bose audio and DVD players are standard, and so is wireless Internet access. Each room also includes a number of invisible features that do their part to reduce the carbon footprints of guests. Curtains are lined with wool to conserve heat, most bulbs are low-energy models, and the bar soaps and mini toiletry bottles that are a staple of hotel room stays have been done away with. Replacing them are bottles of organic soap provided by a local soap maker in Norwich; every bit as effective, and many times less wasteful.

That philosophy can also be found in the restaurant's green kitchen, which recycles its organic waste to create feed for its chickens and compost for growing vegetables. The

THIS PAGE: All of the hotel is fitted with a quirky and eclectic style that never seems out of place.

OPPOSITE (FROM LEFT): Rooms have all been individually designed in a range of themes and styles; the Opium suite has a bathtub located within the bedroom itself for ultimate relaxation.

individually designed bedrooms and suites—slated to increase to 12 rooms and two eco lodges in an upcoming expansion—are subject to change in style and décor. The Red Room is a spacious suite with a private garden, its crimson walls tastefully contrasted with gold trimmings. Intended as a tribute to the powers of love and passion, the room features a working fireplace and a four-poster bed. Opium, on the other hand, is generous duplex restaurant makes and bakes everything on the menu fresh every day; even the after-dinner chocolates are handmade. The kitchen staff, which includes proprietress Vanessa Scott, take pride in using strictly local or homegrown produce for their delightful 'slow food' creations. Mondays to Saturdays, a monthly changing menu is offered at dinner, with tapas being the draw on Sunday nights. As the county was not traditionally involved in cheese making, Norfolk cheeses are a rare delicacy, and an important part of the region's contemporary identity. By cultivating good relationships with local suppliers, the restaurant is able to offer them for most of the year, but should the need to serve any other cheese arise, it is always British in origin. Such is the degree of pride in local food here, that all restaurant staff approach tables already well-versed in the origins of ingredients, and the house makes available a list of all sources and their recipes.

For its contributions to the local economy and for leading the way in ecotourism, the hotel has enjoyed numerous accolades over the years, and in 2007 received a Tourism in Norfolk Awards win for 'Sustainable Tourism', and two Enjoy England Awards for Excellence, amongst others. By adhering firmly to its motto, 'Luxury without sacrifice', Strattons Hotel & Restaurant delivers stylish, modern holidays on par with the best which can be found anywhere else in the world, and at a significantly reduced cost to the environment.

rooms
7 rooms · 5 suites · 2 eco suites

food
modern English

drink
restaurant · bar in resident lounges

features
wireless Internet access · pet-friendly rooms · maps and information on surrounding areas · local produce shop

nearby
fishing · horse riding · cycling · Extreme Adventure high-ropes course · go-karting · walking trails · vineyards

contact
Ash Close, Swaffham
Norfolk PE37 7NH, United Kingdom ·
telephone: +44.017.6072 3845 ·
email: enquiries@strattonshotel.com ·
website: www.strattonshotel.com

broad house hotel

Nestled in 10 hectares (24 acres) of beautiful parkland in the expanses of Norfolk Broads National Park, Broad House Hotel is a country getaway with a touch of five-star luxury. Run by a couple with many combined years of experience in the hotel industry, the hotel has modernity, classic comforts, and above all, a personal approach to service and hospitality.

The Grade II-listed, 18th-century property first caught the eyes of Philip and Caroline Search in 2006, and the decision was soon made to transform the residential building into Norfolk's first five-star boutique hotel. By the end of 2007, the couple were ready to take the wraps off their £2.4 million labour of love.

The newly refurbished interiors are tastefully furnished in a classic style to feel relaxed, with natural light pouring through large windows which look out onto the splendid grounds.

There are nine guestrooms of varying sizes in all, each one individually designed and decorated to suit a wide range of tastes. Views from the rooms in the Queen Anne wing look out over the lawns down to Wroxham Broad. The others face east and west over the hotel's façade and a peaceful koi pond respectively. Two attic rooms offer an unusual stay with lots of privacy. In honour of Broad House Hotel's former residents, the Traffords, all rooms are named after family members.

rooms
6 rooms · 3 suites

food
Trafford's Restaurant: British

drink
Michael's Bar

features
landscaped gardens · wireless Internet access ·
DVD library · function room and marquee ·
boat rental · airport transfers

nearby
Norwich · Wroxham Broad · Norfolk Broads
National Park · bird-watching · river boating

contact
The Avenue, Wroxham
Norfolk NR12 8TS, United Kingdom ·
telephone: +44.016.0378 3567 ·
email: info@broadhousehotel.co.uk ·
website: www.broadhousehotel.co.uk

Bernard's Room and Harry's Room are the two attic accommodations. The former has an all-glass shower stall in lieu of a bathtub, and twin arched windows that face the south and west. The latter is more spacious with higher ceilings and a super-king-sized bed. It also features an en-suite bathroom with two baths, two washbasins, and a separate glass shower that can accommodate two.

The Abbotts Room is defined by a large cast-iron soaking tub set in a corner of the bedroom. Right beside the bath, a window perfectly frames a view of the meadow, a pair of armchairs conveniently placed before it. The room also has a full en-suite bathroom with shower. If one's tastes lean toward the exquisite, Aunt Diana's Suite is a rich affair at the front of the original building, with a separate sitting room that joins into an elegantly appointed bedroom.

Trafford's Restaurant is quintessentially British, and uses only fresh ingredients, many vegetables coming from the kitchen's own garden. For relaxing with friends, there's the plush Michael's Bar, a cosy library with books and newspapers, an airy drawing room in the heart of the house, and plenty of room out on the lawns and terrace.

Throughout the seasons, this boutique hotel has loads to offer the Norfolk visitor. Where others focus on the achievement of a welcoming atmosphere or the provision of contemporary pleasures, Broad House Hotel succeeds admirably in delivering both.

tuddenham mill

Set over a stream on the outer edges of the Suffolk Brecks, Tuddenham Mill is a building with an extraordinarily long history. There has been a mill on the site for over 1,000 years, the fast-flowing water providing power for the grinding work. The current building was erected in 1775, with the 16-m (53-ft) chimney being added later so steam could be used to increase its grinding capacity. The mill only ceased operations in 1954 and lay derelict before being converted into a restaurant in 1972.

Following a sympathetic refurbishment, Tuddenham Mill has recently been transformed into a unique boutique hotel and restaurant.

Renovation work was completed at an estimated cost of £1.2 million, and included a thorough cleaning and excavation of the stream, restoring natural life to the area by encouraging the return of local flora and fauna. The original water mill, with its three bedrooms, has now been joined by a new annex containing 12 flawlessly appointed guestrooms and suites.

Every aspect of Tuddenham Mill's revival was carefully guided by a team of architects, conservation planners, and interior designers to ensure that its classic charm would not be lost. The effort has paid off handsomely—guestrooms proudly feature the mill's original exposed beams, and outdoor balconies or picture windows provide lovely views of the mill pond. The exterior is a charming, weathered mix of brick and siding. In the heart of the building, the original water wheel has been fully restored, now sporting a beautiful glow from lighting installed at its base, and can be observed behind the glass panels of a stylish new bar.

Across the flowing stream, a glass walkway connects the bar to the Race Room, a private dining area with much of the old machinery on view. In warmer months, outdoor seating by the pond is a popular choice, although the window-side tables in the upstairs restaurant, overlooking the pond, remain romantic in any weather. To complement the view, Head Chef Gordon McNeill has fashioned a contemporary menu inspired by the cuisines of Scotland, Italy,

rooms
11 rooms • 4 suites

food
restaurant: Scottish, Asian and Italian fusion

drink
bar

features
2 private dining and function rooms • 24-hour room service • pet-friendly rooms • DVD library • wireless Internet access

nearby
Newmarket • Cambridge • Bury St Edmunds • Ely • Grimes Graves • Thetford Forest • vineyards • quad-biking • clay shooting • walking trails

contact
High Street, Tuddenham, near Newmarket Suffolk IP28 6SQ, United Kingdom • telephone: +44.016.3871 3552 • email: info@tuddenhammill.co.uk • website: www.tuddenhammill.co.uk

and Asia. Wherever possible, ingredients are sourced locally, or made fresh in the kitchen. Seafood is caught off the coast, bread is freshly baked, and even the organic goat cheese recipe once belonged to Gordon's grandmother.

Private dining events and meetings may be hosted in either The Race Room, which accommodates up to 12 guests, or The Terrace Room, a larger private dining space for parties of up to 25. True to its name, it features a private outdoor terrace overlooking the water.

The 11 guestrooms and four Loft Suites are furnished to the highest of standards with Italian furniture, comfortable sprung mattresses fitted with luxurious Egyptian cotton, and matchless views of the tranquil nature surrounding the mill. The bathrooms are especially extravagant affairs, with some featuring huge stone baths large enough for three people, separate walk-in showers, and even exclusive, naturally fragranced toiletries from Jo Malone. The brand name pedigree extends to sound systems by Bose and brilliant flat-screen televisions by Loewe; only the best were considered for these rooms.

These and a number of other thoughtful considerations have given rise to a holiday destination suited to quiet weekend retreats as well as extended explorations of the East Anglian countryside. Quality and comfort are placed above all else on the list, and the charming location is likely to ensure the continued popularity of Tuddenham Mill for another century, if not a millennium.

thenorth

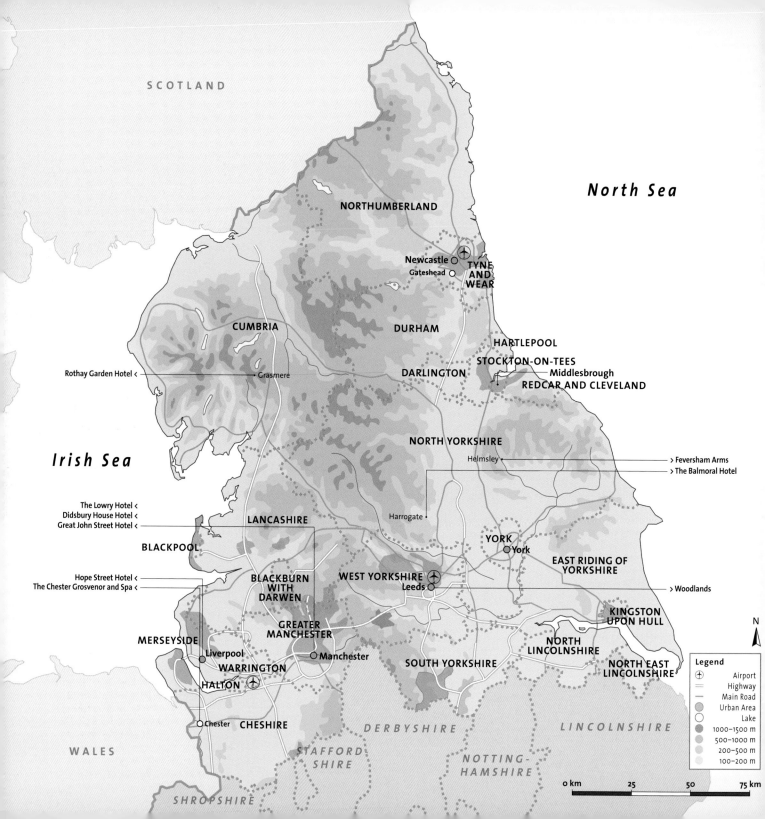

SCOTLAND

North Sea

NORTHUMBERLAND

Newcastle ⊕
Gateshead ○ TYNE AND WEAR

CUMBRIA

DURHAM

HARTLEPOOL
STOCKTON-ON-TEES
DARLINGTON ○ Middlesbrough
REDCAR AND CLEVELAND

Rothay Garden Hotel ⟨──────── ● Grasmere

Irish Sea

NORTH YORKSHIRE

Helmsley ⟨──────────── ⟩ Feversham Arms
⟩ The Balmoral Hotel

The Lowry Hotel ⟨
Didsbury House Hotel ⟨
Great John Street Hotel ⟨──────

Harrogate ○

LANCASHIRE

BLACKPOOL

YORK
○ York

EAST RIDING OF YORKSHIRE

Hope Street Hotel ⟨──────
The Chester Grosvenor and Spa ⟨

BLACKBURN WITH DARWEN

WEST YORKSHIRE ⊕
Leeds ○ ⟩ Woodlands

KINGSTON UPON HULL

MERSEYSIDE

GREATER MANCHESTER

● Liverpool
WARRINGTON
HALTON ⊕

● Manchester

SOUTH YORKSHIRE

NORTH LINCOLNSHIRE

NORTH EAST LINCOLNSHIRE

N

○ Chester CHESHIRE

DERBYSHIRE

LINCOLNSHIRE

WALES

STAFFORD SHIRE

NOTTING- HAMSHIRE

Legend
⊕ Airport
≡ Highway
— Main Road
⬤ Urban Area
○ Lake
■ 1000–1500 m
■ 500–1000 m
200–500 m
100–200 m

SHROPSHIRE

0 km   25   50   75 km

the north

the north awakens

They're different up North. Stretch an imaginary line from the River Dee, on the west (separating Wales from the loaf-shaped peninsula known as The Wirral), to places such as Grimsby and Cleethorpes (at the mouth of the River Humber), on the east. Above it, reaching all the way to the Scottish border, is a part of England that is culturally and temperamentally distinct from the South. And along the dividing spine of the Pennines, distinct in East and West.

More important than geographic and historically cultural differences, in the 21st century, the North of England is a changed place. The old stereotypical world of poverty, of flat, flat vowels and flat expectations, failing industries and unemployment—popularised by generations of grim 'Eh by gum it's tough up North' films and television dramas, is about as relevant an image of the modern North as an 18th-century costume drama.

Technology, services and retailing, media and sport are the new creative engines of the North. The grim factory villages with their rows of tiny, flat-fronted cottages stained by soot and pollution, are rapidly becoming smart bedroom communities with rising property prices, filled with young professionals from the powerhouse cities of the North—Leeds, Liverpool, Manchester, Newcastle, Sheffield. Fueled by growing university populations, the northern arts and music scenes literally explode with energy, while such Northern charmers as York, Chester and Harrogate offer a variety of attractive lifestyle options to affluent baby boomers.

You can love it or hate it, but Anthony Gormley's monumental sculpture, The Angel of the North is unlikely to inspire ambivalence—it is a statement of the new Northern confidence and style that is making itself known. The 20-m- (65-ft-) high statue, spreading its jumbo-jet-wide wings over the A1 Motorway near Gateshead, honours the region's industrial past but marks its transition to the affluent information age.

THIS PAGE: Manchester's Salford Quays, where the brash and new rise up out of the old.

PAGE 200: Anthony Gormley's Angel of the North stands tall, outstretched against a celestial flock of hot air balloons.

a western revival

The cities of the Northwest have had their knocks. In Liverpool, they'll tell you that when the city was named European Capital of Culture for 2008, only a few disgruntled southerners were surprised. In fact, this is a place that had been rebuilding its reputation for decades.

Once one of the most important seaports in the world, the city had been cruising by on its ineffably touristic reputation as the birthplace of the Beatles for far too long when a complicated series of economic and political scandals in the 1980s shook it up and woke it up. Liverpudlians have not looked back since.

Its docks on the Mersey were, in 2004, given UNESCO World Heritage status as Liverpool—Maritime Mercantile City, recognising the their role in Britain's Age of Empire. The area that was once was hub of the slave trade, an emigrant departure point for America, and a centre of shipping and the cotton industry is today a lively museum and café quarter. Contemporary art lovers flock to the area for exhibits at The Tate Liverpool, home of the National Collection of Modern Art in the North of England and the UK's largest contemporary art gallery outside of London. A huge, multi-million pound, luxury cruise terminal opened in 2007 and the kinds of upmarket, swanky restaurants that follow affluence and style are now everywhere. Dress up for 60 Hope Street, a restaurant, bar and bistro in a double-fronted Georgian house. Alma de Cuba, a Caribbean/South American restaurant, bar and salsa club, in a spectacularly converted church on Seel Street, attracts a hip, young international crowd.

Manchester, England's second-largest city, was the 18th-century cotton-making capital of the world. Its wealthy industrialists and tycoons endowed it with museums, galleries, theatres and Victorian civic architecture. Then, in the mid 1990s, a shocking IRA bomb destroyed a huge swathe of the city centre.

The impulse to rebuild eventually spread outside the centre to other underused and tired districts, such that Manchester is now one of the UK's most important showcases of 21st-century architecture. In the heart of the 1996 bombed area, Urbis, by Ian Simpson, is a triangular slice of mirrored glass and one of Manchester's (and indeed, the country's) most recognised buildings. The symbolic sculpture that is Daniel Libeskind's Imperial War Museum North, in the Salford Quays area

THIS PAGE: Urbis is a landmark of Manchester's hectic city centre.

OPPOSITE: A playful installation is exhibited at the Tate Liverpool.

(connected to the rest of Manchester by the Millenium Footbridge), has three linked buildings shaped as shards of a broken globe.

the cities of the northeast

Leeds, in Yorkshire, is England's fastest-growing city and the UK's most important legal services centre located outside of London. Media—both traditional publishing and new media, as well as new technology-based financial services support Leeds's booming economy. In a city that once thrived on tailoring and textiles, fashion manufacturing still makes an important contribution. So it's not surprising that Leeds is a cosmopolitan and sophisticated urban centre with a reputation for fine dining, great nights out, a wealth of cultural activities and terrific shopping—including the first Harvey Nichols opened outside of London—in stylish new city centre malls and atmospheric Victorian arcades.

Beyond the polite and lovely enclaves of medieval York and Regency Harrogate, Newcastle and its across-the-Tyne partner, Gateshead, are hip and gritty places with edgy nightlife and a talent for reinvention through public art. One of the latest Newcastle-Gateshead projects is Nocturne: the Light on the Tyne, a huge, changing colour and light installation, by artist Nayan Kulkarni, on the QEII Metro Bridge. The patterns and colours of the work, reflected on the bridge and the water below, are determined by digital images sent in by members of the public.

peaks, lakes and dales

With so many urban delights for the chic traveller, it's easy to forget that this region also has some of the most beautiful and empty landscapes in England. From the stark, dramatic Peak District, that rises above the Midlands, there are no less than five National Parks. The Yorkshire Dales are 1,800 sq km (685 sq miles) of hills and woodlands, straddling the Pennines and very popular with walkers. The North York Moors, wind-scoured landscapes of heaths and moorlands, have inspired generations of artists and writers. Only about 2,000 people occupy Northumberland National Park, along with long stretches of Hadrian's Wall. The Lake District, the playground of northern tycoons since the first fortunes were made in Liverpool and Manchester, has England's highest peak, it's longest, deepest lake, and an outdoor lifestyle of walking and watersports interrupted by breaks for fine dining, exclusive golf and vintage steamboat cruises.

THIS PAGE: Leeds, West Yorkshire's fashion and retail capital.

OPPOSITE: Hadrian's Wall marked the northern boundary of the Roman Empire, from Newcastle to the northwestern coast.

...some of the most beautiful and empty landscapes in England.

northern style

Ever since Liverpool's biggest export, **The Beatles**, put Mod fashions into the international spotlight, many of England's hippest and most anarchic style directions have bubbled up out of the world of popular music—Punk, New Romantics, Techno, to name a scant few. That must make England's northern cities, generators of wave after wave of new music, among the hippest places in the kingdom.

Take Sheffield, for instance. From Joe Cocker to Jarvis Cocker (no relation), England's steel city has sent such bands as **Def Leppard**, **Pulp** (fronted by the charismatic Jarvis Cocker), **The Arctic Monkeys**, **Little Man Tate** and **The Human League** to international audiences. The city is studded with unparalleled venues for live music. One of the newest, **Carling Academy Sheffield**, opened in April 2008 with local funk rock indie band **Reverend and the Makers**.

Top music venues have always been a part of Manchester's strength—dating all the way back to 1946 when broadcaster Jimmy Savile was credited with inventing the modern DJ by using two turntables, welded together for continuous play, at the **Manchester Ritz**. The Ritz, a live music venue on Whitworth Street, has been around since 1927 and was topping 'Best' bar and venue lists as recently as 2007.

Gigs at the **Manchester Academy** complex (Academy 1, 2 and 3 and Club Academy), a group of venues within the grounds of Manchester University, include all the latest in the sounds of Manchester. The complex was closed for much of 2007 for refurbishment, but has since reopened with added features and capacity.

And it's an indicator of new music's importance to Manchester that a group of highly noteworthy national organisations—including The National Lottery Heritage Fund, the Arts Council England and the Manchester City Council—have raised nearly £4 million to transform the historic **Northern Quarter** venue **Band on the Wall** (25 Swan Street) into a 21st-century centre for new talent and global music. Beginning as a pub in 1865, it became a live music venue in 1937. Over the years, the club has showcased local groups ranging from **Joy Division** and **Simply Red** to post-punk rockers, **The Fall**, and revived new wave band, **The Buzzcocks**, along with a roster of talented British and international musicians. **Art Blakey**, **Richie Havens** and **Bjork** are just some of the famous names who have appeared there. The redeveloped club is scheduled to open by early 2009.

It's a vibrant art scene, in addition to the music, that plays a major role in setting the post-millennial tone of the newly rebranded conurbation, NewcastleGateshead. The city that gave the world **Dire Straits**, **Sting** and hip progressive house beats is now sending out Turner Prize contenders from its two universities, Northumbria and Newcastle, and from its acclaimed knockout art space, the **Baltic** on Gateshead Quays. Shows there often have the same ironic and iconoclastic spirit as modern indie music. As if to further blur the line between the visual and aural art media, the **Baltic** occasionally features the work of artist-cum-musicians. **Brian Eno**, who pioneered modern ambient music, exhibited his installations in the

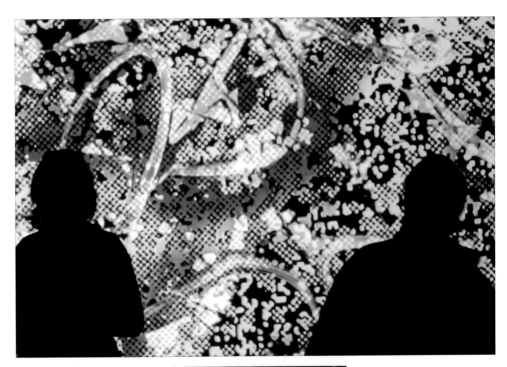

gallery. The photography of **Patti Smith**, icon of punk rock, has also made an appearance.

Art enthusiasts excited by the Newcastle aesthetic can head for **The Biscuit Factory** on Stoddart Street, a huge gallery and 'original art store'. At least 100 artists exhibit their work there, in a 3,251-sq-m (35,000 sq-ft) space which spans two floors. The gallery's offerings, which run a wide range from painting, photography, drawing, sculpture, prints, ceramics and glass, are all first-class and the selection changes frequently. Every three months, the gallery holds an 'Opening' event to showcase work by its newest artists.

THIS PAGE (FROM TOP): Artwork by Brian Eno is a riot of colour and mood; Big breaks and great bands take centrestage at The Ritz Manchester.

OPPOSITE (CLOCKWISE FROM TOP LEFT): Pub bands down at the local will often show surprising talent and polish; Punk—style, sound and attitude; The New Romantic look bubbled up out of a music scene in flux.

buy it!

THIS PAGE: The Rows are medieval, multi-level and galleried shopping streets that are unique to Chester.

OPPOSITE: : Faïence, stained glass and mosaics at the County Arcade, part of Leeds' exclusive Victoria Quarter.

The pristine medieval city of **Chester**, completely surrounded by walls begun by the Romans, is one of England's great shopping playgrounds. This pretty city in the northwest is packed with so many perfectly preserved half-timbered (or black and white) buildings, it looks a bit like a film set.

They are all real. And what's more, they are Chester's unique shopping feature. **The 'Rows'** are long parades of black and whites which date back to the 13th century, and resemble nothing more than a medieval shopping mall. The best part is that, while Chester's main shopping district may look a bit like a theme park, these ancient shops are stuffed with one tempting boutique after another—at least 1,000 in Chester's pedestrian heart.

There are Rows all over the city centre. The best for browsing are **Watergate**, **Eastgate** and **Bridge Street**, where the shops range from trendy one-offs and specialist dealers to the usual tourist tat. Men do particularly well at **Tessuti** (14-20 Watergate) a superstore of European designer kit for guys. Chester's shops are like a pile of wrapped presents under a tree. They may not all contain treasures but part of the fun is simply diving in.

More serious shoppers head for **Leeds**, a city that has historically been associated with English fashion manufacturing. It has been called the Knightsbridge of the north and is undoubtedly its retail capital. The **Victoria Quarter** houses the most exclusive shops, arranged in grand Victorian arcades and Grade II listed buildings full of mosaics, faience and stained glass atria.

Among the 75 top international shops, the Victoria Quarter houses **Louis Vuitton** (98-99 Briggate), **Paul Smith** (17-19 King Edward Street), **Vivienne Westwood** (11-17 County Arcade), **Mulberry** (3-5 County Arcade) and **Harvey Nichols** (107-111 Briggate). Independent designer retailer **Aqua Couture** (36 Queen Victoria Street) features the best of London Fashion Week and new northern designers. **Firetrap** (28-30 County Arcade) has youthful punk-inspired clothes and **Jeffery-West** (21 County Arcade) does sharp and stylish men's shoes. The cutting-edge **All Saints** (33-35 Queen Victoria Street) shapes denim, jersey, tailored pieces and leathers for chic men and women with attitude.

One of Leeds' best-kept fashion secrets is not in Leeds at all but in the otherwise unremarkable town of Barnsley, about 26 km (16 miles) to the south. **Pollyanna** (14-16 Market Hill), founded by Rita Britton in 1967, has been hailed by the Victoria and Albert Museum as one of the leading shops in the world. First in the UK to stock designs by **Comme des Garçons, Issey Miyake, Junya Watanabe** and **Yohji Yamamoto**, the focus at Pollyanna is 'austere modernism'. Customers from all around the world value her judgement and stop in when they're nearby to see what Britton has sifted from the latest collections.

northern elegance

THIS PAGE: An aerial view of the York, centred on the York Minster, the largest consecrated Gothic space in Europe, with a stained-glass window as big as a competition tennis court.

OPPOSITE: Cream teas at Bettys are an establishment in York and Harrogate; fancy hats come out for the elegant Ebor Race Meet at York Racecourse; lawns and herbaceous borders at RHS Harlow Carr Gardens in Harrogate.

Away from the north's industrial centres of engineering, manufacture, shipping, steel and mining, **York** and **Harrogate** are exclusive residential enclaves, surrounded by farmland and sandwiched between the Yorkshire Dales and the North York Moors.

Besides the obvious difference of their urban architecture—York is a walled, medieval city, Harrogate a Georgian and Victorian spa town— the two communities share visible

signs of affluence. Here too, the slow-moving, flat-vowelled Yorkshire speech is less pronounced.

Both York and Harrogate are quintessentially English. And what could be more English than an old-fashioned tea shop? In both Harrogate and York, visitors enjoy high-priced, very English, cream teas and fancy cakes in the apparently very English **Bettys Café Tea Rooms**, founded, as it happens, by a Swiss confectioner.

york

The occupying Romans called the city Eboracum—place of the yew trees— and held it from the first to the fifth centuries. The foundations of their fortress are still visible in the crypt of **York Minster**. The Anglo-Saxons came next. They called the place Eorforwic, until the Vikings arrived at about 800, named it Jorvik and never really left. When the Normans arrived after 1066, this area was one of the last holdouts.

One of the pleasures of York is that it wears its history, visible at every turn, lightly, accommodating modern pastimes with style.

Outside the city walls, the **York Racecourse** is one of England's best venues for the monarch's favourite sport, and hosted Royal Ascot in 2005 when the Ascot course was closed.

York is also the perfect place to spend the Christmas season. Almost every outdoor space is transformed into **Yuletide York**, the city's enormous Christmas Market. **York Minster**, the largest enclosed gothic space in northern Europe, is bathed in a lovely light show throughout the season.

Explore York along its passages, and alleys to find hidden corners and lots of small, independent boutiques,. Along **The Shambles**, a street dating back to the 14th century, buildings on either of the street slope toward each other until they nearly touch.

One of York's most famous stores, **Sarah Coggles**, was founded as a market stall by Victoria Bage (Sarah Coggles was rumoured to be her ex-husband's mistress). The large store on Low Petergate, full of designer brands, is a popular stop for fashionistas.

harrogate

Mineral springs were discovered here in the 16th century. By the 19th, Harrogate was a fashionable spa resort. Victorian grandees promenaded along its tree-shaded avenues. Today, they're lined with exclusive shops. Look at contemporary art, ceramics, sculpture and jewelry at **Godfrey & Watt** (7-8 Westminster Arcade) or scout the boutiques along the cobbles of the **Montpellier Quarter**.

feversham arms

THIS PAGE (FROM LEFT): *The hotel fare is uncomplicated yet satisfying; the intimate lighting and deep soaking tubs set an ideal stage for a warm and relaxing bath.*

OPPOSITE (FROM LEFT): *All the rooms have unique furnishings, colour schemes and design touches; Feversham Arms is located in four provincial stone cottages.*

North Yorkshire's unbroken miles of quaint villages and countryside, with its moors and dales, make it a favourite destination for walkers, photographers, and nature-lovers in general. The small market town of Helmsley is the preferred starting point for many, conveniently located a half hour from York and Harrogate, and is a relaxed and quieter alternative to many fussier country retreats.

Preferring to offer a balanced blend of simplicity and sophistication, the 33-room Feversham Arms hotel eschews the designer pretensions that too often lead down the road of style over taste. Yet, all modern comforts are provided, and the service is polite, professional, and faultless—warm, without veering into the realm of bucolic cliché. Originally a coaching inn built by the Earl of Feversham in 1855, the hotel occupied a single Yorkshire stone cottage until the latter half of the 20th century, when it was expanded by new owners to include three adjacent cottages. A series of renovations followed, adding a pool, tennis court, and gardens, making it a singularly attractive property for visitors to Yorkshire.

Every room and suite exhibits a unique character, having been individually designed to the point of displaying custom colour schemes, motifs, and lighting systems, so no two guests will share the exact same experience. Studio Double rooms all have queen-sized beds, except for the romantic Room #4, which forgoes a bathtub for a

luxurious king-sized bed set amidst lush, deep-red décor. One shouldn't consider it a compromise, however—the large walk-in shower is its own pleasure. Six more spacious King Size Double rooms are also available. Room #18 features a lovely roll-top bath, and even a separate dressing room.

The 12 suites each have unusual and evocative names such as Halcyon, Elysium, and Sanctum. Halcyon is decorated in warm, gentle colours, whereas Elysium features the cleaner, crisper use of off-white and oatmeal tones with unusual textures. Both are equipped with sofa beds in the generous living areas. Sanctum, a Junior Suite, fits perfectly with the countryside with exposed oak beams and an open fireplace.

As their names suggest, the remaining nine Poolside and Garden Suites have inward-facing views, with most offering convenient access to the heated outdoor pool. Some have their own patios and gardens, while others

...no two guests will share the exact same experience.

rooms
11 rooms • 22 suites

foods
The Restaurant: English

drink
cocktail bar

features
spa • meeting rooms • outdoor heated pool • garden • private dining rooms • fireside lounges • secure parking

nearby
North York Moors National Park • Harrogate • York • gardens • walking • cycling • racing • shops • steam railway

contact
Helmsley
North Yorkshire YO62 5AG, United Kingdom • telephone: +44.0.1439.770 766 • facsimile: +44.0.1439.770 346 • website: www.fevershamarmshotel.com

include wood-burning stoves, double-ended baths, and separate children's bedrooms, ideal for a family stay. All guestrooms and suites benefit from best-of-breed amenities such as L'Occitane toiletries, televisions by Bang & Olufsen, and a selection of CDs and DVDs in each room. The soft beds are embellished by sheets of Egyptian cotton and billowy duck-down duvets for comfort.

For most, breakfast in bed is an irresistible indulgence, and every room includes a breakfast table for good measure, but meals at the Feversham Arms hotel can be served in a variety of locations. The Restaurant is an ideal venue for lunch in the summer. Coffee, tea and fresh pastries are served throughout the day in the lounges, and in fine weather, one may even enjoy a pre-dinner drink on the poolside terrace. The signature flavour here is that of the local land, with fresh game, shellfish, poultry, and cheeses sourced from nearby farms. Servings are well portioned, and simplicity rules the design of everything that finds itself on a plate. Much like the hotel itself, the kitchen takes pains to uncomplicate the complicated. The result is dining that truly satisfies, and a getaway that relaxes and refreshes not just the body, but the spirit.

woodlands

A mere 5 km (3 miles) from the populous and modern city of Leeds is a quiet retreat that exemplifies all of the charms associated with the Yorkshire countryside. Woodlands, a historic three-storey country manor built in 1871, originally belonged to a wealthy mill owner who made his fortune in the thriving local textile industry. Restored in 2004 as an exclusive boutique hotel and restaurant, Woodlands pays tribute to its beginnings with 17 individually designed bedrooms, each named after a type of fabric.

With evocative names such as Damask, Samite, and Pashmine, accommodation at Woodlands is anything but common. Each room a singular creation, the guestrooms and suites are draped with luxurious materials in harmonious colours, and handpicked furnishings give them all identities of their own. Large windows look out to the impressive landscaped grounds and let in showers of golden sunlight, especially beautiful in the summer and fall. In the midst of this natural serenity, modern comforts such as a movie library and pillow menu make it possible to enjoy more than just a good night's sleep. Every room is also equipped with a flat-screen television, DVD player, high-speed Internet access, and a well-stocked bar.

The hotel has much to offer in and around the main building, with all corners fitted for comfort by celebrated Leeds interior

THIS PAGE (FROM TOP): Savour English cuisine with a hint of Europe, created with fresh seasonal ingredients from Yorkshire; all of the rooms are fittingly named after luxurious fabrics.

OPPOSITE (FROM LEFT): Woodlands is perfect for a quiet getaway; have a relaxing soak in the antique claw-footed bathtubs.

rooms
17 rooms and suites

food
Bentley Rooms: cutting-edge rustic

drink
Arnage Bar: relaxed fireplace setting

services
24-hour room service • complimentary high-speed Internet access • meeting and wedding facilities • parking

nearby
Harewood House • Harrogate • Leeds • York • Yorkshire Dales • football and cricket grounds • museums • theatre

contact
Gelderd Road
Leeds LS27 7LY, United Kingdom •
telephone: +44.113.238 1488 •
facsimile: +44.113.253 6773 •
email: enquiries@woodlandsleeds.co.uk •
website: www.tomahawkhotels.co.uk

designers Browning and Baize. The reception area, for instance, has been made more striking by a series of large paintings by the New York-based artist, Sammy Dent. Their luminous appearance plays off the white, airy space and elegantly understated wood and leather couches. More examples of unique art can be found by simply taking a walking tour of the well-kept grounds. Six impressive metalwork sculptures, designed by John Coombes, have been installed at various places around the hotel.

The artisanal experiences continue in the kitchen of John Lyons, head chef of the Woodlands' 70-seat Bentley Rooms, comprised of three dining rooms. Serving English cuisine made with fresh Yorkshire ingredients and a hint of European influence,

the establishment and its attached Arnage Bar have become favourites with locals, with the dining room voted the 'Best Fine Dining Restaurant in Leeds' in 2005. Enjoy a view of the gardens from inside, or venture out in the warmer months for al fresco dining. The menus are wont to change with the seasons, so one always gets a taste of the local country to go with the splendid views.

The picturesque Woodlands is also well-suited for that perfect romantic wedding. The Brooklands room is licensed to host ceremonies and a spectacular marquee tent easily accommodates 120 guests under its high ceilings. Those looking for a romantic weekend—or just a chance to get away from busy city life—will surely find Woodlands an ideal spot for special breaks of any kind.

the balmoral hotel

THIS PAGE: *Rooms are appointed with opulent details such as chandeliers and designer chairs.*

OPPOSITE (FROM LEFT): *Savour old British classics at the elegant Harrogate Grille restaurant; the hotel mixes Old World aesthetics with thoroughly modern design influences.*

Emerging from an extensive refurbishment exercise, The Balmoral Hotel infuses opulence with a modern spirit while staying true to a name and tradition that evokes the very archetype of royal splendour. Nestled in the heart of the picturesque Yorkshire Dales, the hotel occupies a stately stone building. Over a century old, the exterior remains reassuringly Victorian, even as it welcomes guests with a futuristic glass portal leading to the utterly modern lobby, decked out in red and black.

The building's original antique fittings have been retained wherever possible, and The Balmoral Hotel mixes and matches classic lines with modern fabrics and designs suited to contemporary tastes. A signature Matthew Hilton chair sits pretty in the lobby, amidst the elegant black Louis V-style chairs and plush loungers. In the guestrooms, vivid colours predominate, with striking designer wallpaper and bright handmade quilts on the beds. Everything, from the crystal chandeliers to the ornate mirrors, is bold, beautiful and absolutely oozes luxury.

Each room is distinctive, with its style and size determined by the hotel's original layout and characteristics. Some are cosy studios, while other rooms are large enough to accommodate a king-sized four-poster bed. Suites offer an additional lounge area with plasma television, and throughout all the rooms and suites, wireless Internet access and high-definition media-interface LCD screens place the latest technological conveniences at one's fingertips. All the little details are taken care of, down to the chic Italian toiletries and mineral water from the local spa.

Guests also enjoy full use of the nearby Academy Spa, which offers a well-equipped gym and pool as well as a menu of indulgent therapies. With Harrogate just minutes away, The Balmoral Hotel is the perfect choice for visitors. Its striking interpretation of the boutique experience celebrates at once the best of old and new world indulgences.

rooms
20 rooms • 3 suites

food
The Harrogate Grille: classic English

drink
The Harrogate Grille

features
Academy Spa with gym and pool

nearby
Harrogate International Centre • Harrogate town centre • Yorkshire Dales • shopping • spas

contact
The Balmoral Hotel
16–18 Franklin Mount, Harrogate
North Yorkshire HG1 5EJ, United Kingdom •
telephone: +44.0.1423.508 208 •
facsimile: +44.0.1423.530 652 •
email: info@balmoralhotel.co.uk •
website: www.balmoralhotel.co.uk •

The Harrogate Grille
telephone: +44.0.1423.565 800 •
facsimile: +44.0.1423.790 019 •
email: contact@grillerestaurants.com •
website: www.grillerestaurants.com

Like the newly refurbished Balmoral Hotel, The Harrogate Grille takes classics to a whole new level, pairing hearty favourites with a stylish new setting. Run by the same team which launched The Hoxton Grille restaurant in London, it takes its cue from the bistros of New York and Paris, where a simple, well-made meal goes a long way.

The Harrogate Grille occupies a generous restaurant space that spills out to the terrace in good weather. Minimalist elegance is the byword here: timeless wooden floors, classic furnishings and soft lighting create a cosy ambience suited to relaxation.

The offerings on the restaurant's menu are familiar yet fresh. The chefs have combined quality ingredients and culinary ingenuity to make old classics, such as steak and chips, even better. Far from being predictable, the menu is updated every four months to take advantage of seasonal produce.

The extensive wine list also exhibits impressive range and taste. Besides enjoying them by the bottle, guests can select from over 20 wines served by either the glass or the carafe. Whatever one's dining preferences, The Harrogate Grille is versatile enough to deliver it with its characteristic aplomb.

didsbury house

THIS PAGE (FROM LEFT): *The rooms are lit with soft and cosy colours; the décor mixes contemporary style with Victorian touches.*

OPPOSITE (FROM LEFT): *Couples may enjoy a romantic bath together; features such as the original fireplace have been maintained; have a slow drink at the Cream Lounge or the Walled Terrace.*

Just a stone's throw from the hustle and bustle of Manchester city centre lies the fashionable Didsbury district, popular amongst the young and hip for its trendy bars and cafés. It is here where one may find the charming Didsbury House, a luxury townhouse hotel set in the tranquil environs of a Victorian villa.

Upon entrance through its doors, the chic hotel proudly displays its historical pedigree. A grand central staircase, carefully restored from the original building, leads to the hotel's centrepiece—a magnificent stained glass window radiating with warmth from the modern atrium beyond. The rest of the hotel's public spaces are similarly impressive. With their plush sofas and stunning fireplaces, the Cream Lounge and Blue Room are ideal for relaxing, while the small bar is perfect for drinks at the end of a busy day. In fine weather, the outdoor Walled Terrace provides another charming option with its subdued lighting and the soothing sound of trickling water.

With its 23 bedrooms and four suites, all in varying sizes and styles, Didsbury House offers options to suit all budgets and tastes. Thoughtful extras such as butler trays with fresh milk, CD/DVD players with access to a borrowing library and Temple SPA toiletries are standard in every room, making every stay just that little bit more special.

The 10 Classic bedrooms are the smallest and vary in shape and size. They are decorated in calming tones with lush fabrics, soft lighting, and crisp linens. All rooms have en-suite bathrooms with an unusual luxury: double-ended bathtubs big enough for two and an overhead rain shower. Slightly larger are four Villa bedrooms. Fitted with restful colours, soft fabrics, and the same bath facilities as Classic rooms, they cast an air of intimacy, making them well suited for couples.

Just as lushly appointed are five Eclectic rooms. True to their name, they all enjoy individual designs, and have bathtubs in the bedroom area itself for an unusual experience.

For a hotel stay with a difference, the Duplex Rooms and Duplex Junior Suites are more like glamorous loft studios than hotel rooms. Their layouts vary: Duplex Rooms have their bedroom downstairs and a bathroom overhead, while the Duplex Junior Suites offer

rooms
27 rooms and suites

food
Breakfast Room: international breakfast • Bar & Lounge: canapés • room service

drink
Bar & Lounge • patio wall garden

features
complimentary parking • The Blue Room • DVD library • spa • gym • boardroom for up to 20 people • wireless Internet access • patio wall garden

nearby
Didsbury Village • Manchester airport • city centre • Bridgewater hall • Deansgate • GMEX and MEN arena • Granada studio • Opera house • Manchester United • Old Trafford • city stadium • Museum of Science and Industry • Harvey Nichols • Selfridges • Trafford Centre

contact
Didsbury Park, Didsbury Village Manchester M20 5LJ, United Kingdom • telephone: +44.016.1448 2200 • facsimile: +44.016.1448 2525 • email: enquiries@didsburyhouse.co.uk • website: www.didsburyhouse.co.uk

a seating area downstairs with a staircase leading to the sleeping area and a large cast-iron bath overlooking the lounge.

Keeping in line with the intimacy and comfort of the rest of the hotel is the Boudoir Loft Suite. Set in the eaves of the villa, this suite has been developed with creature comforts in mind. The cosy lounge boasts an array of comfortable furniture, providing the ideal environment for leisure or work.

The hotel's pièce de résistance is surely the Opus Loft Suite. The largest and most lavish of all the rooms, it stands in stark contrast to its original use as servants' quarters. The bathroom features twin cast-iron roll-top bathtubs, allowing for decadent 'his and hers' bathing, and a separate double steam shower.

For guests wishing to host an extra-special wedding, party or event, the hotel is available for hire and can accommodate up to 100 attendees. Complete with a small gym, private event rooms, and treatment room, Didsbury House offers all the luxuries of a larger hotel, but its exclusivity and and distinct sense of style help it stand apart from the others.

great john street

THIS PAGE: *The roof garden has a gym, heated verandah, and large hot tub for relaxing in.*

OPPOSITE (FROM TOP LEFT): *The décor is a charming mix of modern and Victorian design styles; the Oyster Bar & Lounge offers cocktails in an elegant setting.*

In the heart of Manchester's city centre, overlooking the set of the longest-running English soap opera, Coronation Street, and in the very heart of the city's theatre and shopping district, lies the Great John Street hotel. Originally a Victorian schoolhouse, the building has been cleverly converted into an extremely chic, luxurious boutique hotel—

ideal for those visiting on business or looking for a break in a city that has everything on offer. With the world's biggest football club and some of Britain's best restaurants and bars, Manchester is a mecca for fun-loving, party-seeking shopaholics from all over Europe.

Boasting 30 individual rooms and suites—all designed by owner Sally O'Loughlin—the hotel is the epicentre of off-kilter style. Many of the building's original features have been retained and sit comfortably alongside rich, warm fabrics, extravagant colour schemes and hand-carved period furnishings. Somehow it all comes together and works.

There are five styles of rooms and suites, all with Temple Spa toiletries, CD/DVD players and butler trays. The duplex baby grand rooms are on the first and second floors with high, airy ceilings. Bathrooms are overhead, featuring solid oak floors, rain showers and a romantic bath for two.

Slightly larger are the eight Boudoir Grand rooms which retain original schoolhouse features such as exposed brickwork and steel beams. Like the baby Grands, they too have overhead bathrooms and—best of all—king-sized beds with crisp white linens ensuring the sweetest of dreams.

For an unforgettable—and maybe unpredictable—stay try one of the 10 Classical Grand Junior Suites. They vary from simplex to duplex layouts but all are beautifully appointed and designed to make sure you won't want to step outside to make

The furnishings are opulent, stylish and extremely comfortable...

rooms
30 rooms and suites

food
Oyster Bar & Lounge: canapés • room service

drink
Oyster Bar & Lounge • Rooftop Lounge during fine weather

features
Roof Garden • hot tub • DVD library • event and meeting rooms for up to 150 • gym • valet parking • wireless Internet access

nearby
Bridgewater Hall • Deansgate • GMEX and MEN Arena • Granada Studios • Harvey Nichols • Old Trafford • Opera House • Selfridges • Trafford Centre • Manchester city centre • city stadium • Museum of Science and Industry

contact
Great John Street, Castlefield Manchester M3 4FD, United Kingdom • telephone: +44.016.1831 3211 • facsimile: +44.016.1831 3212 • email: info@greatjohnstreet.co.uk • website: www.greatjohnstreet.co.uk

the most of Manchester's many attractions, not even on a Saturday night when the city is jumping. The four Eclectic Grand and two Opus Grand suites are the pick of the bunch so make sure you put in a special request for one of these glamorous duplexes. In its previous life the space was a classroom; it now evokes a chic New York loft apartment. It retains the high windows of the old school, flooding the room with an abundance of natural light. Most second-floor bathrooms hold twin bathtubs and washbasins with walk-in rain showers that double up as personal steam rooms.

The grandest of all are the Opus Grand suites—size matters here. The furnishings are opulent, stylish and extremely comfortable, feeling like a designer apartment rather than just another hotel room.

After all this, if you really do want to venture outside your suite, head to the rooftop lounge and garden—you might even spot an episode of 'Corrie' in production down below. Ideal for sunbathing, a summer evening barbecue or a dry martini in the hot tub, this rooftop space is unique in the city. Alternatively, cocktail time in the Oyster Bar and Lounge exudes charm and elegance.

In every way, Great John Street is out of the ordinary, providing an experience beyond that of a night away in a big city. To experience modern-day Manchester, make a beeline for this unique hotel that has redefined urban chic. Celebrate your next birthday by booking the whole property, or entertain clients there with a party for up to 200 people. If it's good enough for the biggest football club on earth, it's good enough for you.

the lowry hotel

When The Lowry Hotel opened in April 2001, it enjoyed the distinction of being the first five-star hotel in the Greater Manchester area. Shortly after, the stylish property received a number of impressive reviews, and was even voted as one of the '32 Coolest Hotels in the World' by *Condé Nast Traveller*.

Located in one of Manchester's newest and most vibrant areas, Chapel Wharf, the glass-fronted hotel building is set on the banks of the River Irwell, giving the interiors a bright openness and providing a marvellous natural view from many rooms. Striking architecture and bold interior designs are hallmarks of the Lowry concept, and its curved structure fits right in with the recently developed area. Nearby, the distinctive Trinity Bridge designed by Santiago Calatrava provides walking access to the city centre's attractions and wealth of shopping options.

The 165 guestrooms and suites enjoy panoramic views of the hotel's surroundings and feature contemporary décor by Olga Polizzi, who has designed many hotels for the Rocco Forte Collection. Adhering to a philosophy of cleanliness and simplicity in her designs, the rooms are above all comfortable, and each offers a multitude of thoughtful amenities. Every room has two phone lines, voicemail, and high-speed Internet access for business travellers. For the enjoyment of all, satellite TV channels, high-fidelity sound systems, well-stocked minibars and en-suite marble bathrooms are also standard features.

Those desiring a room at the top will be drawn to the six Deluxe Riverside Suites and the Charles Forte Penthouse Suite. With separate lounge, dining, and pantry areas, the Riverside Suites are suited to those with large families, or guests wishing for the privilege of enjoying the hotel's extensive in-room dining menu in private. Boasting the best views of Manchester and Salford, the Penthouse Suite is tremendously spacious, with a reception lounge perfect for entertaining, large double

rooms
158 rooms • 7 suites

food
River Restaurant: modern British

drink
River Bar and Lounge

features
Lowry Day Spa • Sleep Doctor service • bath butler • business centre • fully-equipped gym • 8 meeting rooms • wireless Internet access

nearby
Bridgewater Concert Hall • Granada TV studios • Manchester cathedral • Manchester city centre • Manchester International Convention Centre • railway station • shopping

contact
50 Dearmans Place, Chapel Wharf Manchester M3 5LH, United Kingdom • telephone: +44.161.827 4000 • facsimile: +44.161.827 4001 • email: reservations.lowry@ roccofortecollection.com • website: www.roccofortecollection.com

bathroom, walk-in wardrobe and dining area complete with baby grand piano. A dedicated butler and private chef are also on hand to assist with any requests.

Down by the water, the award-winning River Restaurant serves modern British cuisine with a European twist. Diners may choose a spot on the outdoor terrace, then come inside for a post-dinner drink at the adjacent Bar and Library Lounge. In addition to excellent cuisine, The Lowry Hotel is also renowned for having one of the 'UK's Best Day Spas', as confirmed by *Condé Nast Traveller* magazine. The Lowry Health Spa is made up of six luxurious treatment rooms offering Carita, E'spa, and Ishi therapies to help soothe and unwind tired bodies.

Located just steps from the city centre and 16 km (10 miles) from Manchester Airport, The Lowry Hotel is privy to all happenings in the UK's second-largest urban zone. Whether they are travelling for business or leisure, visitors will surely find nothing lacking in and around the city's most fashionable hotel.

the chester grosvenor + spa

Housed in a historic listed building complete with a traditional black and white timbered façade, The Chester Grosvenor and Spa is no ordinary city hotel. Owned by and named after the Duke of Westminster and his family, the five-star hotel has accommodated royalty and international celebrities alike for over 140 years. The story of its prestigious address is closely linked to the city's development and vibrant social scene in the 19th century, details of which fill a specially commissioned book available from the hotel.

A series of fine traditions inform the way business is conducted at the hotel, and one of the proudest constants is the Michelin star which has been accorded to the fine dining restaurant, the Simon Radley at The Chester

Grosvenor, for almost 20 years. Originally named Arkle, after the steeplechaser owned by the late Anne, Duchess of Westminster, the restaurant has recently been refurbished and renamed after its long term Executive Chef. Its contemporary dishes are crafted from fresh, seasonal produce and perfectly complement choices from the 1,000-bin cellar. For more relaxed meals and cocktails, La Brasserie offers an elegant take on Parisian dining amidst leather sofas and sleek granite-topped tables.

If one arrives encumbered with all the tension of an international air journey, then The Grosvenor Spa with its five treatment rooms and other facilities should be the first stop after checking in. A menu of therapies, called 'Rituals', promises to knead and soothe

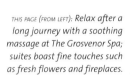

THIS PAGE (FROM LEFT): Relax after a long journey with a soothing massage at The Grosvenor Spa; suites boast fine touches such as fresh flowers and fireplaces.

OPPOSITE (FROM LEFT): The stately hotel building dates back over 140 years to the Victorian era; at La Brasserie, enjoy Parisian-style light meals and desserts.

rooms
66 rooms • 14 suites

food
Simon Radley at The Chester Grosvenor:
fine dining • La Brasserie: Parisian • The Arkle
Bar and Lounge

drink
The Arkle Bar and Lounge: champagnes,
wines and spirits • La Brasserie: cocktails

features
The Grosvenor Spa • complimentary high-speed
Internet • executive boardroom • gymnasium •
meeting suites

nearby
Arley Hall and Gardens • Chester Racecourse •
Chester Zoo • Grosvenor Park • Ness Botanical
Gardens • Blue Planet Aquarium • cathedral •
golf courses • museums • shopping

contact
Eastgate
Chester CH1 1LT, United Kingdom •
telephone: +44.012.4432 4024 •
facsimile: +44.012.4431 3246 •
email: hotel@chestergrosvenor.com •
website: www.chestergrosvenor.com

all manner of complaints from tired bodies, enhanced by the natural properties of premium Molton Brown and Elemis spa products. A steam room, herb sauna, ice fountain, footbath area, and salt grotto round off the list of sublime comforts.

In line with the hotel's dedication to excellence, each of the 66 guestrooms and 14 suites feature unique designs and décor. All rooms are equipped with quality amenities such as Bose CD clock radios, televisions with satellite channels and DVD players, high-speed Internet access, and fully stocked minibars. The Junior, Deluxe, and Master suites feature an in-room music library, and with their large living areas and separate guest bathrooms, are ideal for entertaining. If one wishes to go further in the pursuit of comfort, then only the Presidential Suite will do. The suite's two bedrooms and lounge area are rich, yet understated. Guests are presented with a bottle of Taittinger champagne and canapés upon arrival, and offered full use of a butler service throughout their stay.

As a romantic getaway, or simply a historic gateway to the sights of Chester, The Chester Grosvenor and Spa succeeds not only on the strength of its experience as one of the country's great hospitality providers, but also through its distinguished sense of style.

hope street hotel

THIS PAGE: *The London Carriage Works serves modern food with influences ranging from the Middle East to Southeast Asia.*

OPPOSITE (FROM LEFT): *Rooms boast luxurious details such as heated wooden floors and beds with fine Egyptian cotton sheets; the bathrooms are equipped with lush amenities from REN.*

In wake of being chosen as the European Capital of Culture for 2008, Liverpool has readied itself for an explosion in growth and development. Although Liverpool is well-known as a visual arts city, with vibrant galleries to rival those in London, there were few hotels in the city which offered design-oriented appeal. Some say this changed in 2004—the year that the Hope Street Hotel opened its doors as Liverpool's first luxury boutique hotel.

Occupying a former warehouse in the city centre's trendy Georgian Quarter, the hotel has been renovated with the distinct goal of preserving the 1860 Venetian palazzo-style building's charms. From the restored façade to the exposed brick walls in some rooms, it is history rendered art; style born out of identity. And this is style with no lack of substance, as proven by a string of international awards for its graceful service and quality food. *Condé Nast Traveller* declared it one of the 'World's 50 Coolest Hotels' in 2004, followed by a place on *Tatler*'s '101 Best Hotels' list in 2005 and several *Good Hotel Guide* César Awards.

Hope Street enjoys proximity to some of Liverpool's most popular sights, many of which can be seen from the hotel's 41 rooms and seven suites. Starting with the two cathedrals on either end of Hope Street, down to the clusters of theatres and concert halls around the hotel, and ending with the waterfront—a UNESCO World Heritage site—in the distance, the skyline view is a striking addition to the rooms' list of features.

Each individually designed living space was built with the best available materials and an abundance of fine details. All flooring is made from real birch and oak, and comes with under-floor heating. Tall windows allow natural light to illuminate every corner, giving a bright and airy feel to the uncommonly luxurious rooms. The king-sized beds are covered with Egyptian cotton, and laid in full view of large LCD televisions. Rain showers and fittings by Arne Jacobson Vola create bathrooms that rival the bedrooms for luxury, aided by details such as incredibly soft towels and lavish REN toiletries. Should one wish to send an email or folders of holiday photos to friends, the rooms are conveniently equipped with high-speed Internet access.

Located on the ground floor of the hotel is a restaurant that's certainly worth writing home about. Featuring the award-winning talents of chef Paul Askew, The London Carriage Works serves modern international food from organic and seasonal produce. With a culinary vocabulary honed over a childhood spent in Southeast Asia and the Middle East, Paul Askew's signature cooking style has been called the best in Liverpool by no less than the *Good Food Guide* (2006).

It's hard to fault the hotel's performance over its first four years. The smart integration of classic architecture with clean, modern features makes its rooms more than the sum of their parts, while excellence in service and dining brings guests back time after time.

rooms
41 rooms · 7 suites

food
The London Carriage Works: international

drink
The Residents' Lounge

features
24-hour room service · boardroom and meeting facilities · CD and DVD library · high-speed Internet access

nearby
cathedrals · shopping · concert and theatre halls · waterfront · Liverpool city centre

contact
40 Hope Street
Liverpool L1 9DA, United Kingdom ·
telephone: +44.15.1709 3000 ·
facsimile: +44.15.1709 2454 ·
email: sleep@hopestreethotel.co.uk ·
website: www.hopestreethotel.co.uk

rothay garden hotel

Quiet, secluded, and virtually untouched by the passage of time, Grasmere embodies England's famous Lake District. Geographically and culturally at the heart of the region, the village is an ideal location for enjoying the peaceful scenery and slower pace of life that has inspired many famous writers, including the poets William Wordsworth and Samuel Taylor Coleridge. It is in this idyllic place that Rothay Garden Hotel can be found.

Surrounded by 1 hectare (2 acres) of luxuriant gardens alongside a running river, overlooked by the majestic fells of the valley, the stylish four-star hotel of 30 bedrooms and suites delivers the intimate spirit of the Lake District. Recently refurbished, Rothay Garden lives up to its award-winning name in both service and quality. It has retained two AA Rosettes for over a decade, and enjoys a slew of recognitions, including the Cumbria for Excellence 'Hotel of the Year' award and the *Les Routiers* 'National Hotel of the Year' award.

Three grades of guestrooms are available, beginning with the Langdale Rooms, followed by the lovely Grasmere Rooms and the new Loft Suites, which feature sweeping views of the surrounding area, and are some of the best in all of Lakeland. Elegantly furnished,

THIS PAGE: Rothay Garden Hotel is situated in a grand Victorian residence which dates to 1856.

OPPOSITE (FROM LEFT): Loft Suites offer gorgeous views of the English countryside along with a range of luxurious modern amenities; the hotel restaurant enjoys the distinction of two AA Rosettes.

rooms
25 rooms · 5 suites

food
seasonal North English

drink
cognac and whisky bar

features
landscaped gardens · speciality breaks, with details available from website · high-speed Internet access

nearby
Beatrix Potter Trail · Wordsworth House · climbing · historic houses and castles · hot-air balloon rides · lake cruises · leisure centre · sailing · windsurfing · fishing

contact
Broadgate, Grasmere
Cumbria LA22 9RJ, United Kingdom ·
telephone: +44.0.1539.435 334 ·
facsimile: +44.0.1539.435 723 ·
email: stay@rothaygarden.com ·
website: www.rothaygarden.com

suites also enjoy two flat-screen televisions, Bose sound systems and designer toiletries. The hotel is independently owned, and the resulting flexibility allows many rooms to vary in their configuration and décor. All rooms enjoy en-suite bathrooms and amenities such as satellite television channels, welcome trays and plush bathrobes. Unusual for the Lake District, at least half the rooms provide luxurious 2-m- (6-ft-) wide beds.

Any memory of a Lake District holiday is sure to include more than a few mentions of incredible food, and Rothay Garden prides itself on having prompted more than a few guests to return based on fond feelings for the cuisine at its conservatory restaurant. With outdoor views to match the freewheeling tendencies of its creative seasonal menus, the charming candlelit restaurant provides a culinary sampling of the area's best produce.

Head Chef Andrew Burton is a noted Master Chef of Great Britain, one of only 300 in the entire nation, and is renowned for his daily menus, which are tailored to fresh morning-market ingredients, home-cured meats and handcrafted cheeses. With the aid of proprietor Chris Carss, who offers expert wine pairing suggestions informed by his 30 years of experience in the industry, the restaurant also maintains a superb 140-bin wine list that spans the globe and suits every imaginable need.

Guests will find little here to distract them from the true purpose of their visits—to relax and get away from it all. Days in the Lake District tend to start late, with carefree mid-morning risings, and typically end late after a splendid meal, finished with fine cognac by the fireplace. A wide selection of spirits and two cosy lounges means that on that last point, also, Rothay Garden does not disappoint.

index

index

picturecredits

INTRODUCTION

FASHION + DESIGN

A La Mode
10 Symons Street
South Kensington, London SW3 2TJ
telephone: +44.20.7730 7180

Alexander McQueen
4–5 Old Bond Street, Mayfair
London W1S 4PD
telephone: +44.20.7355 0088
www.alexandermcqueen.com

Alice Temperley
6–10 Colville Mews
Notting Hill, London W11 2DA
telephone: +44.20.7229 7957
heatherc@temperleylondon.com
www.temperleylondon.com

Amanda Wakeley
80 Fulham Road, London SW3 6HR
telephone: +44.20.7590 9105
kms@amandawakeley.com
www.amandawakeley.com

Baltic Centre for Contemporary Art
Gateshead Quays, South Shore Road
Gateshead NE8 3BA
telephone: +44.1914 781 810
facsimile: +44.1914 781 922
info@balticmill.com
www.balticmill.com

Beetham Tower
301 Deansgate
Manchester M3 4LQ

Ben DeLisi
40 Elizabeth Street
Belgravia, London SW1W 9NZ
telephone: +44.20.7730 2994
facsimile: +44.20.77302881
www.bendelisi.com

Betty Jackson
311 Brompton Road
Knightsbridge, London SW3 2DY
telephone: +44.20.7589 7884
facsimile: +44.20.7602 3050
ed@bettyjackson.com
www.bettyjackson.com

Bruce Oldfield
27 Beauchamp Place, London SW3 1NJ
telephone: +44.20.7584 1363
facsimile: +44.20.7761 0351
hq@bruceoldfield.com
www.bruceoldfield.com

Caroline Charles
56–57 Beauchamp Place, London SW3
telephone: +44.20.7589 5850
kathy@carolinecharles.co.uk
www.carolinecharles.co.uk

The Design Museum
Shad Thames, London SE1 2YD
telephone: +44.20.7403 6933
www.designmuseum.org/

Harvey Nichols
109–125 Knightsbridge, London SW1X 7RJ
telephone: +44.20.7235 5000
contactknightsbridge@harveynichols.com
www.harveynichols.com

Exchange Square Manchester M1 1AD
telephone: +44.161.828 8888
contactmanchester@harveynichols.com

The Mailbox
31–32 Wharfside Street, Birmingham B1 1RE
telephone: +44.1216 166 000
contactbirmingham@harveynichols.com

107–111 Briggate, Leeds LS1 6AZ
telephone: +44.1132 048 888
contactleeds@harveynichols.com

Imperial War Museum
The Quays, Trafford Wharf Trafford Park
Manchester M17 1TZ
telephone: +44.1618 364 000
facsimile: +44.1618 364 012
iwmnorth@iwm.org.uk
www.iwm.org.uk

Jacques Azagury
50 Knightsbridge, London SW1X 7JN
telephone: +44.20.7235 0799
facsimile: +44.20.7245 9427
solangeazagury@aol.com
www.jacquesazagury.com

Jaeger
200–206 Regent Street, London W1B 5BN
telephone: +44.20.7979 1100
customer.services@jaeger.co.uk
www.jaeger.co.uk

16–18 Brompton Road
Knightsbridge, London SW1X 7QN
telephone: +44.20.7584 2814

145 King's Road, Chelsea, London SW3 5TX
telephone: +44.20.7352 1122

Jimmy Choo
27 New Bond Street, London W1S 2RH
telephone: +44.20.7493 5858
customercare@jimmychooonline.com
www.jimmychoo.com

32 Sloane Street, London SW1X 9NR
telephone: +44.20.7823 1051

John Rocha
15a Dover Street, Mayfair, London W1
telephone: +44.20.7495 2233
shop@johnrocha.ie
www.johnrocha.ie

Joseph Azagury
73 Knightsbridge, London SW1X 7RB
telephone: +44.20.7259 6887
facsimile: +44.20.7245 0748
info@josephazagury.com
www.josephazagury.com

125 Fulham Road, London SW3 6RT
telephone: +44.20.7584 8241
facsimile: +44.20.7823 9382

Kelly Hoppen
175–177 Fulham Road, London SW3 6JW
telephone: +44.20.7351 1910
sales@kellyhoppenretail.co.uk
www.kellyhoppenretail.com

Liberty
Regent Street at Great Marlborough Street
London W1B 5AH
telephone: +44.20.7734 1234
londonstorecustomerservices@liberty.co.uk
www.liberty.co.uk

Lowry Centre
The Lowry, Pier 8, Salford Quays
Manchester M50 3AZ
telephone: +44.8707.875 780
facsimile: +44.1618.762 001
info@thelowry.com
www.thelowry.com

Nicole Farhi
158 New Bond Street, Mayfair, London W1
telephone: +44.20.7499 8368
facsimile: +44.20.7036 7575
sales@nicolefarhi.com
www.nicolefarhi.com

Patrick Cox
129 Sloane Street, London SW1X 9AT
telephone: +44.20.7730 8886
www.patrickcox.com

Philip Treacy
69 Elizabeth Street, Belgravia
London SW1W 9PJ
telephone: +44.20.7730 3992
facsimile: +44.20.7824 8262
studio@philiptreacy.co.uk
www.philiptreacy.co.uk

Stella McCartney
30 Bruton Street, Mayfair, London W1J 6LG
telephone: +44.20.7518 3100
london@stellamccartney.com
www.stellamccartney.com/int/en

Selfridges
400 Oxford St London W1A 1AB
telephone: +44.1133 698 040
www.selfridges.com

Upper Mall East, Bullring
Birmingham B5 4BP

Manchester Trafford
1 The Dome, The Trafford Centre
Manchester M17 8DA

Manchester Exchange Square
1 Exchange Square, Manchester M3 1BD

Tate Britain
Millbank, London SW1P 4RG
telephone: +44.20.7887 8888
visiting.britain@tate.org.uk
www.tate.org.uk/britain

Tate Modern
Bankside, London SE1 9TG
telephone: +44.20.7887 8888
visiting.modern@tate.org.uk
www.tate.org.uk/modern

Tate Liverpool
Albert Dock, Liverpool, L3 4BB
telephone: +44.1517 027 400
visiting.liverpool@tate.org.uk
www.tate.org.uk/liverpool

Tate St Ives
Porthmeor Beach, St Ives
Cornwall TR26 1TG
telephone: +44.1736.796 226
visiting.stives@tate.org.uk
www.tate.org.uk/stives

Terence Conran
Michelin House, 81 Fulham road
London SW3 6RD
telephone: +44.20.7589 7401
facsimile: +44.20.7823 7015
www.conran.com

55 Marylebone High Street, London W1U 5HS
telephone: +44.20.7723 2223
facsimile: +44.20.7535 3205

Tricia Guild
Designers Guild, 267–277 King's Road
London SW3 5EN
telephone: +44.20.7351 5775
facsimile: +44.20.7893 7720
info@designersguild.com
www.designersguild.com

Urbis
Cathedral Gardens, Manchester M4 3BG
telephone: +44.1616.058 200
info@urbis.org.uk
www.urbis.org.uk

Vivienne Westwood
44 Conduit Street, London W1S 2YL
telephone: +44.20.7287 3188
facsimile: +44.20.7437 2203
info@viviennewestwood.co.uk
www.viviennewestwood.com

Westwood Studios, 9–15 Elcho Street
London SW11 4AU
telephone: +44.20.7924 4747
facsimile: +44.20.7738 9655

6 Davies Street, London W1Y 1JJ
telephone: +44.20.7629 3757
facsimile: +44.20.7629 3757
daviesstreet@viviennewestwood.co.uk

World's End, 430 King's Road
London SW10 0LJ
telephone : +44.20.7352 6551
facsimile: +44.20.7352 6551
worldsend@viviennewestwood.co.uk

THE ARTS SCENE

Bestival
Robin Hill Country Park, Isle of Wight
Bestival Ltd, 3rd Floor, 25 Denmark Street
London WC2H 8NJ
telephone: +44.20.7379 3133
hello@bestival.net
www.bestival.net

Cheltenham Jazz Festival
Cheltenham Festivals, 109 Bath Road
Cheltenham, Gloucestershire GL53 7LS
telephone: +44.1242.774 400
www.cheltenhamfestivals.com

Glastonbury Festival
Glastonbury Festival Office
28 Northload Street
Glastonbury, Somerset BA6 9JJ
telephone: +44.1458.834 596
facsimile: +44.1458.833 235
office@glastonburyfestivals.co.uk
www.glastonburyfestivals.co.uk

Glyndebourne
Lewes East Sussex, BN8 5UU
telephone: +44.1273.812 321

IKON Gallery
1 Oozells Square, Brindleyplace
Birmingham B1 2HS
telephone: +44.121.248 0708
www.ikon-gallery.co.uk

Isle of Wight Festival
Seaclose Park, Newport, Isle of Wight
2nd Floor, 55 Fulham High Street
London SW6 3JJ
www.isleofwightfestival.com

Isle of Wight Jazz Festival
IOW Jazz Festival Office, 6 Pier Street
Ventnor, Isle of Wight PO38 1ST
telephone: +44.1983.856 206
info@iowjazz.org
www.jazzdivas.freeuk.com

The Lisson Gallery
52–54 Bell Street, London NW1 5DA
telephone: +44.20.7724 2739
facsimile: +44.20.7724 7124
contact@lissongallery.com
www.lissongallery.com

Nantwich Jazz Festival
Crown Hotel & Restaurant, High Street
Nantwich near Crewe, Cheshire CW5 5AS
telephone: +44.1270.625 283
www.nantwichjazz.com

National Film Library and Film Archives
BFI, 21 Stephen Street, London W1T 1LN
telephone: +44.20.7255 1444
www.bfi.org.uk

National Film Theatre
BFI Southbank, London SE1 8XT
telephone: +44.20.7928 3232

Ronnie Scott's
47 Frith Street, Soho, London W1D 4HT
telephone: +44.20.7439 0747
facsimile: +44.20.7437 5081
ronniescotts@ronniescotts.co.uk
www.ronniescotts.co.uk

Royal Albert Hall
Kensington Gore, London SW7 2AP
telephone: +44.20.7589 8212
www.royalalberthall.com

Royal Opera House Covent Garden
Bow Street, Covent Garden
London WC2E 9DD
telephone: +44.20.7240 1200
onlinebooking@roh.org.uk
www.roh.org.uk

The Saatchi Gallery
Duke of York's HQ, King's Road
London SW3 4SQ
www.saatchi-gallery.co.uk

V Festival
PO Box 34286, London NW5 2XQ
contact@vfestival.com
www.vfestival.com

White Cube Galleries
48 Hoxton Square, London N1 6PB
telephone: +44.20.7930 5373
facsimile: +44.20.7749 7470
www.whitecube.com

25–26 Mason's Yard, London SW1Y 6BU
telephone: +44.20.7930 5373
facsimile: +44.20.7749 7480

SHOPPING

Aquascutum
100 Regent Street, London W1B 5SR
telephone: +44.20.7675 8200
www.aquascutum.com

Biondi
55b Old Church Street
Chelsea, London SW3 5BS
telephone: +44.20.7349 1111
info@biondicouture.com
www.biondicouture.com

Boodles
178 New Bond Street, London W1S 4RH
telephone: +44.20.7437 5050
facsimile: +44.20.7437 3456
www.boodles.co.uk

52 Eastgate, Chester CH1 1ES
telephone: +44.1244.326 666
facsimile: +44.1244.317 040

1 King Street, Manchester M2 6AW
telephone: +44.1618 339 000
facsimile: +44.161.833 1920

Boodles House, Lord Street
Liverpool L2 9SQ
telephone: +44.1512.272 525
facsimile: +44.1512.551 070

Burberry
157–167 Regent Street, London W1B 4PH
telephone: +44.20.7806 1328
customerservice@burberry.com
www.burberry.com

Caroline Groves
37 Chiltern Street, London W1U 7PW
telephone: +44.20.7935 2329
enquiries@carolinegroves.co.uk
www.carolinegroves.co.uk

Jo Malone
150 Sloane Street, London SW1X 9BX
telephone: +44.20.7730 2100
facsimile: +44.2392.594 323
info@jomalone.co.uk
www.jomalone.co.uk

John Lobb
88 Jermyn Street, London SW1Y 6JD
telephone: +44.20.7930 8089
www.johnlobb.com

Links of London
16 Sloane Square, Chelsea SW1W 8ER
telephone: +44.20.7730 3133
facsimile: +44.20.7819 4151
www.linksoflondon.com

Lock & Co Hatters
6 St James's Street, London SW1A 1EF
telephone: +44.20.7930 5849
www.lockhatters.co.uk

Mulberry
41–42 New Bond Street
Mayfair, London W1S 2RY
telephone: +44.20.7491 3900
facsimile: +44.1761.233 436
mail-order@mulberry.com
www.mulberry.com

199 Westbourne Grove
Notting Hill, London W11 2SB
telephone: +44.20.7229 1635

11–12 Gees Court, St Christopher's Place
London W1U 1JN

Mulberry Men's Store, 38 Floral Street
Covent Garden, London WC2E 9DG
telephone: +44.20.7379 9065

Ozwald Boateng
30 Savile Row, London W1S 3PT
telephone: +44.20.7437 0629
shop@bespokecoutureltd.co.uk
www.ozwaldboateng.co.uk

Rigby & Peller
2 Hans Road, Knightsbridge
London SW3 1RX
telephone: +44.20.7589 9293
facsimile: +44.20.7225 4761
knightsbridge@rigbyandpeller.com
www.rigbyandpeller.com

22a Conduit Street, Mayfair
London W1S 2XT
telephone: +44.20.7491 2200
facsimile: +44.20.7491 4209
mayfair@rigbyandpeller.com

roubi l'roubi
13 Norton Folgate
Bishopsgate, London E1 6DB
telephone: +44.20.7247 4311
roubi@roubi.eu
www.roubi.eu

Swaine Adeney Brigg
54 St James's Street, London SW1A 1JT
telephone: +44.20.7409 7277
www.swaineadeney.co.uk

EAT + DRINK

The Fat Duck
High Street, Bray, Berkshire SL6 2AQ
telephone: +44.1628.580 333
deborahchalcroft@thefatduck.co.uk
www.fatduck.co.uk

Gidleigh Park
Chagford, Devon TQ13 8HH
telephone: +44.1647.432 367
facsimile: +44.1647.432 574
gidleighpark@gidleigh.co.uk
www.gidleigh.com

Gordon Ramsay
68 Royal Hospital Road, London SW3 4HP
telephone: +44.20.7352 4441
facsimile: +44.20.7592 1366
privatedining@gordonramsay.com
www.gordonramsay.com/royalhospitalroad

J Bakers Bistro Moderne
7 Fossgate, York YO1 9TA
telephone: +44.1904.622 688
www.jbakers.co.uk

The Longridge
104–106 Higher Road
Longridge, Preston PR3 3SY
telephone: +44.1772.784 969
facsimile: +44.1772.785 713
longridge@heathcotes.co.uk
www.heathcotes.co.uk/
collection/longridge

Le Manoir aux Quat'Saisons
Church Road, Great Milton, Oxford OX44
7PD telephone: +44.1844.278 881
facsimile: +44.1844.278 847
www.manoir.com

The New Angel
2 South Embankment
Dartmouth, Devon TQ6 9BH
telephone: +44.1803.839 425
www.thenewangel.co.uk

Rick Stein's Seafood Restaurant
Riverside, Padstow
Cornwall PL28 8BY
telephone: +44.1841.532 700
facsimile: +44.1841.532 942
reservations@rickstein.com
www.rickstein.com

Simpsons
20 Highfield Road, Edgbaston
Birmingham B15 3DU
telephone: +44.1214.543 434
facsimile: +44.1214.543 399
info@simpsonsrestaurant.co.uk
www.simpsonsrestaurant.co.uk

Waterside Inn
Ferry Road, Bray, Berkshire SL6 2AT
telephone: +44.1628.620 691
facsimile: +44.1628.784 710
reservations@waterside-inn.co.uk
www.waterside-inn.co.uk

MUSEUMS + GALLERIES

Ashmolean Museum
Beaumont Street, Oxford OX1 2PH
telephone: +44.1865.278 000
facsimile: +44.1865.278 018
www.ashmolean.org

Birmingham Museum and Art Gallery
Chamberlain Square, Birmingham B3 3DH
telephone: +44.1213.032 834
bmag_enquiries@birmingham.gov.uk
www.bmag.org.uk

The British Museum
Great Russell Street, London WC1B 3DG
telephone: +44.20.7323 8299
facsimile: +44.20.7323 8616
information@britishmuseum.org
www.britishmuseum.org

The Courtauld Gallery
Somerset House, London WC2R 0RN
telephone: +44.20.7848 2526
www.courtauld.ac.uk

The Fitzwilliam Museum
Trumpington Street, Cambridge CB2 1RB
telephone: +44.1223.332 900
facsimile: +44.1223.332 923
fitzmuseum-enquiries@lists.cam.ac.uk
www.fitzmuseum.cam.ac.uk

Kettles Yard House
Castle Street, Cambridge CB3 0AQ
telephone: +44.1223.352 124
facsimile: +44.1223.324 377
mail@kettlesyard.cam.ac.uk
www.kettlesyard.co.uk

The National Gallery
Trafalgar Square, London WC2N 5DN
telephone: +44.20.7747 2885
facsimile: +44.20.7747 2423
information@ng-london.org.uk
www.nationalgallery.org.uk

Victoria & Albert Museum
Cromwell Road, South Kensington
London SW7 2RL
telephone: +44.20.7942 2000
vanda@vam.ac.uk
www.vam.ac.uk

The Wallace Collection
Hertford House, Manchester Square
London W1U 3BN
telephone: +44.20.7563 9500
facsimile: +44.20.7224 2155
www.wallacecollection.org

STATELY HOMES

Blenheim Palace
Woodstock, Oxfordshire OX20 1PX
telephone: +44.8700.602 080
facsimile: +44.1993.810 570
operations@blenheimpalace.com
www.blenheimpalace.com

Castle Howard
North Yorkshire YO60 7DA
telephone: +44.1653.648 444
facsimile: +44.1653.648 529
house@castlehoward.co.uk
www.castlehoward.co.uk

Chatsworth
Bakewell, Derbyshire DE45 1PP
telephone: +44.1246.565 300
www.chatsworth.org

Lyme Park
Disley, Stockport, Cheshire SK12 2NR
telephone: +44.1663.766 492
facsimile: +44.1663.765 035
lymepark@nationaltrust.org.uk
www.nationaltrust.org.uk

Waddesdon Manor
Waddesdon near Aylesbury
Buckinghamshire HP18 0JH
telephone: +44.1296.653 226
bookings.waddesdon@nationaltrust.org.uk
www.waddesdon.org.uk

Woburn Abbey
Woburn, Bedfordshire MK17 9WA
telephone: +44.1525.290 333
facsimile: +44.1525.290 271
admissions@woburnabbey.co.uk
www.woburnabbey.co.uk

THE SEASON

Cartier International Polo
Guards Polo Club, Smith's Lawn
Windsor Great Park, Egham
Surrey TW20 0HP
telephone: +44.1784.437 797
enquiries@keithprowse.co.uk
www.guardspoloclub.com

The Derby
Epsom Downs Racecourse
Epsom Downs, Surrey KT18 5LQ
telephone: +44.1372.726 311
www.epsomderby.co.uk

Glorious Goodwood
Goodwood House, Goodwood
Chichester, West Sussex PO18 0PX
telephone: +44.1243.755 000
www.goodwood.co.uk

Henley Royal Regatta
Regatta Headquarters, Henley-on-Thames
Oxfordshire RG9 2LY
telephone: +44.1491.572 153
facsimile: +44.1491.575 509
www.hrr.co.uk

The Royal Academy of Arts
Royal Academy of Arts, Burlington House
Piccadilly, London W1J 0BD
www.royalacademy.org.uk

Royal Ascot
Ascot Racecourse, Ascot, Berkshire SL5 7JX
telephone: +44.8707.271 234
www.ascot.co.uk

Royal Horticultural Society
80 Vincent Square, London SW1P 2PE
telephone: +44.8452.605 000
info@rhs.org.uk
www.rhs.org.uk

The Royal Windsor Horse Show
Royal Windsor Horse Show Office
The Royal Mews, Windsor Castle
Windsor, Berkshire SL4 1UT
telephone: +44.1753.860 633
info@rwhs.co.uk
www.royal-windsor-horse-show.co.uk

Wimbledon Tennis Championships
The All England Lawn Tennis Club
Church Road, Wimbledon, London SW19 5AE
telephone: +44.20.8971 2473
facsimile: +44.20.8947 8752
www.wimbledon.org

LONDON

UP WEST VS OUT EAST

Annabels
44 Berkeley Square, London W1X 5DB
telephone: +44.20.7629 1096

Chinawhite
6 Air Street, Soho, London W1B 5AA,
telephone: +44.2033 0040
info@chinawhite.com
www.chinawhite.com

The Eagle Gallery/EMH Arts
159 Farringdon Road, London, EC1R 3AL
telephone: +44.20.7833 2674
facsimile: +44.20.7624 6597
info@emmahilleagle.com
www.emmahilleagle.com

Flowers East
82 Kingsland Road, London E2 8DP
telephone: +44.20.7920 7777
gallery@flowerseast.com
www.flowerseast.com

Hoopers Gallery
15 Clerkenwell Close, London EC1R 0AA
telephone: +44.20.7490 3907
contact@hoopersgallery.co.uk
hoopersgallery.co.uk

The Ivy
1–5 West Street, London WC2H 9NQ
telephone: +44.20.7836 4751
www.the-ivy.co.uk

Kitts
7–12 Sloane Square, London SW1W 8EG
telephone: +44.20.7881 5990
info@kitts-london.com
www.kitts-london.com

The Light Bar
Asia de Cuba, St Martins Lane Hotel
45 St Martin's Lane, London WC2N 4HX
telephone: +44.20.7300 5599

Lindsay House
21 Romilly Street, London W1D 5AF
telephone: +44.20.7439 0450
facsimile: +44.20.7437 7349
richardcorrigan@lindsayhouse.co.uk
www.lindsayhouse.co.uk

Maze
10–13 Grosvenor Square, London W1K 6JP
telephone: +44.20.7107 0000
facsimile: +44.20.7107 0001
maze@gordonramsay.com
www.gordonramsay.com/maze

Met Bar
The Metropolitan, Old Park Lane
London W1K 1LB
telephone: +44.20.7447 1047
www.metbar.co.uk

Petrus
The Berkeley, Wilton Place
Knightsbridge, London SW1X 7RL
telephone: +44.20.7235 1200

Rainbird Fine Art
114 Clerkenwell Road, London EC1M 5SA
telephone: +44.20.7608 3333
enquiries@rainbirdfineart.com
www.rainbirdfineart.com

Scotts
20 Mount Street, London W1K 2HE
telephone: +44.20.7495 7309
facsimile: +44.20.7647 6326
www.scotts-restaurant.com

Sketch Restaurants
9 Conduit Street, London W1S 2XG
telephone: +44.20.7 659 4500
www.sketch.uk.com

Tom Aikens Restaurant
43 Elystan Street, London SW3 3NT
telephone: +44.20.7584 2003
facsimile: +44.20.7589 2107
www.tomaikens.com

The Whitecross Gallery
122 Whitecross Street, London EC1Y 8PU
telephone: +44.20.7253 4252
info@whitecrossgallery.com
www.whitecrossgallery.com

The White Cube
48 Hoxton Square, Hoxton, London N1 6PB
telephone: +44.20.7930 5373

25–26 Mason's Yard
St James, London SW1Y 6BU
telephone: +44.20.7930 5373
enquiries@whitecube.com
www.whitecube.com

LONDON THEATRE

Almeida Theatre
Almeida Street, London N1 1TA
telephone: +44.20.7359 4404
info@almeida.co.uk
www.almeida.co.uk

The Donmar Warehouse
41 Earlham Street, London WC2H 9LX
telephone: +44.20.7438 9200
www.donmarwarehouse.com

Haymarket Theatre Royal
Haymarket, London SW1Y 4HT
telephone: +44.20.7930 8890
boxoffice@trh.co.uk
www.trh.co.uk

The National Theatre
South Bank, London SE1 9PX
telephone: +44.20.7452 3000
www.nationaltheatre.org.uk

The Old Vic
The Cut, Waterloo, London SE1 8NB
telephone: +44.8700.606 628
ovtcadmin@oldvictheatre.com
www.oldvictheatre.com

The Royal Court Theatre
Sloane Square, London SW1
telephone: +44.20.7565 5000
facsimile: +44.20.7565 5001
info@royalcourttheatre.com
www.royalcourttheatre.com

Shakespeare's Globe Theatre
21 New Globe Walk, Bankside
London SE1 9DT
telephone: +44.20.7902 1400
facsimile: +44.20.7902 1401
info@shakespeares-globe.com
www.shakespeares-globe.org

TKTS
Clocktower Building, Leicester Square

The Young Vic
66 The Cut, Waterloo, London SE1 8LZ
telephone: +44.20.7922 2922
facsimile: +44.20.7922 2802
info@youngvic.org
www.youngvic.org

LONDON SHOPPING

Alexander McQueen
4–5 Old Bond Street, London W1S 4PD
telephone: +44.20.7355 0088
www.alexandermcqueen.com

ANNA
126 Regents Park Road
Primrose Hill, London NW1 8XL
telephone: +44.20.7483 0411

Asprey
167 New Bond Street, London W1S 4AY
telephone: +44.20.7493 6767
facsimile: +44.20.7491 0384
www.asprey.com

Boodles
178 New Bond Street, London W1S 4RH
telephone: +44.20.7437 5050
facsimile: +44.20.7437 3456
www.boodles.co.uk

Boucheron
164 New Bond Street, London W1S 2UH
telephone: +44.20.7514 9170
london.store@fr.boucheron.com
www.boucheron.com

Breguet
10 New Bond Street, London W1S 3SP
telephone: +44.20.7355 1735
breguet.bondst@uk.swatchgroup.coms
www.breguet.com

Browns
6c Sloane Street, London SW1X 9LE2
telephone: +44.20.7514 0040
facsimile: +44.20.7408 1281
sloanestreet@brownsfashion.com
www.brownsfashion.com

Browns Focus
38–39 South Molton Street
London W1K 5RN
telephone: +44.20.7514 0063
brownsfocus@brownsfashion.com
www.brownsfashion.com

Bulgari
172 New Bond Street, London W1S 4RE
telephone: +44.20.7872 9969
www.bulgari.com

Cartier
40–41 Old Bond Street
Mayfair, London W1S 4QR
telephone: +44.20.7290 5150
www.cartier.com

Chanel
173 New Bond Street, London W1S4RF
telephone: +44.20.7499 0005
www.chanel.com

Chaumet
174 New Bond Street, London W1S 4RG
telephone: +44.20.7495 6303
www.chaumet.com

Chopard
12 New Bond Street, London W1S 3SX
telephone: +44.20.7409 3140
www.chopard.com

Couverture
188 Kensington Park Road
Notting Hill, London W11 2ES
telephone: +44.20.7229 2178
facsimile: +44.20.7221 9058
info@couverture.co.uk
www.couverture.co.uk

David Morris
180 New Bond Street, London W1S 4RL
telephone: +44.20.7499 2200
facsimile: +44.20.7499 3249
info@davidmorris.com
www.davidmorris.com

Dior
31 Sloane Street, London SW1 X9NR
telephone: +44.20.7245 1330
www.dior.com

Donna Karan
46 Conduit Street, London W1S
telephone: +44.20.7479 7900
www.donnakaran.com

Fendi
20–22 Sloane Street, London SW1X 9NE
telephone: +44.20.7838 6288
www.fendi.com

Georg Jensen
15 New Bond Street, London W1S 3ST
telephone: +44.20.7318 3009
facsimile: +44.20.7629 0952
www.georgjensenstore.co.uk

Giorgio Armani
37 Sloane Street, London SW1X 9LP
telephone: +44.20.7235 6232
facsimile: +44.20.7823 1342
www.giorgioarmani.com

Giuseppe Zanotti Design
49 Sloane Street, London SW1X 9LU
telephone: +44.20.7838 9455

Graff
6–7 New Bond Street, London W1S 3SJ
telephone: +44.20.7584 8571
facsimile: +44.20.7581 3415
www.graffdiamonds.com

Gucci
18 Sloane Street, London SW1X 9NE
telephone: +44.20.7235 6707
www.gucci.com

Harry Winston
171 New Bond Street, London W1S 4RD
telephone: +44.20.7439 1109
www.harrywinston.com

Issey Miyake
52–53 Conduit Street, London W1S 2YX
telephone: +44.20.7851 4620
www.isseymiyake.co.jp

Liberty
Regent Street, London W1B 5AH
telephone: +44.20.7734 1234
londonstorecustomerservices@liberty.co.uk
www.liberty.co.uk

Marni
26 Sloane Street, London SW1X 9NE
telephone: +44.20.7245 9520
www.marni.com

Mikimoto
179 New Bond Street, London W1S 4RJ
telephone: +44.20.7629 5300
store@mikimoto.co.uk
www.mikimoto.com

Moussaieff
172 New Bond Street, London W1S 4RE
telephone: +44.20.7290 1536
facsimile: +44.20.7496 2746
info@moussaieff.co.uk
www.moussaieff.co.uk

Nancy Pop
19 Kensington Park Road, London W11 2EU
telephone: +44.20.7221 9797
info@nancypop.com
www.nancypop.com

Nicole Farhi
193 Sloane Street, London SW1X 9QX
telephone: +44.20.7235 0877
www.nicolefarhi.com

The Old Truman Brewery
91 Brick Lane, London E1 6QL
telephone: +44.20.7770 6100
estates@trumanbrewery.com
www.trumanbrewery.com

Patek Philippe
15 New Bond Street, London W1S 3ST
telephone: +44.20.7493 8866
www.patek.com

Paul & Joe
39 Ledbury Road, London W11 2AA
telephone: +44.20.7243 5510
www.paulandjoe.com

Prada
43–45 Sloane Street, London SW1X 9LU
telephone: +44.20.7235 0008
www.prada.com

Ross + Bute
57 Ledbury Rd, Notting Hill, London W11 2AA
telephone: +44.20.7727 2348
facsimile: +44.20.7727 7400
shop@anonymousclothing.com
www.anonymousclothing.com

Tiffany & Co
25 Old Bond Street, London W1S 4QB
telephone: +44.20.7409 2790
www.tiffany.com

Valentino
174 Sloane Street, London W1S 9QG
telephone: +44.20.7235 0719
www.valentino.com

Van Cleef & Arpels
9 New Bond Street, London W1S 3SW
telephone: +44.20.7493 0400
www.vancleef-arpels.com

Vivienne Westwood
44 Conduit Street, London W1S 2YL
telephone: +44.20.7439 1109
facsimile: +44.20.7734 6074
conduitshop@viviennewestwood.co.uk
www.viviennewestwood.com

Walter Steiger
48 Sloane Street, London SW1X 9LU
telephone: +44.20.7245 8480
facsimile: +44.20.7245 8479
waltersteiger01@btconnect.com
www.waltersteiger.com

Yves St Laurent
171–172 Sloane St, London SW1X 9QG
telephone: +44.20.7235 6706
www.ysl.com

HOTELS

51 Buckingham (page 62)
51 Buckingham Gate, London SW1E 6AF
telephone: +44.020.7769 7766
facsimile: +44.020.7233 5014
info@51-buckinghamgate.co.uk
www.51-buckinghamgate.co.uk

Andaz Liverpool Street London (page 54)
40 Liverpool Street, London EC2M 7QN
telephone: +44.020.7961 1234
facsimile: +44.020.7961 1235
info.londonliv@andaz.com
www.andaz.com

The Athenaeum (page 64)
116 Piccadilly, London W1J 7BJ
telephone: +44.020.7499 3464
facsimile: +44.020.7493 1860
reservations@athenaeumhotel.com
www.athenaeumhotel.com

Brown's Hotel (page 56)
Albemarle Street, Mayfair, London W1S 4BP
telephone: +44.020.7493 6020
facsimile: +44.020.7493 9381
reservations.browns@
roccofortecollection.com
www.roccofortecollection.com

The Cadogan Hotel (page 68)
75 Sloane Street, London SW1X 9SG
telephone: +44.020.7235 7141
facsimile: +44.020.7245 0994
info@cadogan.com
www.cadogan.com

The Caesar (page 86)
26-33 Queens Gardens
Hyde Park, London W2 3BD
telephone: +44 . 020. 7262 0022
facsimile: +44 .020. 7402 5099
thecaesar@derbyhotels.com
www.thecaesar.co.uk

The Cranley (page 76)
10 Bina Gardens, South Kensington
London SW5 0LA
telephone: +44.020.7373 0123
facsimile: +44.020.7373 9497
cranley@steinhotels.com
cranley.steinhotels.com

Draycott Hotel (2pp)
26 Cadogan Gardens, London SW3 2RP
telephone: +44 .0.20.7730 6466
facsimile: +44.0.20.7730 0236
reservations@draycotthotel.com
www.draycotthotel.com

The Gore (page 78)
190 Queen's Gate, London SW7 5EX
telephone: +44.020.7584 6601
facsimile: +44.020.7589 8127
concierge@gorehotel.com
www.gorehotel.com

Jumeirah Lowndes Hotel (page 80)
21 Lowndes Street, Knightsbridge
London SW1X 9ES
telephone: +44.020.7823 1234
facsimile: +44.020.7235 1154
jlhinfo@jumeirah.com
www.jumeirahlowndeshotel.com

The Metropolitan (page 66)
Old Park Lane, London W1K 1LB
telephone: +44.020.7447 1047
facsimile: +44.020.7447 1147
info.lon@metropolitan.como.bz
www.metropolitan.como.bz

Number Sixteen (page 74)
16 Sumner Place, London SW7 3EG
telephone: +44.020.7589 5232
facsimile: +44.020.7584 8615
sixteen@firmdale.com
www.firmdalehotels.com

The Royal Park (page 84)
3 Westbourne Terrace, Lancaster Gate
Hyde Park, London W2 3UL
telephone: +44 .020. 7479 6600
facsimile: +44 .020. 7479 6601
info@theroyalpark.com
www.theroyalpark.com

Sofitel St James London (page 58)
6 Waterloo Place, London SW1Y 4AN
telephone: +44.020. 7747 2200
facsimile: +44.020. 7747 2210
H3144@accor.com
www.sofitelstjames.com

Sydney House Chelsea (page 72)
9–11 Sydney Street, Chelse
London SW3 6PU
telephone: +44.020.7376 7711
info@sydneyhousechelsea.
www.sydneyhousechelsea.com

RESTAURANTS

The Landau at The Langham (page 88)
The Langham, Portland Place
London W1B 1JA
telephone: +44.020.7965 0165
facsimile: +44.020.7323 2340
info@thelandau.com
www.thelandau.com

Theo Randall at the InterContinental
London Park Lane (page 90)
1 Hamilton Place, Park Lane, London W1J
7QY
telephone: +44 .020. 7318 8747
reservations@theorandall.com
www.theorandall.com

BARS

Artesian at The Langham (page 92)
The Langham, 1c Portland Place
Regent Street, London W1B 1JA
telephone: +44.020.7636 1000
info@artesian-bar.co.uk
website:www.artesian-bar.co.uk

THE SOUTHEAST

The Artichoke Restaurant
9 Market Square, Old Amersham
Buckinghamshire HP7 0DF
telephone: +44.1494.726 611
info@theartichokerestaurant.co.uk
www.theartichokerestaurant.co.uk

The Bel &The Dragon
High Street, Cookham, Berkshire SL6 9SQ
telephone: +44.1628.521 263
www.belandthedragon.co.uk

Bookers Vineyard
Foxhole Lane, Bolney
West Sussex RH17 5NB
telephone: +44.1444.881 575
facsimile: +44.1444.881 399
sam@bookersvineyard.co.uk
www.bookersvineyard.co.uk

The Charleston Trust
Charleston Firle, Lewes
East Sussex BN8 6LL
telephone: +44.1323.811 265
info@charleston.org.uk
www.charleston.org.uk

Cliveden
Taplow, Maidenhead
Buckinghamshire SL6 0JA
telephone: +44.1494.755 562
cliveden@nationaltrust.org.uk
www.nationaltrust.org.uk/main/w-cliveden

The Crown
16 High Street, Old Amersham
Buckinghamshire HP7 0DH
telephone: +44.1494.721 541
facsimile: +44.1494.431 283
crownres@dillonhotels.co.uk
www.thecrownamersham.co.uk

Denbies Wine Estate
London Road, Dorking, Surrey RH5 6AA
telephone: +44.1306.876 616
facsimile: +44.1306.888 930
info@denbiesvineyard.co.uk
www.denbiesvineyard.co.uk

The Electric Palace Cinema
39a High Street, Hastings
East Sussex TN34 3ER
telephone: +44.1424.720 393
info@electricpalacecinema.com
www.electricpalacecinema.com

Godstone Vineyards
Quarry Road, Godstone, Surrey RH9 8ZA
telephone: +44.1883.744 590
www.godstonevineyards.com

The Kings Arms
30 High Street, Amersham
Buckinghamshire HP7 0DJ
telephone: +44.1494.725 722
kingsarms@zolahotels.com
www.zolahotels.com/kingsarms

Ridgeview Wine Estate
Fragbarrow Lane, Ditchling Common
Sussex BN6 8TP
telephone: +44.1444.241 441
facsimile: +44.1444.230 757
info@ridgeview.co.uk
www.ridgeview.co.uk

Shoreham Airport
Shoreham by Sea
West Sussex BN43 5FF
telephone: +44.1273.467 373
facsimile: +44.1273.467 370
admin@shorehamairport.co.uk
www.shorehamairport.co.uk

The Sportsman
Faversham Road, Seasalter
Whitstable, Kent CT5 4BP
telephone: +44.1227.273 370
contact@thesportsmanseasalter.co.uk
www.thesportsmanseasalter.co.uk

Stanley Spencer Gallery
High Street, Cookham, Berkshire SL6 9SJ
telephone: +44.1628.471 885
info@stanleyspencer.org.uk
www.stanleyspencer.org.uk

BRIGHTON

Brighton Festival
12a Pavilion Buildings, Castle Square
Brighton BN1 1EE
telephone: +44.1273.709 709
info@brightonfestival.org
www.brightonfestival.org

Burning of the Clocks
Same Sky, The Old Post Office
1 College Road, Brighton
East Sussex, BN2 1JA
telephone: +44.1273.571 106
facsimile: +44.1273.606 668
info@burningtheclocks.co.uk
www.burningtheclocks.co.uk

Charlie Barley
17 Meeting House Lane, Brighton BN1 1HB
telephone: +44.1273.774 000
charlie@charliebarley.co.uk
www.charliebarley.co.uk

Copacabana
19 Brighton Place, Brighton BN1 1HJ
telephone: +44.1273.725 550
www.copacabanaboutique.com

Digital
187–193 Kings Road Arches
Brighton BN1 1NB
telephone: +44.1273.227 767
richard.skrein@yourfutureisdigital.com
www.yourfutureisdigital.com

Gresham Blake
20 Bond Street, Brighton BN1 1RD
telephone: +44.1273.609 587
info@greshamblake.com
www.greshamblake.com

Honey Club
214 Kings Road Arches, Brighton BN1 1NB
telephone: +44.7000.446 639
info@thehoneyclub.co.uk
www.thehoneyclub.co.uk

Ju-Ju
24 Gloucester Road, Brighton BN2 9UY
telephone: +44.1273.673 161
info@jujubrighton.com
jujubrighton.com

Noa Noa
37 Gardner Street, Brighton BN1 1UN
telephone: +44.1273.818 133
contact@noanoa.com
www.noanoa.com

Pride in Brighton and Hove
6 Bartholomews, Brighton BN1 1HG
telephone: +44.1273.775 939
facsimile: +44.1273.775 964
enquiries@brightonpride.org
www.brightonpride.org

The Royal Pavilion
Brighton BN1 1EE
telephone: +44.1273.290 900
facsimile: +44.1273.292 871
royalpavilion@brighton-hove.gov.uk
www.royalpavilion.org.uk

PLAYGROUNDS OF THE RICH + FAMOUS

Cowes Week
Regatta House, 18 Bath Road,
Cowes, Isle of Wight PO31 7QN
telephone: +44.1983.295 744
admin@cowesweek.co.uk
www.cowesweek.co.uk

Cowdray Park
The Estate Office, Midhurst
West Sussex GU29 0AQ
telephone: +44.1730.813 257
facsimile: +44.1730.817 314
enquiries@cowdraypolo.co.uk
www.cowdraypolo.co.uk

Goodwood
Goodwood House, Goodwood, Chichester
West Sussex PO18 0PX
telephone: +44.1243.755 000
facsimile: +44.1243.755 005
www.goodwood.co.uk

Guards Polo Club
Smith's Lawn, Windsor Great Park
Egham, Surrey TW20 0HP
telephone: +44.1784.434 212
facsimile: +44.1784.471 336
ticket.office@guardspoloclub.com
www.guardspoloclub.com

HOTELS

Chewton Glen (page 120)
New Milton, Hampshire BH25 6QS
telephone: +44.014.2527 5341
facsimile: +44.014.2527 2310
reservations@chewtonglen.com
www.chewtonglen.com

The Forbury Hotel (page 112)
26 The Forbury, Reading, Berkshire RG1 3EJ
telephone: +44.011.8958 1234
claire.edwards@theforburyhotel.co.uk
www.theforburyhotel.co.uk

The George in Rye (page 106)
98 High Street, Rye, East Sussex TN31 7JT
telephone: +44.017.9722 2114
facsimile: +44.017.9722 4065
stay@thegeorgeinrye.com
www.thegeorgeinrye.com

The Hambrough Hotel (page 116)
Hambrough Road, Ventnor
Isle of Wight PO38 1SQ
telephone: +44 .019. 8385 6333
info@thehambrough.com
www.thehambrough.com

Hotel Pelirocco (page 110)
10 Regency Square, Brighton BN1 2FG
telephone: +44.12.7332 7055
facsimile: +44.12.7373 3845
info@hotelpelirocco.co.uk
www.hotelpelirocco.co.uk

The Wellington Hotel (page 118)
Belgrave Road, Ventnor
Isle of Wight PO38 1JH
telephone: +44.0.1983.856 600
facsimile: +44.0.1983.856 611
enquiries@thewellingtonhotel.net
www.thewellingtonhotel.net

Zanzibar International Hotel (page 108)
9 Everfield Place, St Leonards-on-Sea
East Sussex TN37 6BY
telephone: +44.0.424.460 109
info@zanzibarhotel.co.uk
www.zanzibarhotel.co.uk

THE SOUTHWEST

Boconnoc
Lostwithiel, Cornwall PL22 0RG
telephone: +44.1208.872 507
www.boconnocenterprises.co.uk

Glastonbury Festival
Glastonbury Festival Office
28 Northload Street
Glastonbury, Somerset BA6 9JJ
telephone: +44.1458.834 596
facsimile: +44.1458.833 235
office@glastonburyfestivals.co.uk
www.glastonburyfestivals.co.uk

Jamaica Inn
Bolventor, Launceston, Cornwall PL15 7TS
telephone: +44.1566.86250
facsimile: +44.1566.86177
enquiry@jamaicainn.co.uk
www.jamaicainn.co.uk

Lost Gardens of Heligan
Heligan, Pentewan
St Austell, Cornwall PL26 6EN
telephone: +44.1726.845 100
facsimile: +44.1726.845 101
info@heligan.com
www.heligan.com

Silver Lion
12 Gandy Street, Exeter, Devon EX4
telephone: +44.1392.495 994
info@silverlionjewellers.co.uk
www.silverlionjewellers.co.uk

Toot Garook
19 Queen Street, Exeter, Devon EX4 3SH
telephone: +44.1392.201 660
info@tootgarook.co.uk
www.tootgarook.co.uk

Trebah Garden
Mawnan Smith, Falmouth
Cornwall TR11 5JZ
telephone: +44.1326.252 200
facsimile: +44.1326.250 781
mail@trebah-garden.co.uk
www.trebah-garden.co.uk

Trelissick Gardens
Feock, Truro, Cornwall TR3 6QL
telephone: +44.1872.862 090
facsimile: +44.1872.865 808
trelissick@nationaltrust.org.uk
www.nationaltrust.org.uk

THE REFINED RESORTS OF THE SOUTHWEST

Barbara Hepworth Museum &
Sculpture Garden
Barnoon Hill, St Ives, Cornwall, TR26 1AD
telephone: +44.1736.796 226
www.tate.org.uk/stives/hepworth

The Dressing Room
7 Quiet Street, Bath, Somerset BA1 2JU
telephone: +44.1225.330 563
www.bathshopping.co.uk/dressingroom.htm

Exchange Gallery
Princes Street, Penzance, Cornwall TR18 2NL
telephone: +44.1736.363 715
mail@theexchangegallery.co.uk
www.newlynartgallery.co.uk

Kimberly
Trim Street, Bath, Somerset BA1 1HB
telephone: +44.1225.466 817
kimberly@kimberly.co.uk
www.kimberly.co.uk

Newlyn Gallery
New Road, Newlyn, Cornwall TR18 5PZ
telephone: +44.1736.363 715
mail@newlynartgallery.co.uk
www.newlynartgallery.co.uk

Prey
3 York Buildings, George Street
Bath, Somerset BA1 2EB
telephone: +44.1225.329 933
www.preyuk.com

St Ives Society of Artists
Main Gallery and Mariners Gallery
Mariners Church, Norway Square
St Ives, Cornwall, TR26 1NA
telephone: +44.1736.795 582
gallery@stisa.co.uk
www.stivessocietyofartists.com

Tate St Ives
Porthmeor Beach, St Ives
Cornwall TR26 1TG
telephone: +44.1736.796 226
visiting.stives@tate.org.uk
www.tate.org.uk/stives

Thermae Bath Spa
The Hetling Pump Room, Hot Bath Street
Bath, Somerset BA1 1SJ
telephone: +44.1225.331 234
www.thermaebathspa.com

DINING OUT IN THE SOUTHWEST

Fifteen Cornwall
On The Beach, Watergate Bay
Cornwall TR8 4AA
telephone: +44.1637.861 000
www.fifteencornwall.co.uk

Gidleigh Park
Chagford, Devon TQ13 8HH
telephone: +44.1647.432 367
facsimile: +44.1647.432 574
gidleighpark@gidleigh.co.uk
www.gidleigh.com

The Horn of Plenty
Gulworthy, Tavistock, Devon, PL19 8JD
telephone: +44.1822.832 528
enquiries@thehornofplenty.co.uk
www.thehornofplenty.co.uk

The Moody Goose
The Old Priory, Church Square
Midsomer Norton, Bath
Somerset BA3 2HX
telephone: +44.1761.416 784
facsimile: +44.1761.417 851
info@moodygoose.co.uk
www.theoldpriory.co.uk

Restaurant Nathan Outlaw
The Marina Villa Hotel
Esplanade, Fowey, Cornwall PL23 1HY
telephone: +44.1726.833 315
facsimile: +44.1726.832 779
info@marinavillahotel.com
www.themarinahotel.co.uk/nathanoutlaw

Rick Stein's Café
Middle Street, Padstow, Cornwall
telephone: +44.1841.532 700
facsimile: +44.1841.532 942
reservations@rickstein.com
www.rickstein.com

The Seafood Restaurant
Riverside, Padstow, Cornwall PL28 8BY
telephone: +44.1841.532 700
facsimile: +44.1841.532 942
reservations@rickstein.com
www.rickstein.com

St Petroc's Bistro
New Street, Padstow, Cornwall
telephone: +44.1841.532 700
facsimile: +44.1841.532 942
reservations@rickstein.com
www.rickstein.com

Stein's Fish & Chips
South Quay, Padstow, Cornwall
facsimile: +44.1841.532 942
reservations@rickstein.com
www.rickstein.com

HOTELS

The Bath Priory (page 134)
Weston Road, Bath BA1 2XT
telephone: +44.012.2533 1922
facsimile: +44.012.2544 8276
mail@thebathpriory.co.uk
www.thebathpriory.co.uk

Bovey Castle (page 144)
North Bovey, Dartmoor National Park
Devon TQ13 8RE
telephone: +44.0.1647.445 000
facsimile: +44.0.1647.445 020
booking@boveycastle.com
www.boveycastle.com

Burgh Island Hotel (page 148)
Bigbury-on-Sea, South Devon TQ7 4BG
telephone: +44.015.4881 0514
reception@burghisland.com
www.burghisland.com

COMBE HOUSE (page 136)
Honiton, Near Exeter, Devon EX14 3AD
telephone: +44 .014. 0454 0400
stay@thishotel.com
www.thishotel.com

driftwood (page 152)
Rosevine, Near Portscatho
South Cornwall TR2 5EW
telephone: +44 .018. 7258 0644
facsimile: +44 .018. 7258 0801
info@driftwoodhotel.co.uk
www.driftwoodhotel.co.uk

Gidleigh Park (page 140)
Chagford, Devon TQ13 8HH
telephone: +44.016.4743 2367
facsimile: +44.016.4743 2574
gidleighpark@gidleigh.co.uk
www.gidleigh.co.uk

THE WEST MIDLANDS

Avebury
The National Trust
Avebury near Marlborough
Wiltshire SN8 1RF
telephone: +44.1672.539 250
facsimile:+44.1672.538 038
avebury@nationaltrust.org.uk
www.nationaltrust.org.uk

Aziz Pandesia
1 Folly Bridge, Oxford, Oxfordshire OX1 4LB
telephone: +44.1865.247 775
www.aziz.uk.com

The Boat Inn
Thrupp, Kidlington, Oxfordshire OX5 1JY
telephone: +44.1865.374 279

Cousins of Cheltenham
10–11 Montpellier Walk, Cheltenham
Gloucestershire GL50 1SD
telephone: +44.1242.583 983
facsimile: +44.1242.230 620
acousinsofchelt@btconnect.com
www.cousinsofcheltenham.co.uk

Chiang Mai Kitchen
130a High Street, Oxford
Oxfordshire OX1 4DH
telephone: +44.1865.202 233
www.chiangmaikitchen.co.uk

The Garden
99–100 Covered Market
High Street, Oxford
Oxfordshire OX1 3DY
telephone: +44.1865.240 709

Howard's House Restaurant
Teffont Evias, Salisbury, Wiltshire SP3 5RJ
telephone: +44.1722.716 392
facsimile: +44.1722.716 820
enq@howardshousehotel.co.uk
www.howardshousehotel.co.uk

Le Champignon Sauvage
24–26, Suffolk Road, Cheltenham
Gloucestershire GL53 2AQ
telephone: +44.1242.573 449
facsimile: +44.1242.254 365
mail@lechampignonsauvage.co.uk
www.lechampignonsauvage.co.uk

The Looking Glass
12 Bank Street, Bridgnorth
Shropshire WV16 4AJ
telephone: +44.1746.765 883
facsimile: +44.8701.324 976
info@thelookingglass.co.uk
www.thelookingglass.co.uk

Potteries Museum & Art Gallery
Bethesda Street, Hanley
Stoke-on-Trent, Staffordshire ST1 3DW
museums@stoke.gov.uk
www.stoke.gov.uk/museums

Red Lion Pub
High Street, Avebury, Wiltshire SN8 1RF
telephone: +44.1672.539 266
www.redlion-avebury.com

Rollright Stones
Oxfordshire near Long Compton
Contact English Heritage
telephone: +44.1608.642 299
sitemanager@rollrightstones.co.uk
www.rollrightstones.co.uk

Setonaikai
71 Wyle Cop, Shrewsbury
Shropshire SY1 1UX
telephone: +44.1743-343 517
facsimile: +44.1743.233 014
sales@setonaikai.co.uk
setonaikai.co.uk

The Shroppie Fly
The Wharf, Shropshire Street
Audlem, Crewe, Cheshire CW3 0DX
telephone: +44.1270.811 772
andyandkate@shroppiefly.co.uk
www.shroppiefly.co.uk

Silks
11 The Courtyard, Montpellier
Cheltenham, Gloucestershire GL50 1SR
telephone: +44.1242.221 551
info@silksofcheltenham.co.uk
www.silksofcheltenham.co.uk

Spode Visitor Centre
Church Street, Stoke-on-Trent
Staffordshire ST4 1BX
telephone: +44.1782.572 598
spodeinfo@spode.co.uk
www.spode.co.uk

Stonehenge
Junction of A303 and A344/A360
Wiltshire SP4 7DE
telephone: +44.8703.331 181

The Turf Tavern
Bath Place, Oxford, Oxfordshire OX1 3SU
telephone: +44.1865.243 235
www.theturftavern.co.uk

Wedgwood Visitor Centre
Wedgwood, Barlaston, Stoke-on-Trent
Staffordshire ST12 9ES
telephone: +44.1782.282 986
www.wedgwood.com

HERITAGE + CULTURE IN THE HEART OF ENGLAND

The Dirty Duck
Waterside, Stratford-upon-Avon
Warwickshire CV37 6BA
telephone: +44.1789.297 312
7716@greeneking.co.uk
www.dirty-duck.co.uk

Kenilworth Castle
Kenilworth, Off B4103
Warwickshire CV8 1NE
telephone: +44.1926.852 078

The Machado Gallery
9 Wellesbourne Road
Barford, Warwick CV35 8EL
telephone: +44.1926.624 061
www.machadogallery.co.uk

The Shakespeare Birthplace Trust
Shakespeare Centre
Henley Street, Stratford-upon-Avon
Warwickshire CV37 6QW
telephone: +44.1789.204 016
facsimile: +44.1789.296 083
info@shakespeare.org.uk
www.shakespeare.org.uk

GLITTER + GLAM

Artfull Expression
23–24 Warstone Lane
Hockley, Birmingham B18 6JQ
telephone: +44.1212.120 430

Bicester Village
50 Pingle Drive, Bicester
Oxfordshire OX26 6WD
telephone: +44.1869.366 300
facsimile: +44.1869.323 201
bicester@bicestervillage.com
www.bicestervillage.com

The Mailbox
Wharfside Street, Birmingham B1 1XL
telephone: +44.1216.321 000
info@mailboxlife.com
www.mailboxlife.com

Silverstone Circuit
Northamptonshire NN12 8TN
telephone: +44.8704.588 200
facsimile: +44.8704.588 250
enquiries@silverstone.co.uk
www.silverstone.co.uk

SP Green & Co Ltd
34 Warstone Lane, Hockley
Birmingham B18 6JB
telephone: +44.1212.120 370
facsimile: +44.1212.365 768
info@spgreen.co.uk
www.spgreenjewellers.co.uk

HOTELS

Barnsley House (page 172)
Barnsley, Cirencester
Gloucestershire GL7 5EE
telephone: +44.12.8574 0000
facsimile: +44.12.8574 0925
info@barnsleyhouse.com
www.barnsleyhouse.com

Cotswolds88hotel (page 176)
Kemps Lane, Painswick
Gloucestershire GL6 6YB
telephone: +44.014.5281 3688
facsimile: +44.014.5281 4059
reservations@cotswolds88hotel.com
www.cotswolds88hotel.com

Cowley Manor (page 174)
Near Cheltenham
Gloucestershire GL53 9NL
telephone: +44.012.4287 0900
facsimile: +44.012.4287 0901
stay@cowleymanor.com
www.cowleymanor.com

Gee's Restaurant (page 178)
61 Banbury Road, Oxford OX2 6PE
telephone: +44.018.6555 3540
info@gees-restaurant.co.uk
www.gees-restaurant.co.uk

Le Manoir aux Quat' Saisons (page 164)
Church Road, Great Milton
Oxford OX44 7PD
telephone: +44.018.4427 8881
facsimile: +44.018.4427 8847
www.manoir.com

The Old Bank Hotel + Quod Restaurant
(page 168)
92-94 High Street, Oxford OX1 4BN
telephone: +44.018.6579 9599
info@oldbank-hotel.co.uk
www.oldbank-hotel.co.uk

The Old Parsonage Hotel (page 170)
1 Banbury Road, Oxford OX2 6NN
telephone: +44.018.6531 0210
reception@oldparsonage-hotel.co.uk
www.oldparsonage-hotel.co.uk

SPAS

C-side Spa at Cowley Manor (page 180)
Near Cheltenham,
Gloucestershire GL53 9NL
telephone: +44.012.4287 0902
facsimile: +44.012.4287 0901
relax@cowleymanor.com
www.cowleymanor.com

THE EAST

Flannels by Paul Smith
34–36 Bridlesmith Gate
Nottingham NG1 2GQ
telephone: +44.1159.476 466

Lowestoft Porcelain
Redgrave House, Battery Green Road
Lowestoft, Suffolk NR32 1DE
telephone: +44.1502.572 940
facsimile: +44.1502.583 827
general@lowestoftporcelain.com
www.lowestoftporcelain.com

The Norfolk Broads Yachting Company
Southgate Yacht Station, Lower Street
Horning, Norfolk NR12 8PF
telephone: +44.1692.631 330
facsimile: +44.1692.631 133
info@nbyco.com
www.norfolk-broads.com

Paul Smith
Willoughby House, 20 Low Pavement
Nottingham NG1 7EA
telephone: +44.1159.685 990

10 Byard Lane
Nottingham NG1 2GJ
telephone: +44.1153.506 712
customerservices@paulsmith.co.uk
www.paulsmith.co.uk

Sutton Hoo
Tranmer House, Sutton Hoo
Woodbridge, Suffolk IP12 3DJ
telephone: +44.1394.389 700
info@suttonhoo.org
www.suttonhoo.org

EAST ANGLIA

Aurora
Francis House, Redwell Street
Norwich NR2 4SN
telephone: +44.1603.756 231
info@aurora.org.uk
www.aurora.org.uk

By Appointment
25–29 St Georges Street, Norwich NR3 1AB
telephone: +44.1603.630 730
puttii@tiscali.co.uk
www.byappointmentnorwich.co.uk

Caley's Cocoa Cafe
The Guildhall, Gaol Hill, Norwich NR2 1NF
telephone: +44.1603.629 364

Castle Acre Priory
English Heritage, Castle Acre
Norfolk PE32 2XD
telephone: +44.1760.755 394

Colman's Mustard Shop
15 Royal Arcade, Norwich NR2 1NQ
telephone: +44.1603.627 889
facsimile: +44.1603.762 142
avril.houseago@unilver.com
www.colmansmustardshop.com

The Grapevine
109 Unthank Road, Norwich
telephone: +44.1603.760 660
www.grapevinegallery.co.uk

Marr's
6 Royal Arcade, Norwich NR2 1NQ
telephone: +44.1603.766 299
norwich@marrsleather.co.uk
www.marrsleather.co.uk

Norwich Arts Centre
St Benedicts Street, Norwich NR2 4PG
telephone: +44.1603.660 387
boxoffice@norwichartscentre.co.uk
www.norwichartscentre.co.uk

Norwich Castle
Castle Meadow, Norwich NR1 3JU
telephone: +44.1603.493 625

The Ostrich Inn
Stocks Green, Castle Acre, Norfolk PE32 2AE
telephone: +44.1760.755 398
crownath2wf@supanet.com
www.ostrichinn.com

River Studios and Summer Theatre
River Road, Westacre, Norfolk PE32 1UD
telephone: +44.1760.755 800

Sainsbury Centre for Visual Arts
University of East Anglia, Norwich NR4 7TJ
telephone: +44.1603.593 199
scva@uea.ac.uk
www.scva.org.uk

The Sandringham Estate
Estate Office, Sandringham
Norfolk PE35 6EN
telephone: +44.1553.612 908
facsimile: +44.1485.541 571
visits@sandringhamestate.co.uk
www.sandringhamestate.co.uk

Tatlers
21 Tombland, Norwich NR3 1RF
telephone: +44.1603.766 670

Walsingham
The Shrine of Our Lady of Walsingham
Walsingham, Norfolk NR22 6BW
telephone: +44.1328.820 255
facsimile: +44.1328.824 206
accom@olw-shrine.org.uk
www.walsinghamanglican.org.uk

CAMBRIDGE

Café Jello
13 Magdalene Street, Cambridge CB3 OAF
telephone: +44.1223.312 112
david@cafe-jello.com
www.cafe-jello.co.uk

Ely Cathedral
The College, Ely, Cambridgeshire CB7 4DL
telephone: +44.1353.667 735
facsimile: +44.1353.665 658
receptionist@cathedral.ely.anglican.org
www.elycathedral.org

Ian Stevens
28 Magdalene Street, Cambridge CB3 OAF
telephone: +44.1223.304 100
info@ianstevenscambridge.co.uk
ianstevenscambridge.co.uk

Jockey Club Rooms in Newmarket
101 High Street, Newmarket
Suffolk CB8 8JL
telephone: +44.2071.893 800
enquiries@jockey-club-estates.co.uk
www.jockey-club-estates.co.uk

Kings College Chapel
King's College, Cambridge CB2 1ST
telephone: +44.1223.331 100
info@kings.cam.ac.uk
www.kings.cam.ac.uk

Midsummer House
Midsummer Common, Cambridge CB4 1HA
telephone: +44.1223.369 299
facsimile: +44.1223.302 672
reservations@midsummerhouse.co.uk
www.midsummerhouse.co.uk

The National Stud
Newmarket, Suffolk CB8 OXE
telephone: +44.1638.663 464
facsimile: +44.1638.665 173
tours@nationalstud.co.uk
www.nationalstud.co.uk

Newmarket Racecourses
Westfield House, The Links
Newmarket, Suffolk CB8 OTG
telephone: +44.1638.675 500
www.newmarketracecourses.co.uk

Restaurant 22
22 Chesterton Road, Cambridge CB4 3AX
telephone: +44.1223.351 880
facsimile: +44.1223.323 814
enquiries@restaurant22.co.uk
www.restaurant22.co.uk

Scudamore's Punting Company Ltd
Granta Place, Mill Lane, Cambridge CB2 1RS
telephone: +44.1223.359 750
enquiries@scudamores.com
www.scudamores.com

St Bene't's Church
Bene't Street, Cambridge CB2 3RD
telephone: +44.1223.845 062
office@stbenets.org.uk
www.stbenets.org.uk

The Stained Glass Museum
The South Triforium, Ely Cathedral, Ely
Cambridgeshire CB7 4DL
telephone: +44.1353.660 347
facsimile: +44.1353.665 025
info@stainedglassmuseum.com
www.stainedglassmuseum.com

Topshop
Grand Arcade Shopping Centre
22 St Andrews Street, Cambridge CB2 3AX
telephone: +44.1223.367 499

HOTELS

Broad House Hotel (page 196)
The Avenue, Wroxham, Norfolk NR12 8TS
telephone: +44.016.0378 3567
www.broadhousehotel.co.uk

Strattons Hotel and Restaurant (page 192)
Ash Close, Swaffham, Norfolk PE37 7NH
telephone: +44.017.6072 3845
enquiries@strattonhotel.co.uk
www.strattonhotel.com

Tuddenham Mill (page 198)
High Street, Tuddenham near Newmarket
Suffolk IP28 6SQ
telephone: +44.016.3871 3552
info@tuddenhammill.co.uk
www.tuddenhammill.co.uk

THE NORTH

60 Hope Street
60 Hope Street, Liverpool L1 9BZ
telephone: +44.1517.076 060
facsimile: +44.1517.076 016
info@60hopestreet.com
www.60hopestreet.com

Alma da Cuba
St Peter's Church, Seel Street
Liverpool L1 4BH
telephone: +44.1517.027 394
info@alma-de-cuba.com
www.alma-de-cuba.com

Imperial War Museum North
The Quays, Trafford Wharf Road
Manchester M17 1TZ
telephone: +44.1618.364 000
facsimile: +44.1618.364 012
iwmnorth@iwm.org.uk
north.iwm.org.uk

The Tate Liverpool
Albert Dock, Liverpool L3 4BB
telephone: +44.1517.027 400
visiting.liverpool@tate.org.uk
www.tate.org.uk/liverpool

Urbis
Cathedral Gardens, Manchester M4 3BG
telephone: +44.1616.058 200
info@urbis.org.uk
www.urbis.org.uk

NORTHERN STYLE

Band on the Wall
25 Swan Street, Northern Quarter
Manchester M4 5JZ
telephone: +44.1618.341 786
development@bandonthewall.org
www.bandonthewall.org

The Biscuit Factory
Stoddart Street
Newcastle Upon Tyne NE2 1AN
telephone: +44.1912.611 103
facsimile: +44.1912.610 057
art@thebiscuitfactory.com
www.thebiscuitfactory.com

Carling Academy Newcastle
Westgate Road (junction of Clayton Street)
Newcastle-Upon-Tyne NE1 1SW
telephone: +44.1912.602 020
facsimile: +44.1912.604 650
boxoffice@newcastle-academy.co.uk
www.newcastle-academy.co.uk

Carling Academy Sheffield
37–43 Arundel Gate, Sheffield S1 1DE
telephone: +44.1142.537 777
facsimile: +44.1142.537 772
mail@sheffieldacademy.co.uk
www.sheffieldacademy.co.uk

Manchester Academy 1
Oxford Road, Manchester M13 9PR
www.manchesteracademy.net

**Manchester Academy 2, 3 and
Club Academy**
Manchester University Union
Oxford Road, Manchester M13 9PR
telephone: +44.1612.752 930
www.manchesteracademy.net

Manchester Ritz
Whitworth Street West
Manchester M1 5NQ
telephone: +44.1612.364 355
info@ritznightclub.com
www.ritznightclub.com

BUY IT!

All Saints
33–35 Queen Victoria Street, Leeds LS1 6BD
telephone: +44.1132.432 424
info@allsaints.co.uk
www.allsaints.co.uk

Aqua Couture
36 Queen Victoria Street, Leeds LS1 6AZ
telephone: +44.1132.433 336
info@aquacouture.co.uk
www.aquacouture.co.uk

Firetrap
28–29 County Arcade
Victoria Quarter, Leeds LS1 6BN
telephone: +44.1132.468 723
firetrap.leeds@wdt.co.uk
www.firetrap.com

Harvey Nichols
107–111 Briggate, Leeds LS1 6AZ
telephone: +44.1132.048 888
facsimile: +44.1132.048 889
contactleeds@harveynichols.com
www.harveynichols.com

Jeffery-West
21 County Arcade
Victoria Quarter, Leeds LS1 6BN
telephone: +44.1132.443 588
www.jeffery-west.co.uk

Louis Vuitton
98–99 Briggate, Leeds LS1 6NP
telephone: +44.1133.863 120
facsimile: +44.1133.863 122
www.louisvuitton.com

Mulberry
3–5 County Arcade, Leeds LS1 6BW
telephone: +44.1132.346 084
mail-order@mulberry.com
www.mulberry.com

Paul Smith
17–19 King Edward Street, Leeds LS1 6AX
telephone: +44.1132.450 728
www.paulsmith.co.uk

Pollyanna
14–16 Market Hill, Barnsley
South Yorkshire S70 2QE
telephone: +44.1226.291 665
facsimile: +44.1226.206 075
enquiries@pollyanna.com
www.pollyanna.com

Tessuti Store
14–20 Watergate Street, Chester CH1 2LA
telephone: +44.1244.312 585
fashion@tessuti.co.uk
www.tessuti.co.uk

Vivienne Westwood Leeds
11–17 County Arcade, Leeds LS1 6BW
telephone: +44.1132.456 403
facsimile: +44.1132.456 404
leedsstore@viviennewestwood.co.uk
www.viviennewestwood.com

NORTHERN ELEGANCE

Bettys Café Tea Rooms Harrogate
1 Parliament Street, Harrogate HG1 2QU
telephone: +44.1423.502 746
www.bettys.co.uk

Bettys Café Tea Rooms York
6–8 St Helen's Square, York YO1 8QP
telephone: +44.1904.659 142
www.bettys.co.uk

Godfrey & Watt
7–8 Westminster Arcade
Parliament Street, Harrogate HG1 2RN
telephone: +44.1423.525 300
mail@godfreyandwatt.co.uk
www.godfreyandwatt.co.uk

Jorvik Viking Centre
Coppergate, York YO1 9WT
telephone: +44.1904.543 400
facsimile: +44.1904.627 097
www.jorvik-viking-centre.co.uk

Little Bettys
46 Stonegate, York YO1 8AS
telephone: +44.1904.622 865
www.bettys.co.uk

Sarah Coggles
91–93 Low Petergate, York YO1 7HY
telephone: +44.1904.611 001
contact@coggles.com
www.coggles.com

York Early Music Festival
The National Centre for Early Music
St Margaret's Church, Walmgate
York YO1 9TL
telephone: +44.1904.658 338
info@ncem.co.uk
www.ncem.co.uk

York Racecourse
York YO23 1EX
telephone: +44.1904.620 911
facsimile: +44.1904.611 071
enquiries@yorkracecourse.co.uk
www.yorkracecourse.co.uk

HOTELS

The Balmoral Hotel (page 218)
16–18 Franklin Mount, Harrogate
North Yorkshire HG1 5EJ
telephone: +44.0.1423.508 208
info@balmoralhotel.co.uk
www.balmoralhotel.co.uk

The Chester Grosvenor and Spa (page 226)
Eastgate, Chester CH1 1LT
telephone: +44.012.4432 4024
facsimile: +44.012.4431 3246
hotel@chestergrosvenor.com
www.chestergrosvenor.com

Didsbury House Hotel (page 220)
Didsbury Park, Didsbury Village
Manchester M20 5LJ
telephone: +44.016.1448 2200
facsimile: +44.016.1448 2525
enquiries@didsburyhouse.co.uk
www.didsburyhouse.co.uk

Feversham Arms (page 214)
Helmsley, North Yorkshire YO62 5AG
telephone: +44.014.3977 0766
facsimile: +44.014.3977 0346
www.fevershamarmshotel.com

Great John Street Hotel (page 222)
Great John Street, Castlefield
Manchester M3 4FD
telephone: +44 .016. 1831 3211
facsimile: +44 .016. 1831 3212
info@greatjohnstreet.co.uk
www.greatjohnstreet.co.uk

Hope Street Hotel (page 228)
40 Hope Street, Liverpool L1 9DA
telephone: +44.15.1709 3000
facsimile: +44.15.1709 2454
sleep@hopestreethotel.co.uk
www.hopestreethotel.co.uk

The Lowry Hotel (page 224)
50 Dearmans Place, Chapel Wharf
Manchester M3 5LH
telephone: +44.161.827 4000
facsimile: +44.161.827 4001
reservations.lowry@
roccofortecollection.com
www.thelowryhotel.com

Rothay Garden Hotel (page 230)
Broadgate, Grasmere, Cumbria LA22 9RJ
telephone: +44.015.3943 5334
facsimile: +44.015.3943 5723
stay@rothaygarden.com
www.rothaygarden.com

Woodlands Hotel (page 216)
Gelderd Road, Leeds LS27 7LY
telephone: +44.0113.238 1488
facsimile: +44.113.253 6773
enquiries@woodlandsleeds.co.uk
www.woodlandsleeds.co.uk

RESTAURANTS

**The Harrogate Grille at
The Balmoral Hotel**
telephone: +44.0.1423.565 800
facsimile: +44.0.1423.790 019
contact@grillerestaurants.com
www.grillerestaurants.com